MW00614617

COSMIC DANCES

of

THE PLANETS

CHOREOCOSMOS
SCHOOL OF COSMIC AND SACRED DANCE

Cosmic Dances of the Planets

Lacquanna Paul and Robert Powell

SOPHIA FOUNDATION PRESS

SAN RAFAEL, CALIFORNIA

THE SOPHIA FOUNDATION OF NORTH AMERICA

3143 Avalon Court
Palo Alto, California 94306, USA

Telephone/Fax 650-494-9900
Email: sophia@sophiafoundation.org
Website: www.sophiafoundation.org

First published in the USA, 2007
By Sophia Foundation Press
An imprint of Sophia Perennis
© 2007 Lacquanna Paul and Robert Powell

Companion volume to *Cosmic Dances of the Zodiac*

No part of this book may be reproduced
or transmitted, in any form or by
any means, without permission

For information, address:
Sophia Foundation Press, P.O. Box 151011
San Rafael, California 94915, USA

Library of Congress Cataloging-in-Publication Data

Powell, Robert.
  Cosmic dances of the planets / Lacquanna Paul, Robert Powell.—1st ed.
     p. cm.
  Includes bibliographical references.
  ISBN 1-59731-150-2 (pbk. : alk. paper)
  1. Planets—Miscellanea. 2. Astrology. 3. Dance. I. Paul, Lacquanna. II. Title.

BF1724.P37 2006
133.5'3—dc22

                                                2006033173

CONTENTS

From the *Acts of John*, 94–97:

He bade us therefore make as it were a ring,
Holding one another's hands,
And himself standing in the midst he said:
Answer Amen unto me.

He began, then, to sing a hymn and to say:
Glory be to thee, Father.
And we, going about in a ring, answered him:
Amen.

Glory be to thee, Word:
Glory be to thee, Grace.
Amen.

Glory be to thee, Spirit:
Glory be to thee, Holy One:
Amen...

Grace danceth:
I would pipe, dance ye all.   Amen.
I would mourn, lament ye all.   Amen.

The number Eight singeth praise with us.   Amen.
The number Twelve danceth on high.   Amen.
The Whole on high hath part in our dancing.   Amen.
Whoso danceth not, knoweth not what cometh to pass.   Amen...

A way am I to thee a wayfarer.

Now answer thou unto my dancing.
Behold thyself in me who speak,
And seeing what I do,
Keep silence about my mysteries.
Thou that dancest, perceive what I do...

What thou knowest not, I myself will teach thee.
Thy God am I...
I would keep tune with holy souls.
In me know thou the word of wisdom.

Again with me say thou:
Glory be to thee, Father;
Glory to thee, Word;
Glory to thee, Holy Spirit...
Amen.

Thus, my beloved, having danced with us, the Lord went forth.

—*The Apocryphal New Testament* (trsl. M.R. James; Clarendon Press, Oxford, 1924)

Cosmic Dances of the Planets

Preface

The tradition of dance to express the sacred mystery of the unknowable, ineffable dimension of life is common throughout the civilizations of the world. It is to this *sacred rite* that we invite the reader, extending an invitation to participate in a living way with humanity's quest to know itself in relation to the cosmic order – to know ourselves as human beings united in community with a higher mystical body – a cosmic body wedded to an *omnipresence* of transformation.

The following is a compilation woven together in story form with the purpose of providing the readers and participants in cosmic dance with a sense of an organic unfolding of which they are a part. The telling of this story seeks to stimulate a growing awareness and wonderment in the perfection of the mirroring of the cosmos in the human being together with a *sense* for the evolution of consciousness which follows upon the cosmic ordering of time and space, thus serving as a fertile seed-bed for further exploration and contemplation.

Descriptions and indications given by Rudolf Steiner concerning these interrelationships are honored as a focus and starting-point throughout the text. Through a continual unfolding, gradually building up, the reader is invited to participate in a process of organic discovery toward an understanding of the archetypal truths inherent in the relationship of the planets to the human being.

The exploration is presented through a process of layering, beginning first with the formative qualities of the planets expressed in gesture and sound, and then further exploration seeking an understanding of the mirroring of the planets as an organizing principle affecting not only the physical organism but also the interrelationships inherent in the flowing of etheric forces, as well as the astral realities apparent in the realm of the psyche, leading to indications toward soul development. Finally, there is for each planet a brief consideration of the scientific/astronomical aspects of the planet itself. And so the story unfolds, breaking open like a pomegranate, revealing the many seeds of each planet's fecundating force, playing a formative, vivifying role in the whole of creation.

Various sources have provided humus toward the telling of this richly textured, multi-dimensional journey of discovery. Hazel Straker's handbook *Astrosophy – Introduction to a Quest for a New Star Wisdom* gives a fine introduction and first look into the planetary dances in cosmic space. Through the warmth of her wise and seasoned telling, the planets become as living beings with unique rhythms and characteristics that are defined by their patterned movement and interrelationships in space.

The work of Thomas Moore with his investigation into the writings of Marsilio Ficino, the hermetic musicologist from the time of the Florentine Renaissance, provides a wonderful support for exploring the soul's relationship to the planets. For the working toward the evolution of consciousness through the development of soul capacities, the writings of Robert Sardello provide great depth and understanding. So, too, Jacques Lusseyran's *Against the Pollution of the I* proves significant to the telling, providing an enlightening and inspiring tribute to the human "I".

For the correspondence between the chakras and the planets toward the development of spiritual faculties, the writings and research of Robert Powell found a rich ground of support in the depth and substance of the work of Rudolf Steiner and Valentin Tomberg, and in the teachings of Peter Deunov (Beinsa Douno), the great Bulgarian spiritual master.

Through the further research of Robert Powell in regard to the planetary locations relating to the life and healing miracles of Christ, we are invited to participate in the reading of the starry script, following the tradition of the three Magi who looked to the stars in order to behold the birth of the child Jesus.

Also from Robert Powell, the research and penetrating assimilation of historical precedents leading toward a modern understanding of the planets and their correspondences provided in the Appendices are a treasure trove of scientific consideration.

For the planetary correspondences to the metals, the research of Nick Kollerstrom proved to be a goldmine of information, bringing an up-to-date look at how these vital substances support modern life. His work is written with great wit and insight – a delightful read!

As for an inquiry into the mirroring of the planets in the human organism itself, there is both a direct look through a scientific observational lens, as well as an exploration of the flowing of etheric substance revealed in the inter-relationships between the organs and how this is affected by the sounding of one's soul and thought content. For this research the ancient classical Chinese medical texts translated by Claude Larre and Elisabeth Rochat de la Vallée proved to be valuable resources.

The final result of this cosmic investigation into the relationship of the planets to the human being reveals itself to be an organic weaving of continual mirroring and unfolding, profoundly echoing the clairvoyant impressions of Rudolf Steiner, who turned his gaze toward the cosmos with the question: Who are we as human beings, and toward what future possibility are we evolving?

It is our hope with this work to introduce the reader to the *dynamic reality* that underlies and enfolds all of creation. Toward this investigation James Miller's *Measures of Wisdom: The Cosmic Dance in Classical and Christian Antiquity* proved to be a seed-bearing ferment in relation to humankind's quest to understand the living connection of the starry cosmos to life on Earth. This search traditionally has found communion largely through the dance of community moving in a circle – mirroring the patterns of the moving stars against the stillness of the surrounding cosmos.

In grateful appreciation of all these fertile fields of inquiry, we invite you to enjoy the journey...

Introduction

The Earth is the third planet from the Sun and is part of a family of nine planets orbiting around the Sun, comprising our solar system. In addition, the Earth has a Moon, so that gazing out into our solar system we see the Moon, the Sun, and the eight other planets circling around the Sun: Mercury, Venus, Mars, Jupiter, Saturn, Uranus, Neptune, and Pluto. The latter three planets, discovered with the aid of the telescope – Uranus in 1781, Neptune in 1846, and Pluto in 1930 – were unknown to the ancients. In line with the knowledge of antiquity down to the eighteenth century, one speaks of the *classical planets* – seven in number – the Sun, the Moon, and the five planets visible to the naked eye: Mercury, Venus, Mars, Jupiter, and Saturn.

In the Choreocosmos School of Cosmic and Sacred Dance, there are dances for the seven classical planets. The newly discovered planets Uranus, Neptune, and Pluto, referred to in Appendix I, have been left out of our consideration in this book, as they have to do with the early phase of cosmic evolution prior to the beginning of the formation of the human being, which began at the Ancient Saturn stage – marked in our present solar system by the orbit of Saturn.

For those readers unfamiliar with the stages of cosmic evolution, Appendix I provides an overview. These stages were known in antiquity – in ancient Egypt – and the naming of the days of the week, which came from the Egyptian mysteries, was in accordance with the stages of evolution. The days of the week thus have planetary names:

Saturday	(samedi)	the day of Saturn
Sunday	(dimanche)	the day of the Sun
Monday	(lundi)	the day of the Moon
Tuesday	(mardi)	the day of Mars, since the Norse god *Tiw* = Mars
Wednesday	(mercredi)	the day of Mercury, since the Norse god *Wotan* = Mercury
Thursday	(jeudi)	the day of Jupiter, since the Norse god *Thor* = Jupiter
Friday	(vendredi)	the day of Venus, since the Norse goddess *Freya* = Venus

(The French names of the days of the week are given in parentheses as they show more clearly than the Anglo-Saxon names the connection with the planets.)

The planetary week, which came into existence around the beginning of the Christian era, is perhaps the most widespread "astrological" conception, as it is used throughout the world. Yet how many people realize what the names of the days of the week (according to the planets) signify? How many people know that the days of the week were named according to the stages of evolution?

The sequence of presentation of the planets chosen in this study material is that of the days of the week, beginning with Saturn – corresponding to the first stage (Ancient Saturn) of cosmic evolution, i.e. the first stage with respect to the beginning of the formation of the human being. While intended primarily for Choreocosmos students, we hope that anyone interested in learning more about the other members (beyond the Earth) of the family comprising our solar system will benefit from the study material presented in this book. It is a vast subject, one that has a rich tradition going back into the mists of time, and only a small part of the knowledge concerning the planets accumulated through the course of time is presented here.

1

Moreover, the knowledge communicated in this work has the purpose of stimulating the reader to further research into this fascinating topic. This research can be on different levels: astronomical, astrological, or astrosophical – the latter pertaining to astrosophy (*star wisdom*), the wisdom of the stars. The knowledge drawn from these different levels can serve as a starting point for further exploration and a deepening through meditation – in particular through cosmic dance as practiced in the Choreocosmos School, which is *meditation in movement*. Through cosmic dance one can come to a *living experience* of the planets, and this is something very precious which cannot be compared with accumulating information and gaining knowledge, valuable though the latter is.

By way of illustration, let us consider the following experience written down by a Choreocosmos student, which she had in connection with the cosmic dance of Saturn:

> Looking at the Saturn form on a piece of paper for the first time in a Choreocosmos workshop, I was strongly reminded of the similarity with the Saturn planetary seal which I once modelled in clay some years ago. Moving to Saturn for the first time in a circle of people, I was concentrating on getting the form and my steps correct and staying in the circle. After that was accomplished, a year later I noticed, when dancing Saturn with a long-lasting piece of music, I went into a meditative state. My crown chakra started rotating and I could see the form (choreography) we were doing from above.
>
> January this year (2005), when moving the Saturn form and doing the Saturn gestures in the inner circle, while the outer circle was moving the Aquarius form and doing the Aquarius gestures, I noticed – when doing the Saturn sound "U" ("oo") with stretched arms and a certain consciousness on the wrists – that a lot of energy flowed into the space between my hands. I also concentrated on the other movement, the planetary gesture of Saturn, in connection with "*Practice Spirit recollection*" of Rudolf Steiner's *Foundation Stone Meditation*, and a memory arose of a former life.
>
> When entering into the circle at the same time with all the participants moving forward, coming closer into the circle with their arms and hands outstretched, I noticed everybody else in my inner circle actually *holding their own karma between their hands*. This was a very moving experience. At the same time I experienced the outer circle moving through "*water*", balancing thinking, feeling and willing with the gesture of the "M" sound belonging to Aquarius and also with the zodiacal gesture for the sign of Aquarius.
>
> I feel that Choreocosmos also leads to a lot more. The experience was like a ceremony where the participants are serving each other, *streaming out love and receiving love and supporting each other*. At other times in the past when doing the cosmic dances, whenever I sent loving thoughts to Mother Earth I felt the stream of energy coming from the earth and passing through my heart and sending it out into space, a *vertical* movement. This time I also experienced the *horizontal* movement of being loved and blessed and returning love and blessings.
>
> The wonderful thing about Choreocosmos is that you can send your thoughts from your head into your heart, hands and feet in moving, and you receive the most amazing and unexpected gifts back. *To me, Choreocosmos is a modern path toward initiation - truly modern - because you do not do it on your own as in former lives, secluded in a monastery; instead you grow together with the other participants and you depend on the others as they depend on you.*

(Further Choreocosmos experiences written by participants in cosmic dance are to be found at the end of this book, after the Bibliography.)

Musical Accompaniment

Dance only that music which goes from the soul in mounting circles. (*Isadora Duncan*)

The accompanying music for each of the forms for the cosmic dances of the planets has been chosen from the works of the great composers whose music reflects the inspiration of the *harmony of the spheres*. The music has been selected according to the planetary mood and rhythmical form or pattern of each of the seven planetary dances.

Whenever possible, the dances should be accompanied by *live music* (usually piano or violin) since the etheric "vibrational quality" of the music is a potent and valuable aspect of the eurythmic experience, which brings about an enhancement of the flow of cosmic life forces. However, when *live music* is not possible, the "*Planet Music*" CD, created by concert pianist Sylvia Karpe,[1] can be used for individual practice and for teaching in a group.

Eurythmy and Cosmic Dance

The cosmic dances work with the planetary gestures given by Rudolf Steiner, the founder of eurythmy. On the basis of his highly developed faculty of clairvoyance, Rudolf Steiner was able to perceive objectively the archetypal cosmic gestures of the planets, which he communicated in his lectures <u>Eurythmy as Visible Speech</u> in 1924. The sounds corresponding to the planets are the *vowels* (and the consonants correspond to the signs of the zodiac, as outlined in <u>Cosmic Dances of the Zodiac</u>).

Not only does each planet have an archetypal cosmic gesture, but also a corresponding <u>sound</u>, for which there is a eurythmic gesture. These seven gestures are described in the following material as central to the seven cosmic dances of the planets. In reference to the sounding of a planet, this refers to making the *gesture* of the sound non-vocally, expressing the sound *silently through movement.* By not speaking the sound, a greater intensity of expression goes into the gesture.

In the cosmic eurythmy we can experience that each of these gestures activates an *inner response* which works toward the strengthening of the human being and toward a greater alignment with the divine influences of the cosmic archetypes. To become conscious of this inner *formative* response is one of the goals of the Choreocosmos School. This is the healing aspect of the cosmic dance activity, which can be likened to the building-up of Solomon's temple. The *creative* potency of each sound and gesture *speaks* within the participants as the human physical body becomes a *vessel* for the building-up of a temple of wisdom.

In the cosmic eurythmy participants learn to *sculpt* the gestures and sounds into the atmosphere of the surrounding space. This requires a cultivated awareness of the living substance of the etheric body of the earth. This awareness is cultivated through developing the capacity of inner silence and the activity of appreciation and love for the environment. This creates an attracting of life

---

[1] Sylvia Karpe is a Swedish concert pianist who has specialized in accompanying eurythmy and who is the accompanist for Choreocosmos workshops in Sweden. In addition to her "*Planet Music*" CD, also her CD recording of the Choreocosmos music for the Four Elements (Earth, Water, Air, Fire) is available from the Sophia Foundation. The "*Four Elements*" CD also includes Sylvia's recording of the music by Franz Schubert that accompanies the <u>Prayer Sequence in Sacred Dance</u>.

substance which is then shaped by the participants as a *blessing* for the surroundings and a *breathing back* to the spiritual world.

The choreographies for the seven planets used in the cosmic dances have been developed by Robert Powell on the basis of archetypal eurythmy forms (choreographies) given by Rudolf Steiner.

The music accompanying the choreographies is chosen to reflect the mood corresponding to each planet, so that the whole (music, choreographic movement, planetary gestures, and gestures of the planetary sounds) weaves together in the sense of a *total work of art,* capable of engaging one's whole being and leading one to a spiritual experience of these great cosmic archetypes.

The cosmic dances are thus a special development arising from eurythmy, concentrating upon cosmic eurythmy.   The Choreocosmos School and the teachers of cosmic dance acknowledge their profound gratitude to Rudolf Steiner for bringing eurythmy into the world, thus creating a path – through movement – of coming to an experience of the cosmic archetypes of music and language and of the cosmic archetypes themselves.

Orientation Regarding the Study Material

The following work has been prepared as a guide and format for learning the seven cosmic dances which celebrate the creative streaming of the seven classical planets. The forms and patterns of movement are described and illustrated so that their purpose and inspiring archetype can be readily grasped and understood.

Legends and myths have existed throughout the ages concerning this greater macrocosm of which we are a part and which serves as an archetypal pattern for the forming of the human being. These stories provide an enrichment for our imagination and help to draw us more deeply into a conscious understanding and connection with the living currents (*life body*) of the cosmos, which hold the past as well as the future in a continuum of harmonic wisdom and order.

Through the images we can begin to behold the cosmic realm as a *relational field,* a rhythmic constancy of archetypal pattern (*space*) and purposeful movement (*time*) which draws us ever nearer to the divine purpose of the future.

Astronomical and scientific findings and information are included, as well as other material which has been formulated through observable phenomena over many centuries. This information is offered as an enrichment to help deepen the cosmic dance material.

This material is intended as a *seed* to help *ferment* the process of discovery in finding a *relationship* to the archetypes of the seven planets. Participants find that through the experience of the *communal* dance of the cosmos a strong sense of community begins to build amongst the participants themselves. Conversation and dialogue relating to the experiential discoveries of the participants in the planetary dances is embraced through the common effort and can be most fruitful.

Taken as a whole, through the movement of the dance which requires the engagement of the *will,* the experience of the music which addresses the *feeling* life, and the interactive nature of the discussion time which stimulates the *thinking,* one is brought into an awareness of the beauty, wonder, and magnificence of our human *relationship* with the cosmic realm of our spiritual origin. This is a relationship that may be experienced on a physical, soul and spiritual level.

Cosmic *Eurythmy*

"In the image and likeness…"

*Just as Time, the Cosmic Man has a body made up of the signs of the zodiac,
so too he has mental and emotional facilities, which are the planets.*[2]

The Planets: In Relationship to the Constellations

With the eurythmy zodiacal dance forms we are able to explore the *informing* realities of the **zodiacal** constellations.[3] In this way we can discover through the dancing of gesture and sound the cosmic wonder of harmony and order that resounds in the very **structure** of our being. Wisdom has left her imprint and the harmony of the spheres has given form to the human being.

We might think of the stellar **constellations** (which are visible to the eye) as the *inner* clockwork (time body) surrounding our solar system and embedded within the greater body of the galaxy. These constellations are the groups or communities of stars whose relational fields remain *constant* to one another and are thus referred to as the *fixed stars*. The light emanating from these stars seems to pulse and twinkle while sounding out the chords and octaves of the celestial chorus of which they are a part.

The fixed stars form the *working* bodies for the constellations, which since ancient times have been believed to be the dwelling place for groups of spiritual beings belonging to the heavenly hierarchies. Among all the stellar constellations, the twelve zodiacal constellations are of particular importance, as they serve as the shaping forces for the human being. It is the zodiacal constellations which form the framework for the movements of the planets, whose positions are observed to change in relation to the background of the bodies of these fixed stars – hence the name "planet" (from the Greek, meaning *moving star*). We associate the familiar bodies of the zodiacal constellations with the timing of the seasons of the year and can observe from our earthly perspective that they move in an ordered cadence and in measured steps. Thus, the constellations offer a steady companionship throughout the seasons of our life.

The **planets** do not twinkle like the stars, but emanate a brilliant light which serves as a beacon or *telling* sign for the ordered intelligence and sounds which stream forth from the background of the patterned shapes and forms of the zodiacal constellations that watch like "time sentinels" in the background.

---

[2] Valerie J. Roebuch, *The Circle of Stars*. The Cosmic Man is also referred to as "Adam Kadmon", which according to the *Cabbala* is the Hebrew term for the heavenly representation (form) for the primal archetype of the human being (Adam). The same idea is also to be found in the ancient Egyptian culture, which depicted the archetypal form of the human being stretched around the zodiac with the head in Aries, the feet in Pisces, etc. The ancient Egyptian wisdom concerning the human being's archetypal relationship to the zodiac may have come to the Jewish tradition through Moses, who was initiated into the Egyptian mysteries.

[3] Lacquanna Paul and Robert Powell, *Cosmic Dances of the Zodiac*.

The constellations of the zodiac bear the sounds of the macrocosm, which are mirrored in the **consonants** of language. According to Rudolf Steiner, "*The realities of the macrocosm are the consonants.*"[4] The word *consonance* carries the fullness of the incarnating promise of the sounding of the *consonants*, for this signifies a "recurrence of the same or similar sounds; the sounding of two notes in harmony". This is a telling description of the sounding of the cosmos mirrored both in the human being and in language – an archetypal shaping of divine order and providence in time.

The Planets: In Relationship to the Human Being

> *We have the planets within us.* (Paracelsus)

Now we shall consider the planets, which reflect the <u>inner</u> workings of the macrocosm. It is the planets which resound within the **vowels** of language.

> *The vowels supply everything which one needs to know about the human being. They offer the inner key to the macrocosm.*[5]

The movement of the planets through the constellations brings an enlivening force. Within the human being can be felt a stirring and a magnification of the qualities and harmonies of the planets' unique relationships within the bodies of the constellations. Correspondingly, it is the richness of the sounding of the vowels which ensoul the distinguishing boundaries and shaping forces of the consonants. With this understanding we can experience how language is mirrored in our human existence, for it is the planets which stir the soul forces within the inner life of the human being, bringing their unique influence to magnify and fill the endings, beginnings and intervals of life.

The planets have their own unique qualities and sounds as they dance and weave their beautiful patterns around the Earth and the Sun, and toward the zodiacal constellations beyond. They visit the communities of stars in a timely order which is unique to each of them and, correspondingly, the region of the heavens they attend bears a sounding influence upon the planets' unique qualities, just as our consciousness is influenced by the region and culture to which we are born and will vary according to the changes of environment around us.

Sometimes strong and sometimes quiet, the planets blend their sounding notes upon the keys and measured steps of the constellations, producing an ever-unfolding symphony of harmony and sound, whose melodies vary in temperament, rhythm and tone according to their relational locations within the chords and octaves of the timepiece we call the zodiac.

In this way, the planets serve as organs of perception for the greater body beyond – providing a circulation and a breathing between the inner and outer worlds of our sense of reality.

The planets' soundings pulse within us. They relate to our own inner organs of perception, which will always seek an inner accord and harmony with the heavenly chorus we have come to know as the music of the "harmony of the spheres". The planets lead us to the *inner* sanctum of **Sophia**'s melodies.

---

[4] Rudolf Steiner, *History and Content of the Higher Degrees of the Esoteric School*, p. 246.
[5] Rudolf Steiner, *History and Content of the Higher Degrees of the Esoteric School*, p. 247.

Sophia's Melody

*Now, let us follow the organs of sound, called the **planets***
which flow from the chord to the octave.
They will serve as a mirror to give sound to our feelings.
Each of the zodiacal star fields are living beings –
*with head, heart and will forces known as the **decans**.*[6]
These are the chords for the octaves they play.
The planets move about within this musical score –
sounding out their own unique qualities
like instruments in the greater orchestra.
*Just as our physical **organs** play their own unique part*
as instruments of sound within the human being,
so too the planets enliven creation.
The planets bring all the richness of wine to our living.
Some are dry, some are full bodied –
and their relationship one to another is like wine to a meal,
while the star field serves as the setting.
All things work together as a result of the planets play
upon the keys of the heavenly accord –
*called the **zodiac**.*
Remembering that the word zodiac
*comes from the root word **Zodi**,*
which in Sanskrit means "a way to live",
*some call this the **Royal Way**...*

---

[6] The Egyptian decans, which originally comprised thirty-six constellations *below* the zodiacal belt, subsequently became related to 10° subdivisions of the zodiacal constellations when the zodiac was introduced to Egypt from Babylon. The twelve equal-division zodiacal constellations – the original *signs* of the zodiac – from Babylonian star wisdom were each subdivided into three decans, each decan 10° in length being a subdivision of a sign of the zodiac. Knowledge of the original decans was lost with the disappearance of the ancient Egyptian culture. However, the decans have resurrected in a new form in our time, since each decan can be related to an extra-zodiacal constellation *above* (e.g. Auriga) *or below* (e.g. Orion) the zodiacal belt – see Lacquanna Paul and Robert Powell, <u>Cosmic Dances of the Zodiac</u>, pp. 7-9.

We bring honor to Sophia's wisdom

by remembering that the end is in the beginning...

that to walk in the Royal Way

*means to know that the way is stepped like a ladder (**Jacob's ladder**).*

And that each sign is a living being

with levels which function towards one's <u>forgiving</u>.

For it is true that each one gives to the other –

*working together toward the top of the ladder **(Community)**.*

And then they bear fruit.

Each sign bringing its own unique qualities

to this sacred unfolding of grace, sacrifice, and surrender – then triumph!

When the crown is won, they've lived each measured step.

And the planets have played their song...

Now let us begin with the crown!

Cosmic *Eurythmy*

"In the image and likeness…"

Saturn: *"The Sun behold at the midnight hour" (Rudolf Steiner)*[7]

Chakra:	Crown
Organ:	Spleen
Gland:	Pineal
Metal:	Lead
Color:	Blue
Tones:	G and A[8]

Saturn is the furthermost of the seven visible planets – the word planet meaning *wanderer*. Observation of this unique wanderer reveals that it moves slowly – requiring 29½ years to complete its orbit around the Sun, a rhythm which has quite a profound effect upon the human being's biography – marking times of great transition and destiny decisions.[9]

For these reasons Saturn is often referred to as "Old Father Time" and is imagined as a bearded old man with a scythe in hand, signifying the reaping of the harvest of time. We can see him depicted on the ceiling of the beautiful Wies Baroque church in southern Bavaria – where he is seen fallen exhausted before the steps of the gates of heaven, the sands of time having just run out.

Astrologers often refer to Saturn as the "grim reaper". However, our experience of him in cosmic dance will inform us of a far grander significance. Through the Saturn gesture and sound, we shall discover the nobility of the faculty of memory – which Saturn bestows on our crown. For Saturn's rhythm marks the seasons of harvest in the time spans of our lives, as well as in world destiny, sowing the seeds for new beginnings, requiring a righting of our ways and a realigning with higher order.

The eurythmy gesture for Saturn signifies an etheric connection flowing between the crown chakra[10] of the human being (our connection to the heights) and the spleen, the organ that carries the residue of our unresolved emotions and thought life (representing the depths).

The spleen in the human being can be characterized as the time keeper of the physical organs. The spleen works to harmonize the internal rhythms of the physical body with the purpose to heal that which is out of phase.[11]

---

[7] See the planetary verse for Saturn in Appendix IV: *Music and Verses for the Seven Classical Planets.*

[8] The correspondences are tabulated in Appendix III: *Correspondences to the Seven Classical Planets.* For an in-depth discussion, see Appendix II: *Musical Tones and the Planets.*

[9] See Robert Powell, *Chronicle of the Living Christ.* The Baptism in the Jordan took place when Jesus was 29½ years old, bringing him into alignment with his destiny (Saturn) to serve as the living vessel for the incarnation of the Christ.

[10] The chakras relate to the human astral body, the subtle energy body of the soul. The crown chakra (8 petal lotus or 1000 petal lotus) is the astral organ relating to the top or <u>crown</u> of the head. See Appendix III.

[11] The physical <u>organs</u> are related to the human being's etheric/life body – the subtle body of life energy which surrounds and governs the life forces within the physical body.

The Saturn Sound "U"

The Saturn sound ("U") – spoken "oo" in cosmic dance – gives expression to the "as above, so below" principle of archetypal cosmic patterning in the tracing of the vital connection (generating force) that *breathes* between the heavens and the depths of the Earth (Shamballa).[12]

The orbit of Saturn marks the beginning realm of the working hierarchy of the **Seraphim**, the generating creative connection between the fiery realm of the Father and the "time body" of Cosmic Man.

The eurythmy sound U ("oo") – sounding like "Moon" – expresses a quality of gratitude for the love of the Father (God). Thus, the glyph for Saturn ♄ expresses these profound ideas with the love of God represented by the cross above, and the coming into incarnation from the fiery realm of the Seraphim (Father) through the Moon sphere below. In this way the mystery of human incarnation and Earth evolution has been preserved and remembered by Saturn in the significance of the planetary symbol.[13]

Just as the Saturn glyph has been likened to the shape of the sickle or scythe used for the harvesting of crops, so too the eurythmy *sound* U cuts through to the heart of truth, bringing down the flames of pure love (benediction).

The Eurythmy Saturn Gesture

The Saturn *gesture* cups, holds and cradles as though filling with the heaviness (lead) of earthly experience which flows from the heart into the cupped hands held in the region of the **spleen** (the Saturn organ). Then with a "lifting up" gesture, the cup (now filled with life experience) is raised into the *light* of purified consciousness in the region of the **crown** (the Saturn chakra) to be carried back spiritually as "nuggets of gold" (reconciliation) and *remembered* (cosmic memory) in the planetary realm of Saturn.

In the cosmic dance of Saturn we imagine ourselves immersed in the *heavenly* color of light **blue**. An ethereal quality of mood envelops us as we dance the form to music expressing the Saturn qualities: Bach's "Air" from the Orchestra Suite No. 3 in D major or Chopin's Prelude No. 6 in B minor.

---

[12] "*Is the primeval sun of Ptolemy, which he perceived in the center of the earth as the creative ground of the world, the golden fairyland Shamballa?*" Rudolf Steiner: "*Yes – and midnight conceals it.*" See Johanna von Keyserlingk, *The Birth of a New Agriculture*, p. 87.

[13] See Appendix I: *Planetary Stages of Evolution* for further discussion.

Saturn *Eurythmy* Form

Begin first with the measured stepping of the form, generally four (but sometimes six) steps moving diagonally forward to the right and then four (but sometimes six) steps moving diagonally backward to the right. The number of steps depends upon the *time signature* of the piece, e.g. 4/4 indicates four steps, and 3/2 indicates six steps. One always begins with the right foot and does not close the feet together with the fourth step but rather leaves them open. Through practicing measured stepping, one attunes to the rhythm and flow of the music.

After the stepping of the form has been mastered, repeat the form adding the sound gesture only, followed by a repetition of the form with the planetary gesture only. Then combine the two, sound and gesture – alternating with the sound gesture moving in toward the center of the form and the planetary gesture moving out toward the periphery of the form. See the next three pages, especially p. 14.

Cosmic Dance of Saturn

"Connecting with the heights and the depths"

The mood of Saturn is one of solemnity and sacredness. One contemplates the incredible gift and responsibility of incarnation. The body posture is one of steady uprightness. By connecting with Heaven through the crown chakra and the Earth through one's feet, the dancer becomes a living conduit of divine love.

Movement:
Stand with weight balanced evenly between the feet. Connect with the heart of the Earth through the soles of the feet, *creating a connection between the heights and the depths.*

Saturn Sound: U ("oo")
"Connecting with the heights"
Raise arms straight up above head (arms parallel in line with legs). Feel the etheric connection of the feet with the Earth and also flowing between the hands.

Move diagonally *forward* to the right, bringing the "U" gesture down. *Imagine the fiery realm of the Seraphim beaming love to the Earth from the realm of the Father.*

"Connecting with the depths"

Arms parallel to each other, lower arms slowly (palms facing, maintaining the etheric connection between the hands). This is a gesture *of incarnation, coming down to Earth.*

Reverse direction, now moving **back** diagonally to the right, bringing the "U" gesture up, *returning to the fiery realm of the Father.*

Continue Form:
Moving diagonally *forward* (lowering arms) and then diagonally **back** (raising arms), the whole circle moving counter-clockwise to the right, forming a star pattern.

While moving back, slowly return arms (parallel to each other) to position above head (palms facing). *Drawing remembrance of redeemed deeds back to the cosmic realm.*

Alternately lower arms while moving forward and then draw arms up above head while moving back.

Cosmic Dance of Saturn

"The outer has triumphed"

Movement:
Begin by standing erect with weight balanced between the feet, *allowing divine love to flow to the center of the Earth through the soles of the feet.*

Saturn Gesture:
Arms form a closed "O" at the level of the crown, with palms overlapping and facing down, thumbs touch to form an inverted cup.

Move diagonally *forward* to the right, while lowering the arms, *taking in the world, committing it to memory.*

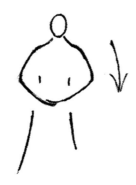

Keeping the Saturn gesture, slowly lower arms from the crown in an arc down to the region of the spleen (Saturn organ), while moving in toward the center of the circle (Earth), *bringing down the memory of the heavenly realm.*

Move diagonally *back* to the right while raising arms.

Keeping the Saturn gesture, raise arms slowly as you return back to the periphery, *bringing life experience to full consciousness.*

Continue Form:
Moving diagonally *forward* to the right, while lowering arms; then diagonally *back* to the right while raising arms, forming a star pattern.

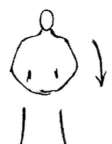

Alternately lower arms while moving forward and **raise** arms, while moving back.

Cosmic Dance of Saturn

"The outer has triumphed"

Movement:
Begin by standing erect with weight balanced between the feet. Connect with the heart of the Earth through the soles of the feet. Extend awareness from the crown up toward heaven.

Move diagonally *forward* to the right, toward the Earth, while lowering the arms, imagining the process of incarnation, coming down to Earth – picturing the planet Earth at the center of the circle.

Move diagonally *back* to the right while forming the Saturn gesture, returning to the periphery of the circle, imagining that one is moving back toward the heavenly realm.

Continue form:
Alternately: Forming the Saturn **sound**, while moving diagonally *forward* toward the Earth (incarnating) and the Saturn **gesture** (remembering) when moving *back* diagonally toward the realm of the Father.

Continue moving to the right, the whole circle moving counter-clockwise, forming the star pattern of the Saturn form.

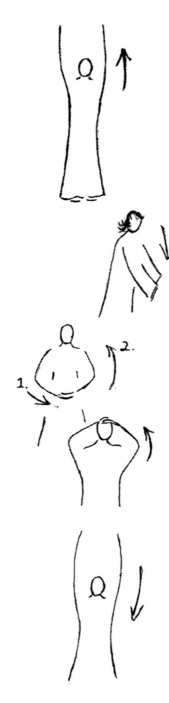

Saturn Sound: U ("oo"):
Slowly raise arms straight up, parallel in line with legs, *connecting with the heights.* Palms facing in, feel the etheric connection which flows between the hands. Finger tips receive cosmic streaming to beam down toward Earth.

Connecting with the depths, lower arms slowly with the "U" gesture, *(Imagine the fiery realm of the Seraphim beaming Love from the realm of the Father.)* Palms facing each other, maintaining the etheric connection between the hands.

Saturn Gesture:
Arms form a closed "O" at the level of the spleen with palms overlapping, thumbs touching, forming a cup. Slowly raise cupped hands up to the crown while moving back *toward the heavenly realm.*

Maintaining an awareness of openness beneath the shoulder caps allows the heart forces to flow into the cupped hands – as in *"My cup runneth over"* – forming a gesture of benediction.

Arms open parallel above head readying to make next Saturn U **sound,** while moving *forward.*

Cosmic *Eurythmy*

"In the image and likeness…"

Saturn: Chronos and the First Stage of Evolution[14]

In the first stage of Earth evolution the primordial gases of what is now known as planet Earth extended out to the orbit of **Saturn**. This was the formative stage for the archetypal *architecture* of the human being relating to the bony substance which we call the skeleton. The skeleton of the human being provides a sacred housing for the bone marrow, the fluid coding for life which flows in the color blue. Saturn thus provides the structural foundation of our existence, which is exquisitely and profoundly formed through Saturn's crystallizing force.[15]

When we say, "*I can feel it in my bones*" or "*My bones just know…*", we are thinking along with **Chronos**, the great cosmic architect who according to the ancient watchers of the stars conceived the thoughts that keep the heavens in order, designing and maintaining the planetary orbits which in antiquity were referred to as the "Golden Chain".

The work of Chronos can be thought of as a *constant* and therefore timeless activity. And because Chronos set the stars in movement, he is considered to be the "***Choreographer***" of the divine plan for the "Monad of Time".

Chronos inspires the work of *conscience* in the human being. The orbital constancy of moving into life's activity and revolving back for reflection allows the light of reason to *dawn* in the heart.

The Choral Dance of Chronos

> *If you truly wish to see the "was" and the "will be" as forms or unchanging aspects of Chronos… then consider in its entirety a complete revolution and choral dance of Chronos… that takes place among the things in the mutable world of **Becoming**.*
>
> (Proclus, *In Timaeum* III, 38)[16]

Pythagoras taught that the ancient philosophers defined time as a ***choral dance*** of the "*now*", a dance of "*Psyche around Nous*" – the Pythagorean etymology of the word "*nous*" meaning "Chronos" or the "***Eternal now***".

When we say, "*all things in right timing*", we are thinking with Chronos, the underlying root of the words *chronological* and *chronicle* (as in the *Akasha Chronicle*, which is the cosmic memory of all that takes place).

---

[14] See Appendix I: *Planetary Stages of Evolution* for further discussion.

[15] Thus it is possible to grasp the meaning of the words relating to the Saturn form in eurythmy, "*The outer has triumphed*" – see the heading of the previous page.

[16] Quoted from James Miller, *Measures of Wisdom*, p. 436.

Plato's explanation of the name **Chronos** indicates a *"child of the pure and undefiled intellect"*, deriving from the word *"koros"* meaning pure (virginal) intellect.[17] Furthering this idea, the neoplatonist Proclus (fifth century AD) described the origin of the name Chronos in his commentary upon Plato's timeless work *Timaeus*:

> *The word chronos is from "choreia", "choral dance" because it is a movement existing essentially in the world of Becoming... The wise, by gazing steadfastly at the nature that is always moving and at the nature that is always at rest, were the first to acquire knowledge of eternity.*
>
> (Proclus, *In Timaeum* III, 9)[18]

This gives us a picture of the wise striving to see the whole truth before jumping to hasty conclusions. Thus, the eurythmy gesture for Saturn instructs us toward the path of clear thinking with the universal order.

In antiquity *"choreia"*, the heavenly chorus, was celebrated in dance as a kind of schooling. The dancers in the cosmic chorus moved around in a circle with hands joined together in a cycle of *regeneration*. This gave expression to the physical world dancing in unison with the vital energy of the vast womb of the cosmos endlessly giving birth to new images.[19]

The Birth of Choreocomos: the School of Cosmic and Sacred Dance

Toward this cycle of regeneration in the world of **Becoming** we discover the streaming of inspiration for the birth of Choreocosmos, *the School of Cosmic and Sacred Dance*. As with all true spiritual initiatives, the genesis and founding principle comes from Chronos, the pure intellect (*"nous"*) which is *remembered* by **Saturn.**

With this endeavor we give expression to the *"nous"* or *"eternal now"* of Pythagoras and can actively *live into* an understanding of the mystery of Teilhard de Chardin's *"noosphere"*:

> *... the tremendous power of divine attraction ...the specific effect of which is ... to make man's endeavors holy.*[20]

The **Becoming** of the "noosphere" of Teilhard de Chardin points to the realm of inspiration from which the birth of Choreocosmos has taken place – both in the ancient understanding (particularly that of the Greeks) of cosmic dance in antiquity and in the modern understanding through the re-emergence of cosmic dance in our time. The ideal regarding this inspiration can be traced to the stream of regeneration from the teachings of **Hermes Trismegistus** set forth in the sacred book entitled *Kore Kosmu* ("The Cosmic Virgin" or "The Eye-Pupil of the World") wherein the student is guided toward knowledge as *a holy endeavor in order to praise God – offering a true service to the world.*[21]

---

[17] Plato, *Cratylus* 396b, quoted from James Miller, *Measures of Wisdom*, p. 443.
[18] Quoted from James Miller, *Measures of Wisdom*, p. 444.
[19] Ibid. p. 447.
[20] Pierre Teilhard de Chardin, *Le Milieu Divin*, p. 65.
[21] See *Meditations on the Tarot*, pp. 186-188.

Saturn: The Orbital Gateway to Cosmic Memory

Following upon the hermetic teaching regarding the "Cosmic Virgin" or the "Eye-Pupil of the World", the star watchers of antiquity characterized Saturn's unique orbital dance. On the one hand Proclus states:

> *If Chronos truly is a Dancing Intellect, then he dances while remaining at rest …and because he remains at rest his choral dances are infinite in number and return to their starting point,* and on the other hand he says, *Those who had seen Chronos with their own eyes testified that the Dancing Intellect was spiral-shaped.*
>
> (Proclus, *In Timaeum* III, 20 and 28).[22]

The form (choreography) for the cosmic dance of Saturn, combining the extension of the line with the continuous curve of the circle, tells the story of continuity – the constancy of endings and beginnings in time. Thus, the spiral of Chronos unites the *revolution* of movement in a <u>circle</u> with the linear movement of *evolution*, resulting in a <u>spiral</u>.

We experience this ***Dancing Intellect*** of Chronos in the choreography of the eurythmy forms of the planetary dances which begin with the dance of **Saturn** and the progression of the straight line as one moves around the circle.

To the inner eye of Proclus, who was both mathematician and astronomer, the spiral movement revealed multiplicities of unique patterns which led him to discover Chronos as the archetypal HELIX:

> *If Proclus had been divinely blessed with prophetic insight into the realm of chromosomes and amino acids discovered by modern geneticists, he would doubtless have perceived the double helix of the DNA molecule as a microcosmic image of the spiraliform Chronos.*[23]

Further observation of the orbit of Saturn in relation to the ***Golden Chain*** of the ***Planetary Orbital Dance*** revealed the swiftness of all the other planets in relation to the slow-moving Saturn, since "the swiftest overtook the slowest". Therefore the orbit of Saturn's unique path becomes the "time-keeper" that marks the endings and beginnings of the planetary journeys through time. Correspondingly, Saturn's orbit bears great influence upon the biographical journey of each human being.

The archetypal example of Saturn's ordering influence is in the life of Jesus, who became united with the Logos (Christ) at the Baptism in the Jordan when he was 29½ years of age – 29½ years being the orbital period of Saturn. This is a *crowning* example of the harvesting of time, with 29½ years marking the completion of one full orbit of Saturn around the zodiac, the time when Saturn returned for the first time to the same location as at the time of the birth of Jesus of Nazareth.[24]

We can think of the words of Christ, *"The last shall be first, and the first last"* (<u>Matthew</u> 20:16) as a heralding of Saturn's orbit at the gateway of all endings and beginnings, receiving all that has been redeemed in the nature of each human being's biography.

---

[22] Quoted from James Miller, <u>Measures of Wisdom</u>, p. 414 & p. 449.
[23] Ibid. p. 450.
[24] Robert Powell, <u>Chronicle of the Living Christ</u>, p. 424 ff.

29½ years

Saturn Forces in Human Biography

Rudolf Steiner describes the journey of the soul after death as a journey through the planetary spheres, undergoing a gradual expansion, a cleansing and purification of the content of the astral body's soul memory – progressing through appropriate teachings in each planetary sphere – so that only the truth of redeemed soul nature enters into Saturn's annals of cosmic time.[25] There was in ancient times a myth which sought to bring to expression the mysteries that live at the gateway of Saturn's realm as "time keeper" and guardian of the threshold. In this story Chronos uses his scythe to castrate his heavenly father Ouranos (Heaven), because Ouranos had offended his wife Gaia (Mother Earth) by shoving her children (all the unredeemed soul nature) back into her womb. The ancient myth thus describes Saturn's realm as the "cut off" (castration) point for the loss of our cosmic/karmic memory which occurs with incarnation and the mystery of the Earth Mother receiving back into her womb all that seeks redemption in the incarnating soul of each human being.

Thus, Saturn's realm (orbit) serves as the guardian at the gate of heaven. Now, we can think back to the true significance of the depiction of "Old Father Time" on the ceiling of the Wies Baroque church sprawled before the gates of heaven with scythe in hand – the "harvester of time" – reaping the "nuggets of gold" from the journey of each human soul.

As the planet of cosmic memory, Saturn becomes the bearer of the memory in a cosmic sense, of the higher will forces or most sacred intentions of the human being's journey in time.

Saturn's Influence in the Shaping of Destiny

Higher Will Forces

In *Meditations on the Tarot* the author describes the five currents of the *will* in relation to the principle of the pentagram as a significant image in the understanding of the five wounds of Christ. By analogy it is **Saturn**'s relationship to the crown chakra in the human being that bears the *thorns* of <u>objectivity</u> bringing <u>conscience</u> to thought.[26]

Thereby the head becomes the *willing* limb of the heart, which is the activating principle of thought. Saturn's call for conscience (*con-science* = *"with knowing"*) entails a thinking with divine order – requiring the marriage of **fire** (cosmic will) and **water**, wherein the *waters* of daily thought and emotional life become <u>stilled</u> (become virginal). Only then can the **Word** (Logos) become incarnate.

This thought brings forward a revolution and evolution (Chronos) from the teaching of Hermes Trismegistus in *Kore Kosmu* – the "Cosmic Virgin" or "Virgin of the World" – calling for the *virginal* "pure intellect". Reintegrated consciousness re-establishes the state of consciousness before the Fall, recalling the words spoken from the Cross, *"Father, into thy hands I commend my spirit."* This is the baptism of fire and water.

---

[25] Rudolf Steiner, *Life Between Death and Rebirth*.
[26] *Meditations on the Tarot*, p.110.

18

With this understanding we can appreciate the significance of the Saturn gesture, with the <u>lifting up</u> of the cup filled with the activity of the spleen (which becomes heavy with the burdens of human thinking and emotional life) to the inspiring call for conscience in the crown chakra. In this way **Saturn** fashions our character and corrects mistakes.

Saturn: In Relationship to the Constellations

Ruler of Capricorn and Aquarius

Saturn is all about the principle of form, structure, and stability, and is the ruler of both <u>Capricorn</u>, the frugal hard-working *Sea-Goat*, and <u>Aquarius</u>, the *Water Bearer*, who heralds the future. Saturn brings the quality of common sense or "good horse sense" and a sense of caution to the chaos of impending change which gives birth to the future – bringing prudence, patience, and economy to the measure and flow of time.

In antiquity the horse signified the ability to maintain thinking, will and purpose in good order – hence the term "good horse sense" well describes the ordering influence of Saturn.

We can understand the importance of Saturn's influence toward the purpose and divine intention of Capricorn, whose work is to bear the *sacrifice* of the head (hardened thinking from the past) in order to think with the heart. Through suffering the wound of *Sagitta*, the *heavenly arrow* and bearer of the Logos (the Sagitta constellation is located in the region of the central *heart* decan of Capricorn), the thoughts and frozen patterns of the past can be freed in order for the *willing limb* of the heart – this being the crown chakra – to *wisely* serve the future.

Likewise, the grace-filled waters of the future which pour forth from the Waterman's Urn of <u>Aquarius</u> must be *tempered* with the wisdom to create new forms of structure and stability inspired by <u>conscience</u> and the working hierarchy of the <u>Seraphim</u>, who inspire deeds which are forged from the flames of pure love.

Saturn and the Pineal Gland

There is an interesting correspondence with the form and function of the **pineal gland**, the gland associated with Saturn, and the working challenges of the two constellations which are ruled by Saturn. The pineal gland is a small endocrine gland in the center of the brain, reddish-gray in color and about the size of a pea. Its function within the wisdom of the endocrine system is toward the production of the sleep-regulating hormone *melatonin*, thus having an obvious relationship to *light* and the rhythms of day and night. The gland becomes stimulated and nourished through the practice of meditation, or "inner listening" that occurs through the seeking of higher guidance, which is an act of the human will being given over to the *light* of *conscience*.

The gland is located at the mid-line between the two hemispheres of the brain and is believed to be important toward the working together of the creative, imaginative faculty of the right brain hemisphere *with* the more practical linear faculties of the left brain hemisphere, bringing balance to one's creative capacity to serve the world.

The pineal gland in the human being can be traced back evolutionarily to the lantern-like organ in reptiles and birds, which in some cases was a fully developed eye. In some animals there was a light-permeable membrane in the scalp, the function of which was to give these animals the use of *light* as a prime *time-giver* in their biological clocks. Could it be that the evolved function of this gland in the human being has to do with the taking in of *supersensible light* in connection with Saturn's function as "time-keeper" for the sacred rhythms of human biography?

With the working challenge of Capricorn being the "overcoming of the *hardened thinking* of the past", it is interesting to note that in plain skull X-rays, the pineal gland is often found to be calcified.[27]

Saturn's Exaltation

Is it any wonder that over time, watchers of the heavens observed that the place of Saturn's *exaltation* is in <u>Libra</u>, in the region of the **Balance Pans** representing the law of Justice? The place of Saturn's exaltation (21° Libra) coincides with the star α Librae (Zubenelgenubi at 20½° Libra) in the first degree of the third decan of Libra. The Arabic word *Zubenelgenubi* means *"the price deficient"*.[28] **Saturn** approaches this place of exaltation – already increasing in strength and influence – when located in the *heart* (central decan) of Libra, in the region of the heavens where <u>Corona</u>, the **Northern Crown**, resides and in the southern hemisphere, the **Southern Cross.**

In the central decan of Libra, Saturn's light shines as a beacon and telling sign of *remembrance* – for the <u>Moon</u> was full in this decan of Libra during the Crucifixion on the Cross. Thus, Christ crucified on the Cross received the *Crown of Heaven* (<u>Corona</u>), the crown of immortal glory, after suffering the *Crown of Thorns*, the will of the heart toward sacrifice, which Saturn *remembers* as sacred.

> *Hold fast to what you have, so that no one may seize your crown.*[29]

This admonition to the Church of Philadelphia reminds us of the heavenly archetypal presence of the constellation of <u>Ophiucus</u>, the **Serpent Bearer,** holding firm the head of the **Serpent** as our responsibility to hold back the serpent forces which rise up to take the crown. For <u>Corona</u>, the **Northern Crown,** like the crown chakra in the human being, represents the crowning achievement of the working *heart* of <u>Libra</u> toward sacrifice, balance, fairness, and justice.

Saturn's exaltation at 21° <u>Libra</u> demonstrates the **Dancing Intellect** of Chronos and serves as a *telling* sign toward the steadying of each human journey. This can be observed in human biography with the Saturn rhythm of 29½ years serving as a threshold time when the shaping force of Saturn's influence comes to bear in the calling forth of true destiny.

Saturn brings a deep-rooted ambition to actualize the potentials inherent at birth. Toward this end Saturn evokes an unrelenting determination to be honest with oneself, allowing no room for self-deception, escapism, or rationalization. Thus Saturn's influence has been likened to "cosmic hands" which bring the capacity to remold one's way of being.[30]

---

[27] Pineal gland – Wikipedia, the free encyclopedia, http://en.wikipedia.org/wiki/Pineal_gland
[28] Joseph A. Seiss, *The Gospel In The Stars*, p. 35.
[29] *The Revelation to John* 3:11 – admonition to the Church of Philadelphia.
[30] Jacques Dorsan, *The Planets in the Houses, The Twelve Astrological Houses must be counted clockwise*.

Saturn and Psyche: Workings in the Soul

Here we have the expression of everything which is most profound, the contemplative, meditative element. The human being is here turned upon himself; I will describe it as deep contemplation.[31]

Saturn is often associated with the soul conditions of melancholy and depression – thereby playing an important role in the economy of the psyche. Freud described melancholy as a time of external inactivity and internal labor – a time when the ability to focus attention upon the outer world dissipates. The cure, according to Marsilio Ficino, is to give oneself over with heart and soul to divine contemplation.[32]

This is an appeal for the **reason of light** rather than the light of reason – a recommendation brought to expression by Marsilio Ficino, the Renaissance "astro-musicologist" referred to as the "Physician of the Soul" by Thomas Moore in his book *The Planets Within*. Ficino described the "reason of light" as the "crowning element" of the psyche and its prime spiritual nourishment. Light comes first, then our intelligence, because our powers of reasoning are only a participation in a higher intelligence.[33]

The Saturn gesture beckons us toward the process of inner reflection, requiring an emptying (becoming unbiased) in order to reflect with the reason of light (conscience). This is a promise which brings imaginative appreciation to the process of the endings and beginnings of life's journeying. For in truth both are a movement and a continuation – frozen and defined only in the dead thinking patterns from the past.

The Well-Tuned Interval: the Alchemy of the Black Sun

The ancient idea of harmony as the "well-tuned" interval brings a new perspective to life's *turnings* – bringing the fluidity of movement as a ready prescription for the wholeness of possibilities – the process of **Becoming,** which has much to do with Chronos. Marsilio Ficino characterizes the contemplative influence of Saturn as evoking *"an influence which draws one into the center of each thing to be investigated and stretches to the heights those things to be comprehended."*[34]

Ficino's profound observations shed new *light* on the significance of the Saturn eurythmy sound and planetary gesture which stretch the soul from the depths to the heights in a continuum of movement.

James Hillman, one of the foremost contemporary thinkers and contributors to archetypal depth psychology, describes the activity of the Saturn influence in the human soul as a healing balance to the widespread *"manic activism of the modern world"* and at the same time calls for a *"dying to the wild world of literalism"*.[35] This requires a learning to *behold* the movement and soul content of one's daily life as symbolic imagery which serves as container or *holy* vessel for the redeeming nature of spiritual truth.

---

[31] Rudolf Steiner, *Eurythmy as Visible Speech*, p. 119, describing the quality of Saturn.
[32] Thomas Moore, *The Planets Within, The Astrological Psychology of Marsilio Ficino*, p. 171.
[33] Ibid. p. 91.
[34] Ibid. p. 172.
[35] Ibid. p. 171.

The sanctity of the human soul requires the necessity of turning inward. A *turning* or tilling of the fertile soil of one's secret garden brings a ripening to the harvest of earthly life. The soul becomes the container for the *marrow* of deep reflection. Here the imagery of imagination becomes primordial, refined, virginal and sacred.

The higher will forces called forth by the call of Saturn *"offer a way through and beyond the shallowness of the present"*.[36] Our earthly task is to carry, forge and refine Saturn's lead into pure gold – which is the alchemical work of the soul toward transformation.

This work is called the alchemy of the *"Black Sun"*.[37]

Saturn Metal — Lead

Lead, the Saturn metal, mirrors the spiritual qualities of its planetary archetype, having to do with form, boundary, our bony skeletal structure, and memory in the recording of the passage of time. Further images reminiscent of "Old Father Time" reveal themselves in reference to the accumulative effects of the Saturn metal upon the environment.

True to Saturn's reputation for inspiring stability in the character of the human being – the Saturn metal **lead** marks the boundary of stability on the Periodic Table of Elements. All elements above lead are radioactive and thus are subject to decay. The natural process of decay stops with the element of lead.

Age, therefore, can be measured according to the proportion of radioactivity to lead isotope content, i.e. lead isotopes in rocks are the *end* product of radioactive decay.

Saturn's steadying influence in the *building* of human character is also mirrored in one of lead's earliest uses. Just as Saturn's "gravitas" working in the soul is helpful toward holding one's balance and uprightness in life – so too the lead weight "plumbum" (Latin word for lead) was used to indicate the plumb-line or vertical line in building.

Lead, which is the "basest" of the traditional seven metals, was the first to be extracted from the earth's ores some 9000 years ago, and so the use of lead has *endured* over many years. Just as Saturn *tempers* the psyche – working to slow down the modern-day "manic" craving for life experience – so too, lead has traditionally been used in gasoline fuel to slow the combustion process, also in house paints to retard deterioration, and even in English pewter (a combination of tin and lead), which is revered for its *enduring* non-tarnish quality.

Alas, for the ale in English pewter drinking mugs, as well as for our own drinking water supply, which has traditionally been carried through lead pipes – for the cumulative effects of lead can be highly toxic and like Saturn definitely have a *sobering* aspect. *"No other metal tends so much to form insoluble compounds."*[38]

Industrial Age illnesses, manifesting themselves with headaches, fatigue, irritability and depression, are all reminiscent of a "saturnine humor". Unfortunately, and owing to a lack of human wisdom, Saturn's quality of enduring strength has sadly led to a poisoning of the atmosphere, resulting in high levels of lead toxicity in the human bloodstream.

---

[36] Quoted from Thomas Moore, *The Planets Within*, p. 171.
[37] Ibid. p. 166.
[38] Nick Kollerstrom, The Alchemy Web Site, *http://www.levity.com/alchemy/kollerstrom_saturn.html* – The information on lead on pages 22 and 23 is a synthesis and paraphrasing of the research given in this article.

With the wisdom of hindsight inspired by Saturn, we now know that lead in the bloodstream impairs the development of the central nervous system during the growth process in early childhood.

When in dismay we say "get the lead out" – perhaps Chronos is speaking through "Old Father Time". Today's "heavy metal" youths could well be the result of the "harvesting of time" – with the cumulative effects of lead resulting in the poor concentration, learning disabilities, instability in social behavior, and hyper-activity so prevalent in school age children today – and paradoxically all are *inversions* of Saturn's steadying influence.

Saturn, as the highest and most distant of the seven classical planets, works to the deepest level – right down to the bony structure of the human being – as does the Saturn metal lead, which stores in the bone tissue. In fact if you could see only that part of a person where lead accumulates, you would see a skeleton. Saturn depicted as Chronos – "Old Father Time" – traditionally appeared as a skeletal figure holding an hourglass, and true to the 29½-year rotational rhythm of Saturn, it takes about 30 years to flush lead out of the system.

Modern-day legislation has resulted in the removal of lead from pipes, paint, and automobile fuel, which has greatly reduced lead in the human bloodstream. However, the accumulation over time continues, and Saturn's metal finds its "ever-ready" use in the durability of batteries, which are wisely recycled (90% in Europe), as well as in cathode ray tubes used to protect the human being from the harmful radiation of today's "memory companions", the television and computer screens. The glass of the cathode ray tube contains 23% lead oxide!

The most prevalent use of lead today is in car batteries which are rechargeable. In California, zero emission electric buses can be recharged up to 50% in five minutes.

If we consider that Saturn, as the "grim reaper for the harvest of time", records and remembers the wisdom of hindsight, as well as the "sobering" effect of Saturn's influence in human biography, perhaps we will become wiser regarding the proper use of lead in the future. For as it stands today, Saturn *leads* the way in warning against metal pollution in the atmosphere and signals us to right our ways to come into a proper alignment with cosmic realities.

Saturn: "The Lord of the Rings"

The name **Saturn** is related to the noun satus (*seed corn*) and the verb serere (*to sow*). The ancient Assyrians referred to Saturn as Lubadsagush which means "oldest of the sheep". The Hindu root word is Sani, meaning "slow". In the Hindu tradition Saturn is the "Son of the Sun God" and is imagined as Chaya, meaning "shadow" and also "King of Dharma". This Hindu imagination of Saturn has been mirrored recently by the newest images of Saturn coming from the Hubble Space Telescope, which reveal that the outermost part of the *shadow* that Saturn casts on its rings is orange, similar to the color of the Moon during a deep lunar eclipse. This latest image sheds light on the clairvoyant gaze of the early star watchers which resulted in the Saturn symbol with the *shadowed* Moon beneath the Cross ♄.

Of the planets in our solar system, Saturn is second only to Jupiter in size. Saturn emits a slightly yellowish light. Like Jupiter, Saturn radiates twice the energy that it receives from the Sun due to slight continuing contractions of the planet's gases, bringing an imagination of the planet as a living being *breathing* in response to the Sun, revealing the planet's respiratory system.

Saturn takes 29.4578 years to orbit the Sun, and true to the ancient star watchers' description of the "winding" planet, Saturn's path is not circular but rather "looped" or "winding". Every twenty years the loop meets Jupiter (conjunction) or is in opposition (on the opposite side of the zodiac from Jupiter). The conjunction is an event that is known to *seed* new cultural impulses, which then come into full *flower* around the time of the opposition some ten years later.

Until the eighteenth century Saturn marked the limit of the planetary system. As the farthest known body, its orbit was imagined to be coiled round and thus enclosed the known moving universe. This conveys the image of the **auroburo**, the symbol for eternity, with the snake biting its tail. It was not until 1656 that it was discovered that the planet itself was wrapped in the coils of its own ring system.[39]

Galileo was the first to view the rings in 1610. However, they appeared to him as two small orbs attached to a large one. Later, when the rings turned edgewise (due to the changing tilt of Saturn's axis) the companions disappeared from view, causing Galileo to lament, *"Has Saturn swallowed his children?"*[40]

The rings of Saturn (seven in number) are among the most beautiful objects that can be seen from a telescope – with a surface texture appearing like snow.[41] Saturn's beautiful rings are what set it apart from the other planets in our solar system. It is the most extensive and complex ring system in our solar system, extending hundreds of thousands of miles from the planet.

Among Saturn's unique features are its numerous moons – the largest being **Titan**, which is the fifteenth of Saturn's 34 moons. Titan, which is larger than the planet Mercury and almost as large as Mars, is the second-largest moon in the solar system after Jupiter's moon Ganymede. The Cassini spacecraft dropped Huygens, a robot probe, through Titan's cloudy atmosphere on January 14, 2005, which then began transmitting data and images back to the Earth. The images of Titan's striking landscape reveal high terrain cut by deep channels – an Earth-like desert topography. Titan's surface is shaped by winds, liquid, and tectonic forces – as is the Earth's surface – but under far more exotic conditions.

On July 26, 2003 Saturn reached **perihelion**, its closest approach to the Sun. Then, on December 31, 2003, the ringed planet was at **perigee** (its closest approach to the Earth) and was in opposition to the Sun. On that date it was 748.3 million miles (1.2 billion kilometers) from the Earth – the closest approach to the Earth than at any time in three decades – and shone at its brightest magnitude -0.5 due to the planet's proximity and the dramatic 25° tilt of Saturn's rings. Among the visible stars only Sirius and Canopus were brighter at that time.

Saturn will not come closer until January 2034. However, on June 27 in 2018 – the time of the next most significant opposition of Saturn and the Sun – Saturn will be 841 million miles from the Earth, almost 100 million miles further away from the Earth than at its closest approach on December 31, 2003.

---

[39] Saturn's rings were discovered by Christiaan Huygens in 1656 and made known in his *Systema Saturnium* in 1659.
[40] http://www.space.com/scienceastronomy/hubble_saturn_030909.html.
[41] *The Solar System*, Scientific American Book, p.105.

Like the Earth, due to its tilt, Saturn has seasons. Observations of Saturn's wind conditions over the past twenty years have indicated a dramatic decrease of 40%.[42] We see this mirrored in the dramatic events of the last twenty years on Earth – signifying the "winds of change" that Saturn has inspired.

"The Sun Behold at the Midnight Hour"   (Rudolf Steiner)[43]

We have a *telling* image with Saturn's appearance opposite the Sun on New Year's Eve 2003. As though bowing to the Sun, Saturn appeared in full radiance between the two stars marking the legs of Gemini. Tilted on his axis, revealing himself to be "Lord of the Rings", Saturn made himself known to be aligned with the archetypal image of brotherhood (Gemini).

This means that on December 31, 2003 in the northern hemisphere Saturn rose in the East just as the Sun set in the West and reached its highest point in the southern sky at midnight – the midnight hour!

> *For the divine Logos dances (<u>choreuei</u>) in a circle, which most men call fortune; and so it flows along, turning from city to city, people to people, land to land, and distributing to some what belonged to others, and to all what belonged to all.*[44]

As above, so below – all things in right timing. Might this be a heralding of the changes we are experiencing in today's world, a change resulting in a redistribution of wealth among the brother/sisterhood of the Earth's peoples?

With these thoughts in mind, the winter of 2003/2004 might be called the "winter of Saturn". For the world is in turmoil after the impulse toward change inspired by Mars during the spring and summer of 2003. At that time Mars made its closest approach to the Earth for some 60,000 years. As Mars was drawing near, the fury of war (the U.S.-led invasion of Iraq) brought the brotherhood of nations to an urgent plea for peace, and the *willing* forces of the human heart were once again awakened.

Saturday: Saturn Day

In brotherhood Saturn bids us to remember the word "quiet", which in Hebrew means "Sabbath". This is Saturday (Saturn's Day) in the Hebrew tradition. The *quiet* that is found in the virginal, pure, inner space of the heart aspires toward the hidden knowledge revealed in the temporal passage of time and thus requires an attentiveness to the "eternal now". Through the opening of the crown chakra, the listening heart comes into connection with Saturn's "reason of light".

Perhaps Saturn's drawing near will resonate within us as a call for deep contemplation, allowing our heart (corresponding to the Sun) to <u>behold</u> – to *be* and to *hold* that which is sacred in the midnight hour.

---

[42] "Hubble Gets Superb View of Saturn and Rings".
   http://www.space.com/scienceastronoms/hubble_saturn_030909.html.
[43] See the planetary verse for Saturn in Appendix IV: *Music and Verses for the Seven Classical Planets.*
[44] Philo, *The Unchangeableness of God*, 176 – quoted from James Miller, *Measures of Wisdom*, p. 125.

Cosmic *Eurythmy*
"In the image and likeness…"

Sun: *"You appear in the heavenly blue"*[45]

Chakra:	Heart
Organ:	Heart
Gland:	Thymus
Metal:	Gold
Color:	White or gold
Tones:	A and C[46]

After the night comes the day. Night consciousness (Saturn), which is associated with our bony fiber, the bare bones or architecture of our essential self – our connection to the realm of the Seraphim and the fiery realm of the Father – is followed by *day consciousness* and the warming rays of the **Sun**.

Following upon the first stage of planetary evolution (now referred to as Ancient Saturn), the next stage of planetary evolution brings the warmth of the Sun. This means that the material substance of our solar system – once voluminous gas that expanded all the way out to the orbit of Saturn – began a process of *inhalation*. As in a birth, there occurred a cosmic contraction and the atmosphere of Ancient Saturn condensed to the orbit of the planet Jupiter. This contraction left behind (*gave birth to*) the planet Saturn and signified the transition from the Ancient Saturn stage to the Ancient Sun stage of evolution. During this stage the Earth, as yet unmaterialized, having been a part of the primal solar nebula which contracted from the orbit of Saturn, remained as an embryo in the womb of a giant, radiant Sun filling the entire space of our solar system up to the orbit now traced out by Jupiter.

These were called the days of **Ancient Sun**,[47] which served toward the creation of the *etheric/life* body of the human being. These days were later mirrored in the early culture of the ancient Egyptians, whose consciousness (at least in earlier times) was oriented toward the *aura* (etheric/life body) of our Sun. *"Aura"* comes from the same root word as *"aurora"* or dawn, signifying the beginning of a new day. The root word *"aur"* coming from the Persian word for light is also related to the Greek word *"aura"* meaning breath.

From this close relationship or attunement to the Sun came the naming of the days of the week, which were named after the planetary stages of evolution by the Egyptian culture and remain so today – with the planetary week which is honored around the entire globe. Thus the great plan of evolution has been preserved for humanity in the naming of the days of the week: Saturn's day, Sun's day, Moon's day, etc.

---

[45] See the planetary verse for the Sun in Appendix IV: *Music and Verses for the Seven Classical Planets.*
[46] The correspondences are tabulated in Appendix III: *Correspondences to the Seven Classical Planets.* See also Appendix II: *Musical Tones and the Planets.*
[47] See Appendix I for further discussion of the Planetary Stages of Evolution.

Now, following the sequence of the days of the week – after the *quiet* stilling of the holy Sabbath, Saturday (Saturn Day) – we arrive at the <u>Sun</u> day of existence (**Sunday**) with the light of cosmic reason (Saturn) now warmed in the birthing womb of the <u>human heart</u>, the physical organ which corresponds to the Sun.

The Eurythmy Sun Gesture

The Sun gesture in eurythmy expresses this archetypal truth. The arms become the wings of the heart as the right arm extends out diagonally forward, reaching up toward day consciousness – the world of **Becoming,** which is attuned to the cosmic realm – while simultaneously the left arm extends diagonally back, reaching down toward the unconscious which holds all the mysteries inherent in our life on Earth. If this gesture would be held without setting both arms into a circulating movement, it would be the eurythmy gesture for the sound "I" (pronounced "ee" in eurythmy). However, with the eurythmy gesture for the Sun, the arms are set in a rotating movement by way of love streaming from the heart chakra, radiating out through the arms and hands, corresponding to the aura of the Sun, raying out love throughout the solar system.

> *You appear in the heavenly blue* [48]

The eurythmy Sun gesture is a living metamorphosis of the formative process of the Saturn sound "U" ("oo"). For now the human being stands fully incarnated upon the Earth, *crowned* by Saturn, with the dance of the cosmos living in the marrow of the bones. Now the "higher will", the divine "I" of human existence, connects heaven and earth, through the power of love streaming from the heart, radiating up through the ***right*** arm moving <u>clockwise</u> and down through the ***left*** arm circling <u>counter-clockwise</u>.

According to the hermetic (Egyptian) teaching *"as above, so below"*, the human heart corresponds to the Sun. Just as the Sun is at the center of the solar system, so the heart is the central organ of the human being.

Through the Sun gesture we *remember* Saturn consciousness, as the human heart becomes the love-filled mediating organ of perception, drawing the light of conscience (Saturn) from the darkness of the "midnight hour" of deep inwardness into the light of day consciousness, filled with unconditional love for all creation. Thus the heart *serves* as guide toward the fulfilling of destiny in the daily walk of life.

There is a building-up process with the Sun gesture, beginning with the firm grounding of the higher will forces of the "I" gesture coming into movement with the harmony of the spheres. Now the straight line and the circle progress into the *alternating* pulse of the spiraling orbital pattern of the choral dance (<u>choreia</u>) of the cosmos, as the arms move in alternating circles – the right arm circles clockwise, attuned to cosmic time, while simultaneously the left arm is moving counter-clockwise. With the alternating circles of the eurythmy Sun gesture, the wisdom from above is "stepped down" into the "daily bread" of existence on Earth.

---

[48] Adapted from Akhenaten`s *"Hymn To The Sun"* – see the planetary verse for the Sun in Appendix IV: *Music and Verses for the Seven Classical Planets.*

The Sun Sound "AU"

The eurythmy gesture for the Sun *sound* "AU" ("ow")[49] brings these two worlds – heaven and earth – together in the human heart. Now the *cup* of Saturn becomes married to the warmth of the human heart. To form the Sun *sound* gesture, which we use to describe the cosmic dance of the Sun, the arms fold in toward the heart chakra. The left hand is held folded and gently cupped facing the heart, bringing the fullness of earthly life to the heart, and the right hand covers the left (as with a soft embrace). Thus one hand gently enfolds the other – expressing the protective *mantle* of our connection to heaven. This "AU" gesture is a sacred gesture that, when held for a time, activates a flow of light and warmth in the heart chakra.

The Midnight Sun: Steiner taught two versions of the "AU" sound, an *inner* and an *outer* expression of the sound. For the cosmic dance of the Sun, we use the inner expression. This is referred to as the "small AU" in eurythmy and expresses the quality of the *inner Midnight Sun.*[50]

Cosmic Dance Form for the Sun

The planetary dance of our Sun weaves a lemniscatory (figure 8) pattern on its journey around the Galactic Center, which takes about 227 million years. As it moves along its path through cosmic space, the Sun alternates in the time span of one year between a movement toward the Central Sun, and a movement away from the Central Sun.[51] Because the Sun is in constant motion, moving clockwise around the Central Sun, the "figure 8" traced out each year progresses in a clockwise direction – creating a progressive lemniscate.

The choreography for the planetary dance of the Sun in eurythmy honors the lemniscatory path of the Sun. When dancing this choreography, the circle that one traces out in the clockwise direction (as one moves back with the Sun gesture) can be inwardly felt as being related to the movement of the Sun as it weaves toward the cosmic realm of the Father, whose heart is identified with the Central Sun in our galaxy. In continuing the lemniscate, the circle that one traces out in the counter-clockwise direction (as one moves forward with the "AU" gesture) can be inwardly experienced as a movement toward the Earth, bringing the light and *regenerative* life gathered from the fiery heart of the galaxy, the Galactic Center, and from the formative archetypal life of the zodiac comprising fixed stars, all receiving that which emanates from the Central Sun.[52]

---

[49] "*Au*" is from the root word "*aur*" as in "*aura*" (surrounding the human being), "*aurora*" (dawn or light bringer) and also "*aurum*" (Latin for gold, which is the metal corresponding to the Sun). In eurythmy "AU" is pronounced "ow" (as in "how").

[50] For the outer gesture of "AU" the extended arms (approximately parallel to one another) circle clockwise over the head from the left to the right and then circle below from right to left, following the movement of the daily rising and setting of the Sun. Except when below, the palms are open and facing forward, radiating the warmth of the Sun toward the Earth, in the spirit of the words "*Feel the whole world*", which relate to the Sun form in eurythmy.

[51] Our Sun, in tracing its progressive lemniscatory orbit around the Central Sun, continually receives light, life, and love from the Divine Heart at the center of our galaxy. See Appendix V: *The Galactic Center* for more information about the Central Sun.

[52] All the stars, including our Sun, rotate in a *clockwise direction* around the Galactic Center (**Central Sun**). This means that all the stars in the heavens, including all the stars comprising the twelve signs of the zodiac, are moving *clockwise*. For this reason the general direction of movement in all the cosmic dances of the zodiac is *clockwise*.

With the Sun form in cosmic dance, as with all the planetary forms, the dancers move in a circle of **community** – circling together in a counter-clockwise direction, following the apparent movement of the Sun through the signs of the zodiac. Therefore with the completion of each "figure 8", the dancers must take care to *progress* further toward the right in the movement around the circle. This lemniscate thus moves in the *opposite* direction to the Sun's path through cosmic space around the Central Sun (Galactic Center). The counter-clockwise movement of the Sun's cosmic dance is in the *same direction* as that of all the other planets, which is the way the Sun, Moon, and planets are observed to move as they progress through the zodiac. On this account all seven planetary forms necessitate a predominate movement to the right in their overall direction.

As we move this lemniscatory path together in practicing the cosmic dance of the Sun, we experience the harmonizing effect of the constancy and measured cadence of the Sun, which has been likened to a "Great Cosmic Sunflower", steadily unfolding the wisdom of the twelve petals of the constellations in the course of the year – living each measured step of the timepiece of the cosmos.

The stepping of the lemniscatory pattern of the cosmic dance of the Sun brings to expression the incarnational path of revolution, involution and evolution as the dancers weave between the cosmic realm, circling back in a clockwise movement in rhythm with cosmic time – forming the Sun gesture – then forward, in toward Mother Earth, now moving counter-clockwise, gathering the richness of earthly life into the warmth of the human heart forming the sound "AU".

In the language of music this is the "well tempered interval" – the function of the human heart toward the "tempering" (harmonizing) of the intervals and turnings of our earthly existence.

Sun *Eurythmy* Form

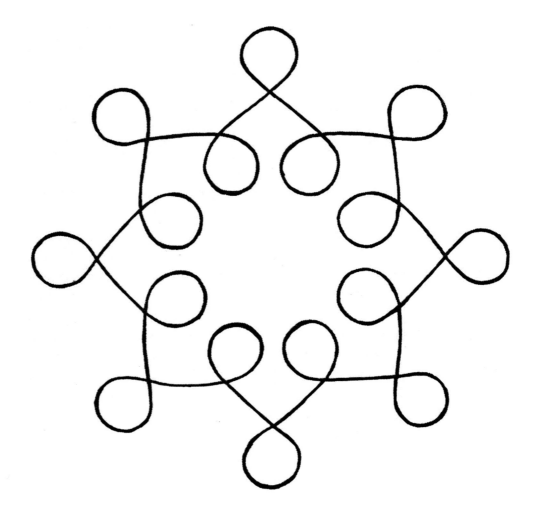

In practicing the stepping of the lemniscatory, figure 8 pattern – the number of steps taken for the completion of the two circles of the figure 8, necessarily depend upon the tempo of the music. In the initial instructing of the form a twelve-step archetype is preferable, with six steps moving clockwise back and around to complete the first circle, followed by a crossover step as the beginning of the six steps moving counter-clockwise forward and around to complete the second circle. (Alternative: eight steps for each circle.)

When practicing without music, an anapest rhythm of short, short, long – short, short, long is appropriate, as its 1 to 4 rhythm corresponds to the rhythm of the human heart and lungs in relationship to the cosmic rhythm of the movement of the Sun.

In all cases it will be necessary to make a crossover step at the midpoint of each circle, front and back, in order to maintain one's forward orientation toward the center of the circle.

Cosmic Dance of the Sun

"Feel the whole world"

The planetary dance of the Sun weaves a lemniscatory pattern around the zodiac moving *alternately* in toward the Earth and back out toward the zodiac and beyond the zodiac to the Great Central Sun, the center of the galaxy.

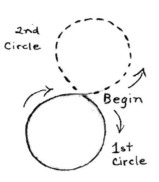

Mastering the form:
Imagine yourself at the center point of the lemniscatory pattern with one circle behind and one in front of you.

Shoulders first!
Trace the pattern of the two circles with your shoulders while standing only. The orientation is always forward toward the center of the form.

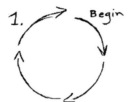

The backward circle, moving <u>clockwise</u>, follows the dance of the Sun as it *circles **back** toward the Central Sun,* the heart of our galaxy.

One traces out the circle behind by leaning first **back** to the right, circling around clockwise to return to the starting point.

Stay attuned to the movement of the shoulders.

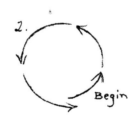

The forward <u>counter-clockwise</u> circle traces the pattern of the Sun as it circles **in** toward the Earth, *raying out life and warmth* drawn by our Sun from the Central Sun.

Now trace the forward circle by leaning **forward** to the right, then circling around counter-clockwise returning back to the center point of the lemniscate.

Stepping the form:
Circle to the right, **back** and around clockwise, coming full circle <u>*slightly to the right*</u> of the beginning point at the center of the lemniscate.

Now circle **forward**, starting to the right and around counter-clockwise, returning <u>slightly to the right</u> of the center point.

Continue the form, stepping in a lemniscatory pattern moving always toward the right.

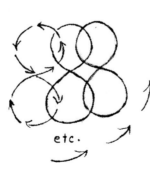

Anapest rhythm:
This can be stepped in an anapest rhythm of short, short long – short, short, long (see preceding description).

The long beat allows time for the cross-over point of the feet when reversing directions forward and back, as described above.

The orientation is always forward toward the center of the dancing circle (the Earth).

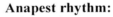
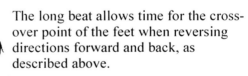

31

Cosmic Dance of the Sun

"Feel the whole world"

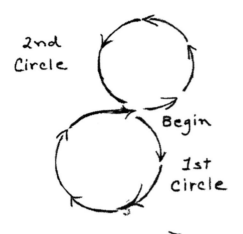

Just as the human heart is the harmonizing organ of the human being, the cosmic dance of the Sun is extremely balanced and has a harmonizing effect. The mood of the Sun's movement, with which we identify in the cosmic dance of the Sun, is that of profound love for all of creation.

The dancers imagine themselves immersed in radiant *white* light while dancing to Bach's music in G major, "Jesus, Joy of Man's Desire" or Bach's "Pastorale in F" transcribed by Dinu Lipatti.

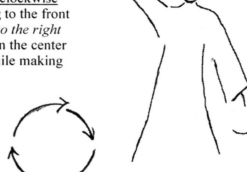

Movement:
Circle *back,* moving <u>clockwise</u> to the right, returning to the front of the circle *slightly to the right* of the starting point in the center of the lemniscate, while making the Sun gesture.

Sun Gesture:
Extend right arm up (diagonally forward) and left arm down (diagonally back); simultaneously rotate arms: right arm clockwise, left arm counter-clockwise (*radiating love* from the heart, connecting heaven and Earth), while circling back around the circle.

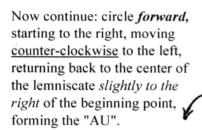

Now continue: circle *forward,* starting to the right, moving <u>counter-clockwise</u> to the left, returning back to the center of the lemniscate *slightly to the right* of the beginning point, forming the "AU".

Continue stepping the form in a lemniscatory pattern, moving always to the right.

Sun Sound "AU"
While circling forward and around, draw hands into the region of the heart, right hand cupped loosely over the left, which is closed softly over the heart chakra (drawing the Earth, creation, and life experience into the human and cosmic heart).

Sun: "The Well-Tempered Interval"

Inner Sun

The forces of the **Sun** work most directly upon the heart and heart chakra of the human being.[53] In the Hindu tradition the heart chakra is referred to as the 12 petal lotus flower, which in number alone suggests an etheric connection to the streamings of the twelve constellations as well as the day and night rhythm of the Sun.

The Sun functions as the heart center of the solar system. Correspondingly, the etheric streamings of the Sun bring vitality to the functioning of the human heart, which is attuned to the rhythm of the cosmic heart (Sun). The 72 beats per minute of the heart correspond to the movement of the vernal point through one degree of the zodiac in 72 years.[54]

In this way the human heart functions as the *inner* Sun for the human being. Just as the Sun is the heart of the solar system, bringing life to the Earth, so too the human heart brings life to the human being through the revivifying process of *receiving* the venous life (oxygen depleted blood) and sending it to the lungs for new breath – then to *receive* it once more to be re-circulated through the arteries and tiny capillary systems, which vivify the human organism.

Cosmic Mirroring

Correspondingly the Central Sun, the fiery heart of our Milky Way galaxy, brings life to our Sun and all the stars of our galaxy, each one of which is a Sun like our Sun.[55] By way of analogy, it is through the *receptive* quality of the Sun that the divine breath of creation is *received* and re-circulated throughout the solar system. This archetypal cosmic process is mirrored in the circulatory movement of the blood, with its center in the human heart.

Following upon this analogy of the heart serving as a vessel, it becomes apparent that in order to *receive* there must be a space, an emptiness to fill. Thus for the *raying* in of spirit, there must be a silent place in the heart. The heart must be made ready in order to be filled. So too with the receiving of the blood. There must be the steady rhythm of emptying the vessel of the heart, in order for the heart to be filled.

The *inner* alchemy of the human heart serves to transform the condition of the blood, to "temper" the incoming *sound* quality (inbreath/venous blood), before breathing out once more, supplying the circulatory system with the *wine* of vitality – freshly oxygenated arterial blood.

---

[53] The chakras are organs within the astral body of the human being. The astral body is the subtle body which is seen clairvoyantly as an aura of color surrounding the human being. The different colors express soul qualities which live in the conscious/subconscious nature of the individual. See Appendix III.

[54] The vernal point is the Sun's location at the vernal equinox (March 20/21), when the Sun is crossing the celestial equator to begin its ascending journey in declination in the Northern Hemisphere. The vernal point is currently located at 5° Pisces and is moving back at the rate of 1° in 72 years towards Aquarius, to enter Aquarius in AD 2375 (= start of the Age of Aquarius).This slow retrograde movement of the vernal point through the zodiac (1° in 72 years) is called the precession of the equinoxes.

[55] See Appendix V: *The Galactic Center*.

The Sun mirrors this process in a constancy of activity which could be likened to breathing – a breathing in of the divine breath from the fiery heart of the Central Sun, while at the same time *tempering* or stepping down the fiery intensity of the Central Sun in the *raying* out of revivifying substance to the whole of the solar system.

What might this mirroring of the functioning of the human heart tell us about the Sun as a receiving vessel, a space – indeed an emptiness? A recent book puts forward the idea that the Sun at its core is an empty space[56], supporting Rudolf Steiner's suggestion that the Sun's core is emptier than that which surrounds it,[57] which is the raying out of the surrounding etheric body of the Sun, expressed in the fluctuations in the Sun's **corona** (aura).

Now, as our understanding of the divine archetype of the Sun as the heart of the solar system becomes more and more apparent, we can begin to envisage the human heart not just as a pump to move the blood, but as the highest entity in human life, which mirrors the divine processes at work in the galaxy. The heart may thus be conceived of as a living being with the purpose to *serve* divine existence.

Respiration: Sun's Corona

The Sun's corona can be seen in all its wonder and magnitude during a solar eclipse, when the disk of the Sun is covered by the face of the Moon, revealing an extraordinary raying out of light, which can be imagined to extend millions of miles beyond the Sun.

Astronomers connect the raying out of the Sun's corona with sunspot activity (which could be likened to the heartbeat or breathing of the Sun) that varies, but seems to normally reveal an 11-year cycle. With each heartbeat or pulsing, the Sun circulates material around the solar system.

In photos these sunspots appear like vortices which disappear into the dark center of the Sun's disk – an image which is similar to clairvoyant depictions of the human chakra system appearing as astral vortices interpenetrating the physical body.

The Sun's corona (aura) has been discovered to have temperatures of up to three million degrees, compared to approximately six thousand degrees on the Sun's disk (photosphere). Thus, the corona is infinitely more active than the disk itself. The activity of the corona indeed indicates the breathing of the Sun in the 11-year cycle of sunspot activity. Thus, the Sun's *in-breath*, when the corona takes on a more or less spherical form, coincides with the maximum occurrence of sunspots, and the *out-breath*, when the corona appears to ray out in all directions, coincides with the minimum occurrence.

Tempering: "Stepping Down the Tempo"

The atmosphere of the Sun's corona (etheric body) is arranged in alternating rings (bands) of positive and negative charged particles which are, according to the NASA Flight Center, *alternately* blown away approximately every eleven years when the solar magnetic field reverses, and the poles switch places – an activity which can be likened to a *"snake shedding its skin"*.[58]

---

[56] Georg Blattmann, *The Sun: The Ancient Mysteries and a New Physics* – see the chapters on the interior of the Sun.
[57] Rudolf Steiner, *Man: Hieroglyph of the Universe*, p. 47: *"The Sun is a hollow space ..."*
[58] John Whitfield, "Solar storms trip magnetic flip," *Nature News Service* (Macmillan Magazines: London, 2003).

Here we can witness the Sun in a constancy of **renewal and becoming**, for the cumulative effect of more than 1000 solar flares a year is to carry the old magnetic field out into space, leaving a new one behind. The charged particles which have been thus ejected from the Sun serve to cocoon the family of planets with charged particles which shield the solar system from harmful rays, reminding us of the eurythmy "AU" gesture in the planetary dance of the Sun.

> *Presenting himself to all, to all equally he offers his embrace.*

> (Gregory of Nazianzus, *Oratio theologica* II, xxix; *Oratio* 28.29)[59]

This is an archetypal example of the Sun's *service* as the heart of the solar system – an exquisite demonstration of the "law of cooperation for existence", which is described in *Meditations on the Tarot* as a complementary perspective to Darwin's theory of the "struggle for existence."[60]

Participating in the Divine Breath

Beinsa Douno, the Bulgarian spiritual teacher who shepherded "Paneurythmy" into the world, describes this activity of *cooperation,* which manifests in the constancy of life-bringing *breath* that weaves between the Earth and Sun and the Central Sun beyond, as an activity of *respiration* which alternates between dawn and dusk, in correspondence to the rhythm of the rising and the setting of the Sun.

Following upon the awareness of the alternating bands of negative and positive charged particles, which comprise the etheric/life body of the Sun, Beinsa Douno describes a process of stepping down that occurs between the Sun and the Central Sun, wherein the Sun *receives* the originating breath of divine love from the Central Sun at the heart of our galaxy, which is then stepped down or *polarized* through the alternating currents of the Sun's etheric field (corona). This yields a current of *regeneration* which is principally positive in charge, and it is this positively charged *breath* which the Earth receives as an *inbreath* during the first hours of a newly born day, with the most intensity at sunrise. This is the time when the Earth's atmosphere is the most receptive, having emptied herself during the night in the absence of the Sun. This divine attraction reverses at dusk when there occurs an *outbreath* of unused charged particles from the Earth, which is received by the Sun and ultimately returns to the Central Sun, where it is purified and made whole once again. And so the dance continues, a *breathing in* and a *breathing out* of the Earth together with the living body of the cosmos.[61]

The Great Cosmic Eye

In an eclipse of the Sun there are moments when the Moon's passage across the face of the solar disk creates an image of the Sun as an enormous cosmic eye looking around his kingdom, an optical illusion which reminds one of the *risus coeli* (the "Laughter of the Sky"). Here we see the Sun as the "eye of heaven" – which Marsilio Ficino, the Renaissance philosopher, calls "the twinkle of the eye of the cosmos" – clued in on the secrets and underlying purposes of existence.[62]

---

[59] Quoted from: James Miller, *Measures of Wisdom*, p. 353.
[60] *Meditations on the Tarot*, p. 208.
[61] Beinsa Douno, *Dans Le Royaume de la Nature Vivante*.
[62] Marsilio Ficino was an astronomer, mathematician, and Hermetic musicologist during the Renaissance, who was highly influential in the Medici "Platonic Academy" in Florence; see Thomas Moore, *The Planets Within*, p. 92.

If we follow this clue further we can discover that the meridian of the human heart has a pathway which passes from the system of the heart up into the *interior* workings of the eye, a pathway of connection between the human heart and brain. Just as the corona of the Sun creates both a brilliance and a radiance, which manifests everywhere, so too it is the liveliness of the human heart which can be seen in the look of the eye.[63]

We gain understanding of the condition of the human heart by remembering the liveliness of the Sun, wherein the *shining* radiance comes not from accumulation but rather a void. Like the Sun, it is within the stillness of the *quiet* which resides within the inner sanctum of the heart that the *light* of true intelligence resides – allowing all the transformations of bodily life which are but a reflection of the inherent aptitude of the wisdom of creation.

Meditations on the Tarot describes the marriage of the heart and head as a partnership which enables the head and heart to *participate* with eternity.[64]

From the void in the heart comes an *inbreath* of spiritual "lumen", which then rays out as an *outbreath* in our actions and daily life. As an example of this divine presence in the heart it is known that saints radiate all the force or strength of the spirit, which has an effect all around them – on vegetation, animals and people. This is true *presence* and, as with the Sun, everyone lives better by these effects.

Sun ☉: The Wisdom of the Heart

> *The nature of God is a circle whose center is everywhere and whose circumference is nowhere…*
>
> (St. Augustine – attributed originally to the Greek philosopher Empedocles, who lived in the fifth century BC)

Following upon the above idea, the sign symbol for the Sun ☉ can be seen to represent the activity of spirit itself, and furthermore, suggests that *everything* is contained within the etheric/life body of the Sun. We can experience from the lemiscatory orbital dance of the Sun both the *gathering* principle – the breathing in of the full *round* of existence and the activating principle which emanates from the stilled interior of the Sun and circulates throughout the solar system. In this way the Sun becomes "*the giving one, the bestower of life*"[65] through the sharing of etheric substance.

It is through the beingness of the Sun in relationship to the human being that wisdom dwells within the inner still point of the human heart. From this point radiates an activity of comprehension which is multifaceted – not limited to a single point of view, but *containing* the whole. This is an activity which is mirrored in the sign/symbol for the Sun ☉ which radiates out equally in all directions, expressing a universality which originates from a beingness which is heart centered.

We speak of the "promptings of the heart" and advise our youth to "follow your heart". What is this mysterious grace which emanates from the quiet discipline of an open "listening heart"? This is a coming into connection with one's **guardian angel**, "*Who envelops the **higher self** or higher consciousness of the individual*"[66] – the true essence of our being, whose activity is connected to the forces (life body) of the Sun.

---

[63] Claude Larre and Elisabeth Rochat de la Vallée, *The Secret Treatise of the Spiritual Orchid*, p. 38.

[64] *Meditations on the Tarot*, p. 207.

[65] Rudolf Steiner, *History and Content of the Higher Degrees of the Esoteric School*, p. 247.

[66] See Valentin Tomberg, *Inner Development* for an inspiring account of the human being's relationship with the guardian angel and the higher self.

The Guardian Angel and the Higher Self

With the Sun we come to the expression of the essence of our being, our connection to our higher self, referred to by Rudolf Steiner as the *"human being in his entirety."*[67]

By way of analogy, because the forces of the Sun work directly on the human heart, it is the "listening heart" that comes into an inner connection with the inspirations of the higher self. The higher self as an emanation from the Sun sphere becomes the source of insight and creativity in the human being.

Valentin Tomberg gives an inspiring account of how a daily practice of "inner listening" in meditation creates a cumulative effect of strengthening the connection to the higher self, which over time gives birth to the higher self within the human heart. *"Just as a snake discards its skin – so a person sheds the lower I."*[68]

Thus the Sun is born within the realm of earthly existence and is then everywhere and in all things as our actions bring the Sun's spirit into every day affairs. Valentin Tomberg describes how we come into a "unity" with our higher self when our activity is in the service of the world.

Robert Sardello bears witness to the importance of listening to the heart in his book *Freeing the Soul from Fear*, indicating that it is through the capacity of the heart that one's true gifts unfold, enabling the essence of individuality to begin to serve the world – and that this knowledge of true identity requires being present to the inner qualities of everyday experience. In this way there is a breathing unity between the inside and outside worlds, offering the possibility of being in *intimate* relationship with an *"ineffable holy presence in the world"*.[69]

Shamballa: Sol Niger (The "Black Sun")

If we hold true to the experience of the eurythmy gesture for the Sun, we must recognize that the human being in his/her entirety (higher I) is connected – through the capacity of the human heart – to *both* the cosmic heart *and* the heart of the Earth.

> *Only he who finds the firm center of support within himself can be a citizen of our planet Earth. In this way the center of his being becomes firmly united with the center of this planet and he finds his own development together with the mission of Earth.*[70]

This brings to expression the importance of our connection to *Sol Niger*, the "Black Sun" in the center of the Earth – corresponding to the Pythagorean understanding of the "vestal fire" burning in the heart of the world.

---

[67] Rudolf Steiner, *Eurythmy as Visible Speech*, p.117. The Sun gesture – expressing *"the whole human being"* – embraces both consciousness (right arm reaching up) and the subconscious (left arm extended down).

[68] Valentin Tomberg, *Inner Development*, p.40.

[69] Robert Sardello, *Freeing the Soul from Fear*, p.43.

[70] Rudolf Steiner, handwritten from Maria Steiner, *Concerning the History and Content of the Higher Degrees of the Esoteric School 1904 – 1914*, p.239.

The Interval — The "Empty Space" Between Two Notes

The Unknown Factor

There is an important "**interval**" between the self-centered, self-serving, self-consciousness of the lower "I" and the birth of the Sun/Christ-centered consciousness, which through the power of unbiased observation is called to the service of all.

Meditations on the Tarot describes this momentous "interval" as the fifth wound. The archetype of the fifth wound is that which Christ received at the crucifixion through the spear of Longinus. In the human being this comes as a penetration from the right side (the will) – a wounding of the heart which gives birth to the quality of *humility*. Thus, the *activating* principle of *living* thought becomes the ability to think with a humble and warm heart.[71]

This is the harmonizing factor of the "eighth force" that the author refers to as the "eighth planet" which brings the influence of the seven forces of the astral body (the chakras related to the seven planets) into a state of equilibrium.[72] He calls this the "unknown factor" which dwells in the *interval* – the void in the center of a *stilled* heart.

The crossing point in the lemniscatory movement of Sun-centered consciousness which connects the cosmic principle to inspired activity in the world results in *sacred* magic. This is the *interval* of a learning to *listen* to the heartbeat and pulsing of love which comes as a *breath* and promise to the waiting heart.

This can *serve* as an antidote to fear which may otherwise manifest in reactive behavior or callous, uncaring actions toward the environment. Robert Sardello observes that the "*center of not knowing is the one place where the forces of fear cannot enter*".[73] A stilling of the heart requires a letting go of bias and preconceived notions in order to listen to the pulse of wisdom and love in the heart.

Give Us This Day Our Daily Bread

In the practice of Christian hermeticism it is known that the access to the cosmic stream is silence. Through becoming inwardly quiet and still, an inflow of *life force* may take place. The heart as container of life and warmth provides a fertile bed for the incarnation of the "living" word – WORD becomes flesh.

> *I wish to set holy souls in rhythm with me…*
> *You who have been moved to become wise have me as a bed.*
> *Rest upon me.* (From the *"Hymn to the Father"*, *Acts of John* 94-97.)[74]

This is the fertile bed "*wherein the mercury of intellectuality undergoes transmutation into the gold of spirituality.*"[75]

---

[71] *Meditations on the Tarot*, p. 111.
[72] Ibid. p. 196.
[73] Robert Sardello, *Freeing the Soul from Fear*, p. 59.
[74] Quoted from James Miller, *Measures of Wisdom*, p. 83.
[75] *Meditations on the Tarot*, p. 605.

Gold — The Sun's Healing Agent

Gold (*aurum* in Latin), the metal associated with the Sun, is known to be quite a healer as well. The eurythmy sound "AU" not only expresses the aura or etheric/life body of the Sun, but also stems from the same root as the word *aurum* (gold), as well as *aurora* (dawn or sunrise). *Aurora* was the Greek name for the goddess of dawn.

Like the forces of the Sun, gold is present in everything. Just as sunlight permeates air, so too gold is diffused through the Earth's crust and is present in all the other metals. The distribution of gold within the human organism reaches the highest concentration in the human heart. Correspondingly, gold is used as a heart remedy – and is known to ameliorate depressive or suicidal conditions, which might be thought of as an eclipse of the Sun qualities in the heart.

Colloidal gold is known to affect the body's warmth mechanism bringing relief for alcohol and drug addiction. Dietary gold – like the warmth of the Sun – is a pain reliever and therefore gold salts are used in arthritic joint injections.

Cows have a high concentration of gold in their horns. Perhaps it was this mystery which the ancient Egyptian culture, whose consciousness was orientated toward the Sun's aura, brought to expression with the image of the rising Sun depicted between the two horns of a cow.

In biodynamic farming the horns of the cow are used for the preparation of fertilizer required for the health of the soil, and the dairy cows' horns are left intact (unshorn) in honor of this great Sun mystery. It is quite revealing to note that in the occurrence of the hoof and mouth epidemic in England, there was not a single biodynamic dairy farm affected.[76]

Sun — The Great Physician

Sunrise is the moment when the Earth and all her beings are the most receptive to the life-bringing, vivifying forces of the Sun. It is at this time that the Sun's influence acts most strongly upon our cranium or crown, pouring in light and refreshing our head forces and central nervous system.

Likewise, the rising of the Sun brings refreshing insights and new perspectives that serve to enlighten and bring a "new dawn" into world consciousness. Beinsa Douno prescribed a faithful watching of the Sun rising over the horizon as often as possible – this having a most potent cumulative effect. Rudolf Steiner indicated as an exercise that one takes in the dawn/sunrise mood of nature, picturing the constellation in which the Sun is located at that time.

Correspondingly, homeopathic medicines and plant juices can be preserved for many years by exposing them to the rising and setting Sun over a definite period of time.

In light of the Sun as the "great physician", Beinsa Douno recommends standing with one's back to the Sun to renew and revivify the vital forces. Further, he referred to the *Sol cure* for all disease: to expose one's chest to the Sun daily for half an hour. In this way one's heart (the harmonizer) comes into an attunement with the regenerative forces of the Sun's corona (life body).

---

[76] This gold discussion is paraphrased from: Nick Kollerstrom, "*The Metal Planet Affinities – Gold*"; http://www.levity.com/alchemy/kollerstrom_gold.html

39

The Secondary Organ of the Heart — The Small Intestine

The secondary organ of the heart is the **small intestine**, which rests within the center of the coiled labyrinth of the intestinal tract. The small intestine receives the finer particles and juices of the digestive system.

Just as the heart refines the spirit and serves as the "**Governor**" for the quality of the blood, so too the small intestine receives the transformed food. Its function is transitional, assuring that the finer qualities of the intake of food provide good quality juices for the vitality of the blood. The work of the small intestine is to _separate_ the *clear* from the *unclear,* and its activity takes care that the food becomes a part of our own body.

Thus, the Sun's movement motivates the circulation of the heart qualities in the *tempering* of the circulation of the digestion system. *"I am the bread of life"* becomes a physical reality with the Sun, the archetypal "I", as the orchestrator of life, health and regeneration.

Sun Psychology — The Interval of Day and Night

In the language of music, the Sun is the living metronome for the life of the psyche as well as the physical realm of existence. From the Sun we learn of the importance of the rhythm of day and night. This strengthens the soul toward the capacity of embracing opposites.

With the interval of day and night, the respiration of divine breath from above (fire) meets the silence of night reflection (water), wherein the spoken word of form (cosmic breath) meets the *"silent radiation"* of memory and realities beyond the threshold."[77]

> *Day to day pours forth speech, night to night declares knowledge.*
> (*Psalms* 19: 2)

This is the inner crossing of the lemniscate – allowing life to organize itself. The crossover point of the interval of day and night describes a threshold of *respiration* which breathes between the *"day activity of human effort (prayer) and the night activity of divine grace (benediction)".*[78]

Becoming conscious of the importance of this breathing between form and reflection builds the strength of soul to develop the capacity of imagination as a breathing between the inner and outer experience of life.

Thomas Moore in *The Planets Within* observes how the alchemy of the Sun, which pulls the seed from the soil and ripens the fruit, also *dries*, withers and decays – each phase being an important season for the nourishment of the soul, bringing the *measure* of change to the *rhythm* of time.

Moore describes how embracing the *polarity* of spiritual and earthly realities enriches one's encounter with daily life (Sun). A life lived too much in the bright light of the spiritual realm without care and attention to the mundane realities of daily existence becomes dry and brittle, *"out of phase"* with the living currents of one's time.

---

[77] Quoted from *Meditations on the Tarot*, p. 102.
[78] *Meditations on the Tarot*, p. 100.

The story of **Icarus**, who in Greek mythology was given wings of feathers bound together by wax in order to fly free, illustrates the challenge inherent in the two extremes. When Icarus flew too close to the Sun, the wax melted, causing Icarus to drown in the sea.[79]

So too, one can experience a certain "drowning" in the sea of the mundane realities of life, if not *tempered* and *lifted* by the inspirations and new perspectives of spiritual light, which engage the will toward creative endeavor in rhythm with one's time.

Sun God Helios / Apollo

Apollo, the god of music, poetry and healing, brings to expression the vivifying qualities of a true Sun psychology in the language of music. According to Thomas Moore, "*Apollo's music interprets for our soul's ear the patterns of life as it moves in time.*" This well describes the soul qualities inherent in the Sun god Apollo's relationship with **Helios**, the Sun god that drives his chariot across the sky. This relationship clearly defines time not only as temporal, but also as music for the soul of the world.[80]

Soul time bears the quality of water. It does not congeal, but rather there is fluidity. Rigid, frozen patterns are a kind of desert for the soul. Unlike **Icarus,** who wants to escape the realities of his life, Apollo's music "*draws us into itself – allowing us to feel the variations of tempo and movement, tension and release – but also the feelings and deeply felt fantasies associated with those movements.*"[81] Thus life's *movements* become *poetry* for the soul.

Sun psychology is as varied in texture as it is moving in time. Yet the *texture* must come from the *inner weaver* of the heart's capacity to hold and to savor the sacred. The mark of being present to the presence or possibility of **becoming** can be a healing antidote to the mechanistic rhythms of the fast-paced, technological realities of the beginning movements of the twenty-first century.

"AU" — The Midnight Sun

The Dark Night of the Soul

In his *New Testament Studies*, Valentin Tomberg brings life and fluidity to the process described by Rudolf Steiner as the *Trial by Air,* which is a Sun mystery.[82]

Tomberg gives as a point of reference the imagination of the 12 petal lotus of the heart center as a single point, a still point surrounded by twelve equal radiating lines coming together in the center of the heart. In this way the human heart center is realized as the spiritual focus of the coming together of the twelve cosmic streamings of the zodiac.

In the process of learning to return to this still point of quiet, the void within the heart, one's awareness of the consciousness of the heart begins to awaken. This is a process which becomes more and more compelling as the *light* of the **higher self** ("I") begins to be born in the heart – the birth of the Christ within.

---

[79] Icarus, according to Greek legend, drowned in the Icarian Sea near Samos on his flight from Crete.
[80] In Greek/Roman mythology Apollo was associated with the Sun on a soul/spiritual level, whereas Helios was the Sun god on a more physical level.
[81] Thomas Moore, *The Planets Within*, p. 89.
[82] See *New Testament Studies*, Chapter IV on the Beatitudes by Valentin Tomberg – in reference to the microcosmic perspective of the macrocosmic occult trials that he describes in his seven lectures in *Inner Development*.

There comes a point in this return to stillness when a zero-point is reached within the soul's experience wherein the heart becomes separated from the inflow of the cosmic rays and the soul feels itself *"plunged into loneliness, darkness and silence."* There arises a *"painful feeling of breathlessness in the soul"*. The work is to maintain the balance of the two feelings – the complete freedom of self reliance *and* the pain of separation from the cosmic realm (inbreath).

The ancient Egyptian culture enacted this Sun mystery of the Trial by Air in the initiation rites in the King's Chamber of the Great Pyramid (Cheops) of Giza – with the initiate being placed into a sarcophagus for three days, plunged into the silence of the soul's long dark night.

This is the dark night of the soul described in the writings of St. John of the Cross, which helps one to realize the profound words from the Cross, *"My God, my God, why hast thou forsaken me?"*

The "void" in the heart now gives rise to a spiritual deed – *"Father, into thy hands I commend my spirit"* – wherein the experience of the soul being held by the *ineffable* realizes the *presence* of love. The magnitude of this event now becomes the *"central motive of life and action"*. As Valentin Tomberg describes:

> *The great change which takes place in the spiritual organism of the heart is that the heart itself begins to shine out into the cosmos.*

Now the motivating principle of love, which is the force of connection between all of creation, gives birth to the faculty of intuition, whereby the forces of the soul reach out in a gesture of communion. This is the sacred activity of redemption.

The fruits of a transformed heart yield the light of *sunlit clarity* far surpassing the light of *reflection*.

> *Thou resting, glowing light.* (Rudolf Steiner)[83]

Sun: Planetary Rulership

The Constellation of Leo

The experience of the transformation of the human heart brings us to an understanding of the Sun's relationship to the constellation of Leo, the ***Lion*** – which is one of *rulership* – for it is the Sun's activity in the heart which manifests the kingly nature of Leo.

We know the constellation of Leo as the cosmic archetype for the forming of the human heart and circulatory system which flows from the heart out to the extremities and back again to the heart.

Thus, the circulatory system of the human being mirrors the spiritual circulation of the transformed human heart, which rays out in an activity of *communion* and returns with the clarity of *sunlit* intuition to the stilled silence of the "listening" heart.

We can recognize the ideas of circulation and the spiritualized heart in the sign/symbol for the constellation of Leo – wherein the longing for communion rises up out of itself and returns to encircle the *waiting* heart which is marked by the star **Regulus,** the heart of the Lion (located at 5° Leo).

---

[83] Rudolf Steiner, *"The Twelve Moods"* – expressing the Sun in Cancer; see Lacquanna Paul and Robert Powell, <u>Cosmic Dances of the Zodiac</u>, p. 115.

This region of the heavens, the first decan (0–10°) of Leo, which corresponds to the "thinking" heart of Leo, marks the memory of three of the healing miracles of Jesus Christ.[84]

The Conversation at Jacob's Well

2½° Leo remembers the **Conversation at Jacob's Well** – a conversation which took place at *midday* on Wednesday July 26, AD 30, the time of day when the etheric/life streaming forces of the Sun work directly on the human heart.

A young woman seeking water found Christ Jesus *waiting* at the well. Jesus spoke to her saying, *"Whoever drinks of the water that I shall give him will never thirst; the water I shall give him will become a spring of water welling up to eternal life"* (*John* 4: 13-14).

This was on a Wednesday (Mercredi), Mercury Day – a day of *healing* and transformation for the *living waters* of life.

The Raising of Lazarus

3° Leo remembers the **Raising of Lazarus** from the dead with the words "*Lazarus come forth*" – marking the birth of the eternal "I" within the heart of Lazarus.

On the day of the raising of Lazarus, there took place a conjunction of **Sun** and **Moon** with the star **Regulus** (the "Heart of the Lion"). This was on July 26, AD 32. It was on a Saturday morning (Saturn Day) – relating to the *crown*. Lazarus *awakened* as if from a sleep. Then Jesus placed his hand on the head (crown) of Lazarus and breathed upon Lazarus seven times, the seven gifts of the "Holy Spirit" – symbolizing *spiritual maturity*. Lazarus had chosen the path leading to the *Kingdom of Light*.

The Healing of the Nobleman's Son

10° Leo remembers the **Healing of the Nobleman's Son** which took place on a Thursday, Jupiter Day. Jupiter was considered by the Babylonians to be the "god of wisdom".

This is the archetypal story of the human "I"/ *Self,* being given over to another human being – a loss which can only be restored by the radiation of the archetypal Sun, the Christ.

Joel, a 14 year old boy, had fallen ill with a fever and was dying. The boy spoke out that only Jesus Christ could heal him. Joel, the son of Selathiel, had been given over to the nobleman Zorobabel for adoption – a *telling* image of the giving over of the *Self* (Sun/I) in order to win favor or to please another.

The *Self* of the father works upon the physical condition of his children. Thus, Joel had not received the proper radiation of the sun-like "I" qualities from his father Selathiel, whose *Self* had become moonlike in his condition of dependence upon another human being, the nobleman Zorobabel. It was Selathiel's faith and will forces which made it possible for Jesus Christ to restore the *Self* (Sun/I) to the father, resulting in a healing radiation to the son, which occurred at the seventh hour.[85]

---

[84] See Robert Powell, *Christian Hermetic Astrology*, p. 303.
[85] Robert Powell, *Christian Hermetic Astrology*, pp. 103-105.

The rulership of the Sun in Leo brings a balancing and healing alchemy to the challenges inherent in the constellation of Leo of both "over inflation" of the lower ego or its opposite pole – the loss of the sun-like "I". The archetypal imprint of the Sun *entrains* the soul and the lower self to return to the *waiting* heart of the deeper essential *Self*, the sun-like "I", which radiates in harmony with the Sun. This is spiritual *kingship*, as in *"Thy kingdom come…"*

There is a curious mirroring in Nature of Jesus' three days in the tomb. When a new lion cub is born, it lies on the ground for three days until on the third day the mother lioness resurrects it by breathing upon it, bringing it to life.[86]

Sun's Exaltation: Aries — Golgotha Mystery

The Sun in Aries the **Ram** or **Lamb** is the heavenly archetype mirrored in the first month of spring, signaling new beginnings. Thus it is not surprising that the Sun finds its **exaltation** point in Aries (19°), the central decan (working heart) of the "Lamb". This is the decan which remembers the **Mystery of Golgotha** – the **Crucifixion** and the **Resurrection** of the archetypal Son of Man, Jesus (the man) Christ (the spirit) of the Sun.

19° Aries, the place of exaltation of the Sun marks the day of the **Conversation with Nicodemus**, when Jesus said, *"Unless man is born of the spirit, he cannot enter the kingdom of heaven."*

This central decan of Aries is ruled by the Sun and shares the etheric body of *Cassiopeia* – the constellation of the **Enthroned Woman**. With the exaltation of the Sun in this decan, Cassiopeia becomes the image of the *"Woman clothed with the Sun"*.

The Mystery of Etheric Life on Earth

This concludes our exploration of the **Sun** and also the **Ancient Sun** evolution. This was the beginning stage of the carrying forth of all that is inherent in the breath of the Creator, which *lives* on in the etheric/life body of every form of creation. Thus, the remembering of the sacred pattern for the wisdom of the inner organic nature of creation came forth as in a cosmic breath into the sounding chambers of the heart. This was the **Sunday** of existence. The following inhalation of the divine breath brought about a further contraction, which left behind (gave birth to) the planet **Jupiter**, whose orbit defines the working realm of the **Cherubim**, *serving* as the bearers of divine wisdom.

All of this is carried in turn as a remembrance of purpose in the sacred vessel of the human heart.

---

[86] Thomas Moore, *The Planets Within*, p. 135.

Cosmic *Eurythmy*
"In the Image and Likeness…"

Moon: *"Lumine thou each hill and vale, shining Moon above."*[87]

Chakra:	Root (base of spine)
Organ:	Brain/sexual organs
Gland:	Gonads
Metal:	Silver
Color:	Violet or silver
Tone:	B[88]

Following the seven days of creation, we come now to the **Moon** day of existence, **Monday.** The Moon brings the light of the Sun to the darkness of night. One might say that the Moon's "soul" purpose is to reflect the light – for true it is that the Moon as the planet nearest the Earth serves as *gateway* and "Grail Maiden" for the passage of each human soul coming into incarnation upon Mother Earth.

The Moon as "Grail Maiden" holds the mystery of birth. Following upon the bestowal of the etheric/life body[89] in the days of the Ancient Sun, the solar nebula experienced a further contraction (condensation) to the realm/boundary of the <u>orbit</u> of the planet <u>Mars</u>. There began the *cosmic day* of **Ancient Moon**, the phase of planetary evolution during which the human being's <u>astral body</u> was formed.[90]

The astral body reflects the activity of the **Dynamis**, known as the *Spirits of Motion*. This sheds *reflective* light upon the words from the *Book of Genesis*, *"… and the Spirit of God was moving over the face of the waters."* For that breath of life which is carried by the etheric body (the watery element) gave birth to *movement*. Correspondingly, the solar wind proceeding from the Sun and the "winding" of the planets are *reflected* in the inner *movements* of the internal organs and glandular system of the human being – reflecting the gift of the etheric body bestowed during the Ancient Sun evolution.

During Ancient Moon evolution the human being received the foundation for the inner *intelligence* of *movement* – relating to the <u>central nervous system</u> conducted through the human brain and spinal column/vertebrae.

Just as the birthing womb within the human being is a water-bearing vessel, so too the Moon's orbit defines and shares the boundary of the Earth's etheric body which is connected to the watery element. Therefore the Moon, as cosmic womb for the soul and *gateway* to the Earth, is the most watery of all the planets due to its proximity in relationship to the Earth's etheric aura.

---

[87] From the Moon verse – see Appendix IV: *Music and Verses for the Seven Classical Planets.*

[88] The correspondences are tabulated in Appendix III: *Correspondences to the Seven Classical Planets.* See also Appendix II: *Musical Tones and the Planets.*

[89] The etheric/life body relates to the inner organs (heart, lungs, kidneys, etc.) and glandular system. The etheric body is essentially a <u>time</u> organism.

[90] The astral body, a subtle body surrounding and interpenetrating the physical body, has seven main centers, which are the seven chakras, and its physical expression in the human being is through the central nervous system and spinal column. The astral body relates to our sense of <u>space</u>. See Appendix III.

We can observe the presence of the Moon's breath in the ebb and flow of the Earth's tides. Water as a known conductor of sound and vibration has an exquisitely responsive nature, bearing the same reflective qualities of the Moon.[91]

So too the central nervous system (the bearer of the human astral body) is exquisitely attuned and responsive to the internal and external atmosphere of the etheric/life body – often bringing its *reflective* nature to bear upon the physical and soul conditions of the human being.

Reflections: The Moon's Form in Cosmic Dance

The form for the cosmic dance of the Moon in eurythmy is a reflection of the *breath* of the Moon as it *moves* within the ebb and flow of the Earth's waters, bringing to expression the pattern of a wave form, a carrier wave for cosmic sound which moves the tides of the waters of life – swelling first in toward the Earth then pulling back (irresistibly) toward the cosmic realm.

The form describes the *interval* or still point between each wave pattern as a rounding back into the center of one's being – rooted deeply within earthly life – like the cresting of a wave. Thus the *movement* of the form gives expression to a gathering of the fullness of time in an interval of reflection and then the inevitable dissolution necessary to the *movement* of time ever forward. This is a reflection of the cosmic outbreath of the Sun (solar wind) mirrored in the phases of the Moon.

It is in the *movement* of the Moon's forces within the face of the waters of "Mother Earth" that the human being is powerfully reminded of the Earth's connection to the starry realm. In this way the Moon *serves* toward the training of the reflective capacity of the human being.

The Moon Sound "EI"

The Moon sound "EI" (pronounced "I" as in "eye") gives voice to the soul qualities of the Moon as the *union* of two vowels (diphthong) pronounced as one sound. The Moon is wedded with the higher purpose of the Sun and in service to the Earth as her constant companion, bringing the light of the Sun into the reflective hours of night.

As the Earth's *companion* the Moon brings the gift of reflection to the human being's striving to become "I" – becoming a true reflection of the Sun's bestowing of the higher Self.[92] The diphthong sound "EI", in bringing to expression the Moon 's relationship to the Sun above and the Earth below, reflects the archetypal qualities of this relationship as true stewardship.

The Eurythmy Sound *Gesture*: "EI"

With the eurythmy gesture for the sound "EI", the "I", the *inner* Sun of existence, which is remembered by Saturn, comes into an intimate (reflective) *relationship* with earthly life. The movement of the "EI" gesture gives expression to the **horizontal** striving toward the **vertical** – through the rhythmic ebb and flow qualities of daily existence.

---

[91] Masaru Emoto, *The Hidden Messages in Water*, p. 33.

[92] The human "I" is "moonlike" at the present phase of evolution but will through Christ become more and more "sunlike" in the course of time, as expressed in the image of the Risen One beheld by John on the island of Patmos.

The movement of the arms reflects the Moon's presence as Grail maiden, tracing the pattern of the crescent Moon, described by star watchers as the "Grail Moon" (the crescent Moon when seen lying parallel to the horizon, forming the shape of a chalice).

Now the arms, as the "wings of the heart", having realized their vertical relationship with the cosmic realm (in the cosmic dance of the Sun), come into the horizontal *feeling* experience of life on Earth. As *midwife* and *cradle* the arms sway first to the right (will) then to the left (heart), as the hands open downward to tenderly *receive* and gently *touch* into the breath of the Earth.

The Ebb and Flow Pattern of the Sound *Gesture*: "EI"

As with the union of the two vowels in the sound "EI", the arms work together to describe the pattern of the wave form. As the right arm opens out from the heart and extends, bringing expression to the flow pattern in toward the Earth, the left hand describes the pull of the tide by stroking the extended arm from the outstretched hand back toward the heart, and then the arms reverse their movement and describe the ebb and flow pattern in the opposite direction as the wave form pulls back away from the Earth (imagining the Earth to be at the center).[93]

The Moon *Gesture*: The Interval

The movement of the form builds in momentum toward the cresting of the wave, which is the *interval* before the beginning of the next wave form. After the two "EI" gestures (first to the right, with the wave pattern flowing in toward the Earth – and then to the left, with the second wave pattern pulling back away from the Earth), the Moon gesture is formed as the form *spirals* around coming to a still point, the interval before the next movement of the ebb and flow pattern.[94]

In forming the eurythmy gesture for the Moon, the arms open out and circle around in a *gathering* gesture, then come together with wrists crossed and hands lightly clenched in a *downward* gesture, bringing expression to the human being's connection to the Earth. Then follows a momentary still point, the interval before the next ebb and flow pattern of the form. The holding of the Moon gesture (giving expression to the interval of the still point) can be experienced *both* in relation to the root chakra *and* as a "taking hold" of the lunar forces streaming down through the legs and feet, both bringing the human being into connection with the Earth.

The Moon gesture mirrors the Moon's gift of reflection, describing a "stilling" of the waters (necessary for true reflection) and a "reining in" of the emotional *waters* of the astral life. This is a coming to rest in the depths of one's being, feeling deeply connected to one's soul purpose toward the Earth.

The mood of the cosmic dance of the Moon is one of tenderness and reverence toward the Earth. As with the higher purpose of nightly reflection, the Moon's dreamlike quality is imbued with the soul's remembrance of the *purpose* to serve.

---

[93] See the eurythmy form for the cosmic dance of the Moon, where the first wave forward to the right expresses the flow pattern of the Moon's orbit moving toward the Earth and the second wave back to the right indicates the ebb of the Moon's path drawing away from the Earth.

[94] See the eurythmy form of the cosmic dance of the Moon: after forming the two "EI's" following the wave form toward the Earth and then pulling away from the Earth, the Moon gesture is shaped while moving around the spiral form following the double wave form.

Moon *Eurythmy* Form

The choreography for the cosmic dance of the Moon is a gentle wave form – recalling the connection of the Moon with water and the tides – flowing forward, then backward to the right, and then circling forward and spiraling around in a counter-clockwise direction.

The Moon sound "EI" is formed twice (once to the right and once to the left) on the wave moving forward and then backward to the right, and the Moon gesture (shaped on the spiral) is completed when the spiral form is finished.

The dancers are "awake" in the dreamlike mood of the Moon, and imagine themselves immersed in the wonder of the color *violet*, while moving to the music – for example, of Beethoven's "Moonlight Sonata" or Chopin's "Berceuse" ("Lullaby").

Cosmic Dance of the Moon

"Look within"

Begin by stepping the form, flowing forward in a wavelike curve to the right, then back flowing further around to the right and then spiraling in, moving forward (counter-clockwise) to the left…

Pause (like the breaking of a wave: the still point in the form). Then continue the pattern once again…

Coming into the etheric flow of the music, allow your shoulders to guide the movement – swaying gently to the right, then back and around to the left.

Moon Sound: "EI"
While curving in a wavelike pattern *forward*, extend the right arm gracefully out to the right, while the palm of the left hand traces the length of the extended arm, gently stroking the outside of the extended arm from wrist to shoulder.

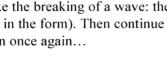

Movement: Form the Moon sound "EI" while moving to the right in a wavelike pattern, flowing first forward and then flowing back…

While curving in a wavelike pattern *back* and further to the right, the left arm extends gracefully out to the left, while the palm of the right hand traces the length of the extended arm, *gently stroking the outside of the extended arm from wrist to shoulder.*

Moon Gesture:
While spiraling *forward* (counter-clockwise), the arms swing open, out and around (palms open and facing down) in a gathering gesture, while spiraling into the center, the wrists cross in the region of the life center (hands lightly clenched). *This is a gathering of creative forces from the subconscious realm below and a reining in or taking hold of the lower will forces and aligning them with one's higher soul purpose.*

Now: Form the Moon gesture while spiraling *forward* in a counter-clockwise direction.

<u>Pause</u> at the center of the spiral, bringing the Moon gesture to completion.

The Moon relates to our astrality, the (lower) astral level of the human being (the subconscious).

49

The Grail Maiden

The receiving one, mirroring...[95]

With the "EI" gesture in the cosmic dance of the Moon, the movement of the arms forms an image of an upturned crescent Moon. We associate the crescent Moon with the *promise* of new beginnings, acknowledging the Moon as receiving vessel for the "seeds" of creation. Just as Saturn's cup of *remembrance* anoints the crown chakra with the *grace* of conscience, the Moon sound "EI" bears the promise of *communion*, the "upturned cup" of receiving. The *communion* vessel for life on Earth is – according to the Grail tradition – "*when the physical body is regarded as the communion body*" with the capacity (through the human being's nervous system) to "*become present to the rhythms of the world.*"[96]

The rhythms of the Moon bring us deeply into connection with life on Earth.

By *becoming* present to the subtle interweaving of world processes, we come into harmony with the creative principle of nature – becoming the body vessel to "*receive its willingly bestowed revelation.*"[97]

In this way the "upturned cup" serves as the generating force for the active human will. With the Moon sound "EI" – the *union* of two potential wills, that of the subconscious (Moon) and that of the true *Self* (Sun), brings a sounding note to the *union* of head and heart, toward the task of aligning head, heart and will – **becoming** creative *movement* in the world.

The lower ego is influenced by the lunar forces of astrality at work in the subconscious of the human *personality,* which is the sense of *self* connected with being incarnated on the Earth – whereas the *individuality* gives expression to the higher *Self* of cosmic origin, associated with the Sun.[98]

As the lower self's sphere of activity, which is anchored in earthly life, is subject to the lunar forces of astrality, it has as its task to come into harmony with the creative principle of nature – "*the receiving one, mirroring...*"[99]

> *Here we have everything in the human being which is creative; it is the capacity for creation.*[100]

This *potential* for *creative* work in the world is one of the gifts arising through our lunar capacity to *receive* nature's revelations. The words "potential" and "capacity" reveal the paradoxical nature of the Moon – for in the activity of receiving we are <u>active</u> rather than passive. This is a *willed* activity, just as the activity of reflection requires the conscious decision to be *wakeful* to all the subtle revelations of daily existence.

The ebb and flow pattern of the Moon's pull upon the tides of the Earth's waters is reflected in the capacity of the human being to *sense* beyond the physical form – to *move* toward (ebb) and to pull back for reflection. This is the work of "*collaboration with life*" which bears the "*fruits of the Tree of Life.*"[101]

---

[95] Rudolf Steiner, *History and Content of the Higher Degrees of the Esoteric School*, p. 247.
[96] Robert Sardello, *Freeing the Soul from Fear*, p. 169.
[97] *Meditations on the Tarot*, p. 68.
[98] See Robert Powell, *Hermetic Astrology*, vol. I, p. 213.
[99] Rudolf Steiner, *History and Content of the Higher Degrees of the Esoteric School*, p. 247.
[100] Rudolf Steiner, *Eurythmy As Visible Speech*, p. 118, describing the Moon's potential influence.
[101] *Meditations on the Tarot*, p. 68.

In the cosmic dance of the Moon the dancers strive toward the conscious <u>activity</u> of *conscience* when forming the eurythmy sound "EI", wherein the *movement* of the force of attraction is uplifted and in union with the higher purposes of the Sun. This union strengthens one's sense of *"moral receptivity."*

Robert Sardello expresses the idea of "moral receptivity" in *Freeing the Soul from Fear* in this way…*"Our moral receptivity weakens the more we separate ourselves from the rhythms of the world."*[102] This would be the <u>passive</u> end of the spectrum which does not <u>respond</u> to the living sound of the Moon as the bearer of the reflective light of the Sun.

According to Sardello, *"Moral receptivity becomes the generating force for creative deeds which reveal the character of our Ego/Higher Self /"I", bringing the unique gifts of our individuality in service to the world."* In this way we live into the significance of the words of Rudolf Steiner describing the spiritual essence of the Moon, *"The receiving one, mirroring."*

The Moon's forces bring *movement* to the four limbs of the human being: the arms which in eurythmy are considered the "wings of the heart" (Sun), and the legs which are the "wings of the will" (Moon). *Eurythmy is a training of the will through the limbs, leading one to one's true purpose.*

The Root Chakra — The 4 Petal Lotus Flower

The fecundating streamings from the lunar rhythms are connected through our astral body to the root chakra which is located at the base of the spinal column. It is through the *rhythmic* flow of the fluids in the spinal column that the root chakra *communes* with the crown. In turn, there is a downward streaming through the chakras from the crown to the heart and from the heart chakra to the root chakra. This circulating current forms an etheric *"egg"* of life-sustaining etheric substance, called the *microcosmic orbit*.

In Hindu tradition the root chakra is referred to as the 4 petal lotus flower. An inner picture can be formed of two of the petals streaming down toward the Earth, and two petals streaming up toward the heart and from there into the two arms. This image describes the "branching of the four limbs" in relation to the four petals of the root chakra. The current of living sound ("EI") serves toward the *union* of the Sun forces in the heart chakra enlivening the arms, with the Moon forces in the root chakra enlivening the legs. The resulting circulatory streaming of life energy encompassing the entire human being from the crown chakra to the feet, including the "branching of the four limbs", is called the *macrocosmic orbit*.

Through the Mystery of Golgotha the root chakra, the center of procreation (reproductive system) and renewal (microcosmic orbit), has been redeemed by Christ's words, *"I am the true vine"*. These words reveal the archetypal divine plan for the root chakra as the astral organ for generation, transformation, rejuvenation, healing and liberation.

---

[102] Robert Sardello, *Freeing the Soul from Fear*, p. 171.

The Healing Miracle of the Wedding at Cana

It is the root chakra in the human being that most strongly comes into connection with the influences of the Earth. This chakra is related to the first healing miracle of Christ, the **Wedding at Cana**. This healing miracle has to do with a mystery relating to the root chakra's current of connection with the crown, which is the gateway to the divine breath. In turn, the divine breath *serves* to spiritualize the blood in working together with the Sun's activity in the heart.

The circulatory *movement* of this current *of connection* describes a *marriage* of the Sun and Moon forces streaming within the human being. In the cosmic dance of the Moon, we work to strengthen this current through the movement of the eurythmy gesture for the sound "EI" – the sounding of the Moon. Through this movement of connection, the spiritualized currents of the crown chakra (Saturn) flow into the branching of the four limbs, and all the way down into the feet, bringing the human being into *communion* with the Earth and earthly life. This is the fulfillment in the human being of the *"washing of the feet"*, through the activity of Christ, starting in the crown chakra, streaming all the way down to the feet.

A spiritualization of the blood occurs through the marriage of the currents of the crown with the etherized currents of the heart. Through the Sun's activity in the heart, the heart chakra being the primary vessel of Christ's working in the human being, the transformation of the waters of life into the wine of eternal life is made manifest, whereby the blood becomes the bearer of light. This is the *fructification* of the marriage of heaven and earth, the uniting of the solar (heart chakra) and lunar (root chakra) life currents which flow within the *communion body vessel* of the human being.

The Mysteries of Birth: Lunar Rhythms

The Moon serves as Grail Maiden and as gateway for the sending down of the spirit seed of the incarnating soul (relating to **conception**) from the Moon sphere. Correspondingly, the human mother serves as "Grail Maiden" and gateway in giving birth to the child. The word month comes from "Moon". We speak of the feminine "moon time" (menses). This is a blood mystery which corresponds to lunar rhythms.

The consciousness of the ancient **Babylonian** culture was orientated toward the mysteries of the Moon. It is through the teachings of the early Babylonian priesthood that our knowledge of the soul's descent through the planetary spheres originates. These teachings describe the taking on of the characteristics of the planets as living templates of ordered life *"before entering into corporeal existence."* Thus, the Moon serves as gateway both for birth and *"after death when the soul makes its journey through the heavens in reverse direction and with the opposite effect."*[103]

Etheric Conception

> *The etheric conception is an event belonging to the Moon sphere, the sphere indwelt by the incarnating human being at the moment of conception, having descended there from the fixed star realm through the seven planetary spheres.* [104]

---

[103] Robert Powell, *Hermetic Astrology*, vol. I, p. 104.
[104] Ibid. p. 282.

In former times, when human beings still had a natural clairvoyant perception of events in the etheric realm, the etheric conception template was beheld as the *"descent of the stork"*.[105]

It is within the Moon sphere that the weaving of the etheric life body takes place. *This is a Moon mystery which can be held in consciousness when doing the eurythmic "EI" gesture in the cosmic dance of the Moon.* The Moon sphere is the realm of the **Angels** who serve as guardians and guiding spirits for the human being's journey through life on Earth. During the time between conception and birth, the **Guardian Angel** weaves the karmic destiny of the incarnating soul into the etheric template by looking back toward the planetary spheres and observing all that remains unfinished in the developing human being's soul nature requiring karmic meetings with redemptive potential.

Seven-year Periods

> *God grants the human being three score years and ten.* (*Psalm* 90: 10)

The Moon has a relationship with the stars which is called the sidereal rhythm, reflecting a rhythm of 27⅓ days, which is the number of days the Moon requires to orbit around the zodiac to return to the same star.

Willi Sucher, who pioneered the work of Astrosophy,[106] observed an important discovery regarding the relationship of this 27⅓-day rhythm of the Moon to the weaving of the etheric body, which takes place during the nine-month cycle of pregnancy. He found a parallel correspondence of the Moon's orbits with the forming of the etheric body in relation to the formation of the physical body during the embryonic period in the womb. Archetypally there are ten 27⅓-day cycles of the Moon's orbit around the zodiac, amounting to 273 days of pregnancy. During each of the ten lunar orbits, the Guardian Angel (within the Moon sphere) weaves the human being's destiny into the etheric body – a destiny which will unfold within the ten seven-year periods of life following the time of birth. During the first orbit of the Moon the weaving of destiny relates to the first seven-year period of life, and so on.

The weaving of destiny which occurs during the nine-month embryonic period of life thus constitutes the cosmic prefiguring of the destiny which unfolds after birth in ten consecutive seven-year periods in the biography of each human life. The unfolding of destiny is *experienced* in reverse order to the soul's incarnating passage descending through the planetary spheres before birth. The first seven years of life reflect the etheric growth processes developed in the Moon sphere during the first 27⅓-day orbit of the Moon. This is the "infancy" phase of life when the child's consciousness is *lunar* and is primarily focused upon its interface with the earthly mother.

The next seven-year period between the ages 7 and 14, relating to the *Mercury* sphere, reflects the concerns of early childhood, when the child is learning to communicate within the greater community of its peers – going to school with an eagerness to learn, as an expression of Mercury's influence.

---

[105] The etheric conception generally takes place within the three day period following the physical coming together of the egg and the sperm. See Robert Powell *Hermetic Astrology*, vol. I, pp. 282-283. The stork was the form appearing to clairvoyant perception of the spirit seed sent down by the incarnating soul as the bearer of the archetypal forces for building up the physical body.

[106] See the biographical introduction to: Willi Sucher, *Cosmic Christianity and the Changing Countenance of Cosmology*, which is concerned with revealing the cosmic dimension of Christianity.

The seven-year period between the ages 14 to 21 bears the concerns of the *Venus* sphere, during which the development of sexuality and the richness of emotional life during adolescence unfolds.

At age 21 the human being enters the ***Sun*** stage of development, which unfolds during the next three seven-year periods – extending from 21 to 42. Age 21 marks the birth of the Self ("I"). Viewed from a higher perspective, a moral training ensues. The human being's strivings in the world seek the resolution of the promptings of the heart – in connection with the Sun forces.

According to *Psalm* 90: 10, "*God grants the human being three score years and ten.*" Here there is an indication that, in an archetypal sense, the human life lasts seventy years. This can be seen as two halves: the first 35 years, and the years following. This division of life holds true for the life forces of the etheric body, whereby age 35 indicates a turning point in the activity of the human life body. After the age of 35 a gradual decline in life energy sets in.

On a soul level the turning point is midway through the Sun period, at age 31½. This results in a mirroring of the previous seven-year periods of life in reverse order: wherein the years 31½ to 42 mirror ages 21 to 31½ (early Sun), followed by the years 42 to 49 (Mars) which mirror the (Venus) years 14 to 21, followed by the (Jupiter) years 49 to 56 which mirror the (Mercury) years 7 to 14, and 56 to 63 (Saturn) mirroring the years from birth to age 7 (Moon).

Thus, the unfolding of destiny in the years which follow the Sun period will not only reflect the concerns and karmic imprinting of the planets which orbit beyond the Sun (Mars, Jupiter, and Saturn), but will also render a folding-back process – a mirroring – which presents a fresh encountering of the karmic patterning from the former years during the Moon, Mercury and Venus periods. The soul – now enhanced with the Ego strength of the Sun – is provided with the opportunity to resolve the issues and questions which have revealed themselves in the earlier seven-year periods.

The seeds of the Grail questions which have been planted in the fertile bed of youth and deepen in the emotional waters of adolescence – *if* allowed to then flower and ripen in the heart during the Sun years, age 21 to 42, *may* in the following years become the *seeds* which bear fruit within the soul. The Grail quest has begun, for it is during these years that the human soul seeks *re-solution*.

The soul can often suffer from *imprisonment* within the frozen patterns of the past which have been woven into the etheric unfolding of destiny. However, when the human being reaches the mature years, following the Sun period, the expanded perspectives of the planets which orbit beyond the Sun (Mars, Jupiter and Saturn) can *inspire* a new mobility and freedom, a fresh breath – allowing for the expression of the true Self. Thus, the seven-year rhythm within the human organism – reflecting the Moon's prenatal sidereal rhythm – is toward *generation, transformation, rejuvenation, healing and liberation.* The creative principle of the "EI" (Moon) sound thus resounds as liberating action in the world, bringing into *movement* that which is enslaved or petrified.

The Fruits of the Harvest

Toward the flowering of the human being's true self, the last seven years of the Sun period (ages 35 to 42) bring the concerns of the higher self to bear upon the youthful strivings of the Sun period of life. Now begins the time of the harvest. The Mars period (42-49) mirrors the adolescent stirrings and emotional issues and questions encountered in the Venus period (14-21). The Mars force brings strength and voice for the impulse of change necessary for the freeing of the soul. *Mars* seeks the truth and inspires right action so that these years can free one toward the fruitful expression of the gifts of true individuality.

Ages 49 to 56 are the *Jupiter* years wherein the enthusiasm for learning awakened in early childhood – the Mercury years (7–14) – becomes a valiant quest for wisdom and the enjoyment of the fruits of the harvest. Now the hunger for learning and concerns related to the young child's peer group undergo a metamorphosis into a *quest* for wisdom and the seeking for one's true karmic stream. Humanitarian concerns often awaken during these years, expressing Jupiter's influence of magnanimity and toward community.

The *Saturn* years (56-63) mirror the events of the first seven years of life. These are the years when conscience comes to bear upon the unfoldment of one's life and the seeking for spiritual resolution and understanding intensifies.

The years following age 63 are related to the realm of the fixed stars, as one's karmic ties associated with the planets have now loosened their hold in the unfoldment of destiny. The soul begins to pulse with the *inner* sounds of the distant starry realms as one exits at age 63 the planetary spheres of destiny unfoldment, characterized by the etheric weavings of the planetary spheres, to return to the realm of influence of the fixed stars.

Perhaps one can then begin to hear the **heart** of creation at the center of the galaxy, the Central Sun around which all the fixed stars (Suns) of our galaxy revolve.[107]

The Re-Membering of the Moon

Regeneration and Renewal

Furthering the purpose of the seven-year rhythm of the Moon's influence upon the unfolding of destiny in the life of the human being, it has been discovered that within each seven-year period the human body (vessel of material substance for the soul) undergoes a complete *renewal* – every cell is created anew. This is a lunar mystery that reveals the healing potential inherent within each seven-year period, suggesting that there is no limit to the renewal and regeneration that can occur on all levels – physically, mentally, and spiritually.

Physical Center of the Seven Lotus Flowers

The coming into manifestation of physical renewal is brought to expression in the cosmic dance of the Moon through the "EI" sound of the Moon, which may be seen in relation to the enlivening activity of the root chakra. The 4 petal lotus flower serves to mediate or bring into connection the cosmic forces which are active in the physical body. As the spiritual organ which is most intimately related to the forces of the physical body, the root chakra can be thought of as the *"physical center"* of the seven lotus flowers.[108]

Through the activating principle of the lunar imprint within the etheric life body of the human being, the human soul memory becomes the living, reflective interface between the *thought life* and the *physical body*. The body is born anew as consciousness is impregnated by the reflected light of spiritual conscience. Spirit then becomes the creative interface between the soul and the world as thinking becomes wedded to the heart.

---

[107] See Appendix V: *The Galactic Center*.
[108] Robert Powell, *Hermetic Astrology*, vol. I, p. 137. See also Appendix III.

In his *New Testament Studies*, Valentin Tomberg describes how the practice of meditation, as a free initiative on the part of the human being, strengthens the current of connection to the higher forces of *conscience* and how, correspondingly, the stream of light from above begins to illuminate the depths of the subconscious. As the Sun ("I") forces awaken in the heart, one's actions in and toward the world and community change. One becomes *awake in the dream* of the past which is imprinted into the fabric of one's own etheric body. One is *clothed* anew with each moment lived in the *reflected* light of truths which can bring refreshing perspectives of new life to the deadened currents of the distant past.

The Brain — The Physical Organ Relating to the Moon[109]

Toward Regeneration and Renewal

The human brain is a lunar organ which functions as a *trinity* in relation to our mental, emotional, and spiritual life.

The reptilian brain which is located at the base of the skull requires repetition and formality for development. It functions toward survival. The constancy of lunar rhythms lives at its core. It dwells in the part of a baby's head which is cradled in the warmth of the hand and nourished by the constancy and rhythms of daily regimens of child care. The developing child's emotional stability and ability to thrive are supported by the repetition of daily rhythms and can suffer when these rhythms are interrupted or become unstable and chaotic. This is the part of the brain that stores our memories and needs stimulation for renewal.

In adult life a daily rhythm of meditation serves as a strong support to this region of the brain, which is most intimately connected to the central nervous system, and thus bears a profound effect on our sense of physical well being and health.

The mid-brain requires *movement* in order to *feel* a *connection* with others. Its concerns are toward socialization, relationship, and community. This part of the brain becomes mis-developed with too early intellectual training. We could say that the mid-brain is linked to the present and to *willed* activity from the heart's inclination toward interconnectedness.

The neocortex (the forebrain) is the last to awaken (around the age of 10-14) and is open to inspiration relating to the future. It is this part of the brain which functions toward *regeneration*.

Through meditation (as the subtle bodies cleanse) the neocortex is nourished and begins to function toward clarity and unity. The *masculine focus* is strengthened to separate the *real* from the *unreal*; while the *feminine focus* receives the inspirations from higher consciousness, becoming a *vessel* for spiritual inspiration.

---

[109] Research of Joseph Chilton Pearce, summarized by Carol Parrish, *The Aquarian Rosary*, pp. 13-15.

The Pituitary and Pineal Glands — The Moon "receiving, mirroring"

The **pineal** gland, which looks like an upside-down pine cone, is located in the center of our cranium and responds directly to the crown chakra. This chakra, corresponding to the planet Saturn, functions toward the reception of the breath of inspiration from above and brings harmony between the <u>nervous system</u> and the <u>blood system</u>.

The **pituitary** gland is located forward of the pineal gland and functions in direct relationship to the chakra corresponding to Jupiter, which is the organ of light known as the Third Eye. The pituitary gland is divided into two parts having to do with the heart and will functions. The function of the heart is changed by the pituitary, which is strengthened through meditation.

The pineal and pituitary glands start to undergo a change once a meditative life has begun. The quality of the blood is affected by the stimulating/nourishing activity of the glands. This in turn affects the functioning of the organs, which undergo a process of *renewal*.

Transmutation

A process of transmutation begins to take place as the subtle bodies cleanse. The etheric counterpart of the physical body becomes clearer and has more impact on the physical body, which receives its vivifying forces from the etheric.

The physical body becomes a reflective vessel for higher consciousness – a light bearer. This is a process of transmutation through which matter turns toward light.

Through the activity of meditation and inner reflection, the individual mind becomes "attuned" to the divine mind. The *feeling* heart and the *knowing* mind begin to function as one. This leads to *gnosis,* which is the *knowing* of the etherized heart. With gnosis a feeling of safety and support bring a sense of stability to enrich the physical life.

The Moon's Relationship to the Constellations

Cancer ♋ – The Crab

In astrology the Moon's influence on the human being is considered to be heightened when the Moon is in the sign of Cancer, the **Crab**, which is ruled by the Moon. This signifies that the starry realm of Cancer especially calls forth the Moon's transformative potential. Just as the crab must change its shell when it has been outgrown, so too the Moon allows for growth and total regeneration within seven years.

The sign/symbol of Cancer gives expression to the spiraling of etheric forces that shape the rib cage within the human being, the *cradle* of cosmic sounding that enfolds the human heart. Thus, the rib cage is seen in correspondence to Cancer. It is through the spiraling forces of the breathing in and the breathing out of Cancer that we attune most deeply to the principles and call of cosmic evolution. The Moon as mediator of the soul's descent into incarnation is especially "at home" in this region of the heavens that was believed by the ancient star gazers to be the *gateway* for the soul's passage into earthly life.

The star cluster known as **Praesepe** is located in the *listening* heart of the starry sign of Cancer. In antiquity this region was imagined as the **Beehive**, where souls enter into earthly life in order to obtain the golden nectar of earthly experience to take back to the Heavenly Queen, Sophia, whose divine feet rest upon the upturned crescent Moon.

Toward Transformation

The shared purpose of both the Moon and Cancer is a *union* of forces toward transformation. Astrologers often refer to Cancer as the "nurturer" of the zodiac, bearing the gifts of the exquisite *feeling nature* that is associated with motherhood. The Moon, as the planet which, by nature of its proximity to the Earth, shares in the watery element of the Earth's aura (etheric body), thereby attends the soul of humanity through the responsive, reflective nature of the cosmic breath within the watery element associated with the central nervous system in the human being. This is the cosmic breath and sound which nourishes the human embryo within the womb of the earthly mother and is a source of reflective influence throughout the length of one's life, primarily through the *feeling nature* of the individuality.

Let us consider the words of Valentin Tomberg describing the phenomena associated with the law of metamorphosis in light of the human potential toward *transformation*; and let us consider this both with respect to our discussion thus far <u>and</u> in relation to the "reining in" or taking hold of one's feeling nature, which comes to expression in a wonderful way through the eurythmy gesture for the Moon in cosmic dance:

> *The phenomena of the law of metamorphosis must be studied in so far as they may be observed in human existence. For such phenomena may be observed in the sphere of the human being's inner life as well as in that of the structure of bodily organs. In both spheres the rule holds good that metamorphosis occurs through the alternation of restriction and freedom. Speech, for example, is a metamorphosis of the faculty of movement by an enhancement of this faculty. The enhancement, however, could not have taken place unless a limit had been set to the outer movement. Suppressed external movements became the concentrated movements of speech. Similarly, the faculty of thought is a further stage of the metamorphosis of the faculty of movement. Thinking is an enhancement of the faculty of speaking when the latter is checked by suppression. In silence, the human being learns to think, as in the bridling of the urge to movement one learns to speak. But this metamorphosis can be carried further. Thinking can be enhanced into a new, higher faculty. This may result from the thought-movement being consciously brought to a stand-still when it is not a question of passivity or of deficiency of thought but of the whole thinking-force being concentrated on one point. Through this concentration, thinking is enhanced and transformed into the faculty of <u>spiritual seeing</u>. This metamorphosis is brought about through the practice of Meditation…*

> *Hence, on the karmic path of Initiation the soul must pass through an inner – and also often an outer – situation in which all the basic forces of feeling and willing are bound…*[110]

---

[110] Valentin Tomberg, <u>New Testament Studies</u>, pp. 158-159.

The Exaltation of the Moon

The Moon finds her place of exaltation at 3° <u>Taurus</u>, marking the region of the ***Pleiades***.[111] The seven stars which comprise the Pleiadian cluster (located at 5° in the neck of the Bull) reveal the true *voice* of Taurus, and were imagined in antiquity as the *Seven Daughters of Atlas* who wept for their father, who had taken on the burdens of the world.

The Hindu system of 28 "**Nakshatras**" which are referred to as "**Lunar Mansions**" <u>begins</u> in the region of the neck of the Bull which contains the Pleiadian cluster. It is quite striking that the star **Atlas** directly adjoins the stars of the Pleiades, the "Seven Sisters", who represent the seven daughters of Atlas. Here we discover a correspondence with the first vertebra of the human spinal column – the atlas bone – which is the first of the seven cervical bones which support the neck and the base of the cranium. As the first vertebra, the atlas bone then bears a clear correspondence to the first Nakshatra, "Krittika" in Hindu astrology, which contains both the star Atlas and the star cluster of the Pleiades.

The 28 Nakshatras are defined by specific stars in the sidereal zodiac. They bear an obvious influence, when visited by the Moon, upon the human astral body, which comes to expression in the nervous system of which the 28 vertebrae are central.[112]

The 28 Lunar Mansions also correspond to the two 14-day periods of the <u>waxing</u> and <u>waning</u> phases of the visible Moon belonging to the ancient myth of **Isis** and **Osiris**, which foretold the future coming of Christ – in particular his death and resurrection through the Mystery of Golgotha.

In this way the Moon's exaltation in the region of the Pleiades remembers the future, for according to Rudolf Steiner, the progress of Earth evolution is headed toward the cosmic *out-breathing* of the Pleiades,[113] moving us toward the "Word of God".

The Maori people of New Zealand start the New Year with the heliacal rising of the Pleiades, or rather with the first <u>New Moon</u> after the appearance (heliacal rising) of the Pleiades in June. The Pleiades are called "Matariki" by the Maori, who say at the start of the New Year: *"Divine Matariki, come hither from the distant heavens; bestow the first fruits of the year upon us."*

Osiris and the Fullness of Time

The ancient **Egyptian** culture (which came into fullness in the Age of Taurus) celebrated the *re-membering* potential of the Moon's forces in the mystery teachings of the **myth of Isis and Osiris**, wherein Isis, the goddess of wisdom, each month lovingly gathers (re-members) the 14 parts of

---

[111] The Babylonians recognized that the Moon's place of exaltation, its most powerful location in the entire zodiac, is when it is located in the star cluster of the Pleiades, in the neck of the Bull. The Babylonians depicted the Moon together with the Pleiades on the cuneiform tablet Vat 7851 – see Ernst Weidner, <u>Gestirn-Darstellungen auf Babylonischen Tontafeln</u>, pp. 5-10. However, they did not specify the stellar location of the Pleiades exactly, indicating it to be 3° Taurus, when in fact the location of the Pleiades is at 5° Taurus.

[112] The 28 Nakshatras are referred to in the Vedas and play an important role in the ancient Vedic astrology. When the zodiac was introduced into India around AD 150, one of the Nakshatras (Abhijit) was dropped, and the remaining 27 Nakshatras were redefined to begin at 0° Aries. This arbitrary change <u>veiled</u> the understanding of the connection of the human being to the stars, since clearly the vertebrae begin with the upper part of the spinal column corresponding to Taurus.

[113] *"The next solar system will take place in the Pleiades. The whole solar system is moving toward the Pleiades"* - <u>Beiträge zur Rudolf Steiner Gesamtausgabe</u> 37/38 (1972), p. 81 (notes written by Rudolf Steiner).

Osiris' dismembered body – Osiris having been slain by his jealous brother.[114] On a conscious level the myth revealed the mysteries of the waxing and waning phases of the Moon. However, in our present-day soul *reflections* we recognize the mirroring of the Mystery of Golgotha and the 14 stages of the Cross.

In the myth, Isis is the primal <u>gathering</u> force that continues to bring the <u>generative</u> forces of <u>Osiris</u> into wholeness. Thus, Isis was recognized and revered as the sustaining force which re-members creation.

As with the "EI" (diphthong) sound of the Moon, this mystery teaching reveals the union of two sounds which sound as one.

The Octave

The octave of the principle of *re-membering* in the Isis and Osiris teaching occurred with the **Ascension** of Jesus Christ, which according to the research of Robert Powell took place on May 14, AD 33, when the ***Sun*** was located at 23° ***Taurus,*** whose sign/symbol ♉, with the upturned arc above a circle, *mirrors* the image and iconography of Isis with the crescent Moon above her head – a reflective image of the Moon gathered into fullness (becoming a Sun) beneath the "Grail Moon" (promise of new beginnings). This is an image of the fulfillment of the new Moon's *promise* of resurrection.

The Ascension — the Fulfillment of the Octave

Gather up the fragments, so that nothing may be lost. (*John* 6:12)

On the day of the **Ascension** the **Moon** was located at 16½° Aries in the heart of the constellation of the "Lamb" – remembering the location of the <u>Sun</u> at 15½° Aries on the day of the **Resurrection**.

It is quite remarkable to note that the **Moon**'s appearance in the heart of Aries (central decan) on the day of the Ascension remembered the **Sun**'s location for seven major events in the life of Jesus Christ:[115]

12° Aries	Mary Magdalene's anointing of the Messiah	April 1, AD 33
13½° Aries	Last Supper/Gethsemane Night	April 2, AD 33
14° Aries	The Transfiguration	April 3-4, AD 31
14° Aries	The Crucifixion	April 3, AD 33
14½° Aries	Jesus' Teaching in the Temple at age 12	April 3, AD 12
15½° Aries	The Resurrection	April 5, AD 33

… and finally, the **Ascension** day itself (May 14, AD 33; Moon 16½° Aries) when the ***Sun*** was at 23° ***Taurus,*** marking the fulfillment of the promise foretold in the myth concerning Isis and Osiris taught in the Age of Taurus.

---

[114] See Robert Powell, *Hermetic Astrology, vol.II: Astrological Biography*, pp. 358-362.
[115] See Robert Powell, *Christian Hermetic Astrology*, p. 234.

The Re-Membering of the Moon

The Subconscious – Hecate – the Cosmic Soul

One could say that the Moon remembers down into the depths of the soul life, whereas Saturn remembers up into the heights of the cosmic dimension of destiny.

As Grail Maiden and maintainer/sustainer of the etheric body of the Earth, the lunar forces accompany and serve the human soul while incarnated on the Earth.

For the Neoplatonists, the lunar realm was understood as the reflective source of reality and was imagined as the Moon Goddess **Hecate**, who represented the Cosmic Soul, the source of all virtue and the ruler of the visible (imaged) world.[116]

As the gateway to the soul's return to the cosmic realm after death, the Moon becomes the repository of the soul conditions of earthly life. In this way the etheric/life body of the Moon becomes the bearer of this imprint and thus remembers the conditions of our soul life.

We experience the constancy of the Moon's reflective influence in the images and symbolic language of our dreamtime, as well as in the patterning and *pre-conditioned* sentiments that live on in the depths of our subconscious.

In this way the Moon's relationship to the human psyche serves to indicate the heart's desires – how we must live in order to be happy. This is where a change in "heart" resuscitates the "good".

The heart's longing, which is remembered by the Moon and mirrored in our dream life, serves as a bridge to the realm of mystical reality. Here the soul's capacity for reflection is confronted with the relationship between the spiritual and material aspects of truth and is required to embrace both. The mystical realm has to do with two opposing realities – spirit and matter – requiring the capacity for paradoxical modes of thought and expression in order to bridge between them.

We approach the paradoxical when we consider the Greek understanding of Hecate as the Moon in her *invisible*, hidden aspect <u>sojourning beneath the horizon</u> in the depths of daytime reality. This reflects the "EI" sounding of the Moon's remembering in the subconscious soul life of the human being.

Hecate — Kamaloca — Soul Karma

Following upon the paradoxical understanding of **Hecate** as "Cosmic Soul" and "bearer of the Good" with Hecate in the *depths,* we encounter the Greek imagination of Hecate as the *"ruler of souls who come into the underworld at death."*[117] As the mistress to the underworld, Hecate was associated with stories of spirits and ghosts taking possession of the living – as well as being responsible for the occurrence of nightmares.

The imagination of the Greeks, of Hecate ruling the souls who come into the underworld after death, acknowledges the Moon's orbit as gateway for the soul's <u>return</u> to the cosmic realm after death.

---

[116] Robert Powell, *History of the Planets*, p. 25.
[117] Ibid.

Kamaloca

There is an esoteric teaching that the content of the soul memory, which has been recorded within the human being during life, is re-experienced in the Moon sphere after death. This is called **kamaloca**, which is an *unwinding* or replaying of images from one's life that occurs as the lower astral body begins to dissolve in the Moon sphere after death in the first period of the soul's passage back through the planetary spheres. This process, which is generally accepted as an esoteric truth, has been highlighted in recent years by accounts of people who have lived through "near death" experiences and afterwards have described having experienced a panoramic flashback of their life.

Thus the Moon can be imagined as the bearer of our soul karma, for it is this that takes possession of the living and also authors the mysterious haunting of our most dreaded nightmares.

The Dark Side of the Moon

> *The Moon is a very polite lady – she never shows us her backside.* (W.J. Stein)

This comment describing one of the unique aspects of the Moon is mirrored in human behavior in the curious phenomenon of *masking*. The whole fabric of the personality becomes a mirror image of the collective notion of what is valued in one's peer group and cultural background. This becomes the *self* that we present to the world. In addition we fashion *identities* for ourselves which over time become hardened shells of automatic posturing and patterns of protection that completely mask the true identity – the real feelings and the deeper prompting of our soul which, were it not for the masking, would normally beckon us toward our true purpose and spiritual calling.

The tragedy of this *lunar temptation* is that often we become the mask – becoming nothing more than an automaton – unable to feel or to perceive the truth of our being.

Thomas Moore in his book *The Planets Within* describes how the lunar rhythms stir a continuous movement of soul and body, giving rise to promptings coming from deeper currents than superficial realities. These promptings are varied, as the Moon's reflections respond to *all* the planets and are therefore capable of orchestrating our life as an *organic* whole. The small ego engaged in ordinary experience moves in a faster rhythm than the deeper levels of psyche which are represented by the other planets. Thus there can be an impatience in the ego with the timing of the soul. *"Without the rhythm of lunar reflection, the ego will drive the soul to the brink of despair."*

The eurythmy Moon gesture is an expression of the call for inner reflection – a coming back to the center of one's true self – and a necessary emptying of ego concerns in order to receive a valid sense of direction toward the next movement in one's life.

> *Lunar watchfulness assures good timing, and a full awareness of body and soul conditions. Over time one is able to perceive the Moon's dynamics in the episodes of personal life – the waxing and waning, fullness and emptiness, beginnings and endings which give shape and tone to one's existence.* [118]

In his book *Freeing the Soul From Fear*, Robert Sardello describes how the modern conditioning of the world sensationalizes everything, so that our lunar sensing which is capable of *reflective touch* becomes desensitized. Our nervous system becomes dulled and overwhelmed with too many

---

[118] Thomas Moore, *The Planets Within*, p. 160.

images – too much, too fast. The soul's promptings and the call of the higher self are therefore not perceived, which results in a paralysis of the higher will. Automatic behavior becomes a convenience as we lose touch with the soul qualities of the world. A life filled with synthetic experiences and sensations lacks inner reflectiveness. In contrast, our lunar feeling nature provides a way of knowing – a knowing, through the soul, of the world.

The dark side of the Moon is a world of <u>inversion</u> to the *living* qualities of sense perception – producing an illusory world of fabricated reality.

The Shadow of the Moon: The Phenomenon of the Double

Following upon the theme of false images, we arrive at the phenomenon of the human double, which operates as a caricature of our true self. This is a subject filled with complexities that cannot be addressed adequately in a work on the cosmic dance of the planets. We will address the subject of the human double briefly in relationship to the eurythmy dance of the Moon. However, for greater depth and understanding, one is well served by the clear reflections of Valentin Tomberg in his book *Inner Development*.[119]

Basically, it is the human being who stands firmly in the stilled center of his existence, who must master the pull (from the left) of the temptation toward escape into an illusory world or the pull (from the right) into the hardening effects of materiality and mechanization.[120]

Both worlds pull upon the inner integrity of the human being, and both worlds are subject to the forces of the repository of our karmic past, which lives on in the fabric of our etheric/life body and astral body.[121] These are caricatures of our unredeemed nature and can result in thoughtless, unconscious behaviors which lack the reflected light of conscience.

"Look Within"[122]

With the "EI" eurythmy sound gesture we feel the pull of the tides of life – first to the right, then to the left. However, there is always the inner tension of the pull back to the heart – a gathering of the images of life's events, to be reflected upon in the stilled silence of the inner sanctum of the heart, reflecting the sovereignty of the human being who stands upright in the center of daily existence.

This place of centrality is the domain of the sovereign "I", the place of freedom from the phenomenon of the double, and thus requires a constancy of return – a daily moment-to-moment awareness of being awake to the call of conscience and a vigilance with respect to the shadow cast by the work of the double, which will automatically take over when there is a lack of consciousness.

---

[119] Chapter 2 of *Inner Development* deals with three aspects of the double. These aspects are also explored in Karen Rivers' study course on "Challenges of Inner Development: Encountering the Double", which is available from the Sophia Foundation of North America.

[120] See Valentin Tomberg, *New Testament Studies*, pp. 145-150.

[121] In Valentin Tomberg's *New Testament Studies* the two-sided tendency in the human being is described as a result of the Fall – with the temptation toward seeking illusion being activated by *shame* and the tendency toward materiality being motivated by *fear*.

[122] These words relate to the Moon form in eurythmy.

The Moon requires confronting self-delusion – one's dark side, or shadow. The Moon gesture in eurythmy allows us to experience the strengthening of the true nature of the Ego, which is able to *take hold* of the astral body's tendency toward unbridled behaviors – having their root cause in the depths of the unconscious.

This strengthening influence from within outwards results in what Valentin Tomberg calls "*bread from heaven*". For when we learn to attune to the soul's deepest yearnings, we awaken the boundless resources of the inner world.

> *When the inside is in order, the outside takes care of itself.* (Goethe)

The Institutional Double

The theme of the double has many aspects and levels which can inspire enlightening conversation and necessarily require deep reflective work. The book *Freeing the Soul From Fear* is helpful toward recognizing the doubling effect which lives as companion to daily life. The author, Robert Sardello, specializing in the spiritual psychology of the soul, suggests that work environments, institutions, marriage, and most creative endeavors all develop over time an energy pattern or thought form which takes on a life of its own and must be encountered with *fresh* perspectives, *human* warmth, and *living* thoughts that have their *genus* in the vitality of spiritual inspiration (inbreath).[123]

One could use the living imagination of the **Moon**, which according to science is a dead planet, as being an example of the Earth's double. However, the Moon *lives* by virtue of *movement* and *reflective* light from the living presence of the **Sun,** and in this way serves toward the revitalization of earthly life.

Lunar Rhythms

Moon's Nodes

In addition to the seven year rhythm in human biography, there is yet another lunar rhythm which affects the unfolding destiny of the human being. This is the rhythm of 18 years 7 months, the time taken by the Moon's nodal points to return to their same location as at the time of one's birth.

The Moon's nodes mark the points of intersection of the orbital path of the Moon with the apparent path of the Sun, which is called the **ecliptic**. The position on the ecliptic where the Moon rises above the ecliptic plane is designated as the ascending node (☊) and the place where it moves below, the descending node (☋).[124] The lunar nodes regress through the zodiac in a certain rhythm.

This rhythm occurs every 18 years 7 months, and is believed to indicate a *gateway* or opening to the greater "whole" – the world of the Sun and planets beyond the orbit of the Moon.

Like the Saturn rhythm of 29½ years, the Moon's nodal rhythm can show up quite prominently in one's biography over the course of one's life. One of the most striking examples of this was in the

---

[123] Robert Sardello, *Freeing The Soul From Fear*, pp. 145-174.
[124] The Moon's elliptical orbit is inclined 5° in relation to the orbit of the Sun, and because of this inclination there are nodes, which are the points of intersection of the two planes.

life of the astronaut Alan Shepard. There are three notable events in his biography which are evidently linked to the rhythm of the lunar nodes. The first is that he made his first flight into outer space at the time of his second Moon node (age 37). Later he was one of the twelve astronauts to walk on the Moon. This second notable event happened when he reached the age of 47, approximately midway between his second and third lunar node (the half rhythm of 9 years 3½ months is also an important rhythm). Thirdly, he died at age 74, which was his fourth Moon node return.[125]

The gateway openings which occur with the return of the Moon's node to its location in the zodiac at the time of one's birth offer a meeting or karmic interface of our soul memories (remembered by the Moon) with the *inspirations* of our higher spiritual calling of destiny, emanating from the realm of the Sun.

The *Transfiguration* of Jesus Christ took place when the Moon's <u>ascending</u> node (gateway to the astral world) was in <u>conjunction</u> with *Aldebaran* (15° Taurus) – known as the "Eye of God". Remembering that the Moon finds her place of *exaltation* in Taurus, we have quite a remarkable image with the Moon's *ascending* node coming into conjunction with Aldebaran – a coming together of the Moon's gateway with Aldebaran, the stellar "Eye of God", at the time of the pouring in of light with the Transfiguration.

Pertaining to Human Biography

The Moon's nodal points move in a retrograde direction around the ecliptic, passing through the center of the zodiacal belt. This movement signifies a gradually changing relationship of the Moon's nodes to the constellations, shifting in a clockwise direction (<u>opposite</u> to the counter-clockwise movement of Sun, Moon and planets through the zodiac). The slow retrograde movement of the Moon's nodes through the zodiac amounts to a shift of just over 1½° each month. A complete revolution of the lunar nodes through the zodiac takes 18 years 7 months, and it is this *return* of the Moon's nodal points to the same zodiacal location as at the time of birth that can be noted as a time of significant change in human biography.

The significance of this rhythm becomes particularly apparent in childhood at the halfway point – around 9 years 3½ months – when the child's lunar relationship with the mother looses its hold and the child begins to see itself as separate from its parents. Now the child seeks a mirroring of itself from the greater peer group in the environment of play and school.

---

[125] Regarding the middle one of the three events referred to here, the exact point in time of 2½ orbits of the Moon nodes is 46½ years of age, and when Shepard landed on the Moon he was 47 years 2½ months old, 8½ months past the exact Moon node return (2½ x 18.61 = 46½). Taking account of the half cycle of 9 years 3½ months, the times of the "gateway openings" of the Moon nodes' returns are: 9 years 3½ months, 18 years 7 months, 27 years 11 months, 37 years 2 months, 46 years 6 months, 55 years 10 months, etc. Since the Moon's nodes can be conceived of as an axis extending from one side of the zodiac to the other, it is apparent that a "gateway opening" occurs not only when the axis has rotated through 360 degrees, but also when it has rotated halfway, i.e. through 180 degrees. With the three events in Alan Shepard's life referred to here, it will be noticed that in each case these events occurred a few months after the exact Moon node return. Just as one first has a thought and then usually some time elapses before the thought is brought to realization in action, so the cosmic event – in this case the return of the Moon's nodes – sows an impulse, which generally is only brought to realization some time later.

The Eclipse Phenomenon

The **Sun**'s orbit intersects the axis of the lunar nodes in a six-month rhythm[126] and the Moon crosses its nodal axis approximately every two weeks. This creates the possibility that from time to time the **Moon** and the **Sun** *meet* at one of the two nodal points. The new Moon is the occurrence of the meeting (conjunction) of the Sun and Moon. When the new Moon occurs at or close to one or other of the Moon's nodes, an eclipse of the <u>Sun</u> occurs. Whereas the Sun is *always* on the ecliptic – by definition the ecliptic is the Sun's path through the zodiacal belt – the Moon crosses the ecliptic only at the nodal points. Only then is the possibility given for the Moon to cover the face of the Sun. Otherwise, at every other new Moon, the Moon is either above or below the Sun and not directly in front of it. Therefore the precondition for a solar eclipse is that the new Moon takes place at, or close to, one of the lunar nodes.

What is the precondition for a lunar eclipse? First, it has to be full Moon, which means that the Moon, the Earth, and the Sun are aligned. Second, for the same reason as in the case of a solar eclipse, it is only when at **full Moon** the Sun and the Moon are *opposite* one another at or near the nodal points that an eclipse of the <u>Moon</u> takes place. Then at **full Moon**, when simultaneously the Sun and Moon are at or close to the Moon's nodes, a total *lunar eclipse* is caused by the shadow of the Earth cast upon the Moon, since the Earth is then *exactly* (or more or less exactly) between the Sun and the Moon on the nodal axis. On the other hand, at **new Moon**, when the Sun and Moon are in conjunction with or sufficiently close to the nodal axis, a total *solar eclipse* is due to the Moon's passage <u>between</u> the Earth and Sun. Partial eclipses occur when the Sun and Moon are within proximity of the Moon's nodes but are not directly at or sufficiently close to the lunar nodes to cause a total eclipse.

There is yet another factor to consider, and that is the distance of the Moon from the Earth. Since the Moon moves in an *elliptical* orbit, it is sometimes nearer and at other times further away from the Earth. When the Moon is at *perigee* – closest to the Earth – the apparent disks of the Sun and Moon are almost exactly the same size, so that at a solar eclipse the Moon's face then completely covers the Sun. However, when the Moon is at *apogee* (furthest away from the Earth), at an eclipse of the Sun, since the disk of the Moon then no longer completely covers the Sun, a rim of light will appear around the darkened face of the Moon. This is called an ***annular eclipse***.

Sidereal —Synodic Rhythms

The Moon has <u>two</u> primary observable rhythms. There is the 27⅓-day rhythm, which is calculated by the Moon's position in front of the <u>fixed stars</u>. The Moon requires this period of time to return to the same zodiacal location. This is called the ***sidereal rhythm***, 27⅓ days being the length of time taken for the Moon, wherein the spoken word of form (cosmic breath) meets the "*silent radiation*" of memory and realities beyond the threshold, to return to conjunction with the same fixed star.

In addition there is the 29½-day rhythm, the ***synodic rhythm***, arising out of the Moon's relationship to the <u>Sun</u> from phase to phase – for example, from full Moon to full Moon or from new Moon to new Moon. In the latter case, due to the Sun's <u>progression</u> through the zodiac, the Moon – after returning to conjunction with the same fixed star after 27⅓ days – requires an <u>additional</u> two days to catch up with the Sun. (This accounts for the brief period of a little over two days after the Moon has returned to the same zodiacal location as at the preceding new Moon, which elapses until the actual occurrence of the next new Moon.)

---

[126] The 6-month rhythm of the Sun's passage through the lunar nodes comes 18½ days earlier each year.

The Phases of the Moon

The four phases of the Moon taking place from one new Moon to the next – first Quarter, full Moon, last Quarter, new Moon – form an approximate cross in space. The **waxing** phase is when the Moon is growing in fullness from new Moon to full Moon, and correspondingly the **waning** phase is when the Moon's fullness is lessening between the full Moon and the new Moon.

The *new Moon* occurs when the Moon is in *conjunction* with the Sun (same zodiacal location), whereas the *full Moon* occurs when the Moon appears on the opposite side of the zodiac to the Sun's zodiacal location. Following these rhythms in daily life, one could consider the new Moon phase as a time of sowing, when a new impulse is given, and the full Moon phase as a time of blossoming, or the coming into full flower of that which was sown at the new Moon.[127]

Lunar Years vs. Solar Years

Yet another lunar rhythm can be found in the calendars of different peoples/cultures around the world who celebrate a lunar year rather than a solar year. For these cultures the day begins at dusk and the length of the month is measured by the movement of the Moon in *relation* to the Sun – new Moon to new Moon.[128]

The twelve months of the lunar calendar are based on the synodic 29½-day rhythm of the Moon, which includes the two-day period required for the Moon – after the completion of the sidereal rotation of 27⅓ days – to catch up with the progression of the Sun in its rotation around the zodiac. Thus, the length of the lunar year – comprising 12 synodic months – amounts to 354⅓ days, falling eleven days short of the 365¼ days in a solar year.

Intercalary Lunar Years

Complications occur when we consider the eleven days which remain at the end of each **lunar** year before the beginning of the next **solar** year. (In a symbolic sense these 11 days or 12 nights are traditionally celebrated as the twelve holy nights between December 25 and January 6 each year.)

Over time it becomes necessary to add (intercalate) an additional month (13th month) to catch up with the rhythm of the solar year.

How and when the varying cultures adjust the **intercalation** of the 13th month differs. For example, the Hebrew lunar calendar adds seven extra lunar months intercalated over a 19-year period. However, the Muslim cultures do not intercalate extra lunar months at all. They adhere to a year comprising twelve lunar months. For example, the celebration of the Fast of Ramadan (lasting for the whole month of Ramadan, the ninth month of the Muslim calendar) shifts back eleven days earlier every year in terms of the solar calendar. Thus it requires 33 years for the Muslim calendar to come back into synchronicity with the solar year, since 34 lunar years (twelve lunar months, each 29½ days long = 12,050½ days) is a

---

[127] Rudolf Steiner's indications reveal an interesting correspondence. He spoke of the new Moon as having an effect upon the human brain, the full Moon upon the base of the spine, and the first and last Quarters upon the middle region in between – Rudolf Steiner, *Man in the Light of Occultism, Theosophy, and Philosophy*, p. 166. Further, he referred to the new Moon as a time of putting questions to the spiritual world and full Moon as a time of receiving answers to one's questions – Rudolf Steiner, *Human Questions and Cosmic Answers*, p. 10.

[128] The lunar calendar of ancient Egypt is an exception, because the Egyptians were basically oriented toward the Sun and began their day at sunrise. Their lunar calendar, therefore, extended from the old Moon, the last visible crescent of the Moon seen at the time of dawn/sunrise, to the next old Moon.

mere 2½ days short of 33 solar years (33 x 365¼ = 12,053 days). Therefore it would be wrong to assume that the month of Ramadan starts on the same day of the year in each solar year.

The Dark Moon (New Moon)

The lunar year is observed by a significant number of cultures in the modern world – Hebrew, Muslim, Chinese, Japanese, and others. In the Hebrew calendar, for example, each lunar month begins with the observation of the first crescent of the *visible* new Moon. The first crescent of the new Moon becomes visible in the evening approximately 18 hours (this time varies depending on conditions) later than the astronomical/*actual* new Moon which is hidden by the Sun's aura when the Sun and Moon are conjunct.

The "dark of the Moon" is the period of time between the disappearance of the last crescent of the Moon (old Moon) and the first visible appearance of the crescent of the new Moon. These days were counted as Sabbath days (days of rest) in some cultures of antiquity.

Lunar Phases in Nature

We can observe how the phases of the Moon work upon the watery element in nature. For example, scientists have observed an increase in the precipitation of rainfall three to five days after the new Moon and also after the full Moon.

Both the Earth's etheric body and the etheric/life body of the human being are strongly affected by the lunar rhythms. We see this in the tides of the Earth's waters and in the movement of fluids in the human **spinal column**. The waxing and waning phases of the Moon appear to also have a subtle effect upon mental activity, due to the stirring of the memory field within the etheric body.

The woman's **menstruation** cycle corresponds to the **synodic** (waxing and waning) rhythm of the Moon. One could say that the rhythm of menstruation corresponds to the dark of the Moon (new Moon) phase, representing the completion of one cycle and the beginning of the next cycle – whereas **ovulation**, the release of the egg from the fallopian tube, would correspond to the full Moon.

With each new Moon phase, the lunar presence serves as vessel and Grail Maiden for the fresh breath of life emanating from the Sun, which enlivens the etheric/life realm of the Earth. Following upon this initial breath of freshness, the gathering force of the full Moon phase (which works upon both the astral and etheric/life body) serves as a reflective force to magnify the astral conditions of the human soul in relation to the world soul – and can as a result bring about an experience of upheaval in the emotional life, if the astral body is out of control.

Lunar Phases in Dreams

The two-day period of the **synodic** rhythm, during which the Moon catches up with the Sun, corresponds to the time required for the **astral body** to *impress* itself into the **etheric body**. We experience this in our dream life, wherein our etheric bodies become imprinted with the content of our astral concerns emanating from the Moon sphere – the realm of our **guardian angel**. Dreams are known to be especially potent around the times of new Moon and full Moon.

Angelic Rhythms — Synodic Month

As discussed earlier, the Moon sphere is the realm of the angels. Keeping in mind that the new Moon works most strongly on the head forces, it is interesting to consider that the <u>dark phase</u> of the Moon (from the Earth's perspective) would correspond to midday for the angels from the perspective of the Moon sphere. At this time the Moon is closest to the Sun and receives the maximum amount of light – analogous to the time of midday on Earth. During this time the angels are active in our <u>thought</u> life, the thinking realm. The Moon is a storehouse of wisdom handed down from generation to generation.

Correspondingly, the <u>full Moon</u> (from Earth's perspective) would be experienced as midnight for the angels, as the Moon is then on the other side of the Earth and is furthest away from the Sun. During this time the angels are very active in our <u>dream time</u>. The full Moon works most strongly upon the base of the spine – the realm of the will and instinctual life, relating to the subconscious level in the human being.

Following the analogy of the lunar cycle with the times of the day as experienced by the angels in the Moon sphere, we can understand the correspondence of "angel sunset" to the first quarter Moon and "angel sunrise" to the last quarter. The phase when the Moon is 90 degrees in relation to the Sun (sunset and sunrise in this analogy) would be experienced more in the region of the heart and lungs – thus affecting the rhythmic system in the human being.

Selene and the Phases of the Moon

> *Horned Selene waxed bright ...And led the way as shepherdess of the nocturnal gods.*
> (*Orphic Descant on the Resurrection*, Hymn IX, 35-38)[129]

The Greek imagination of the Moon was threefold – represented by three goddesses: Selene, Artemis, and Hecate. Each embodied a different aspect of the mysteries inherent in the movement of the Moon.

Unlike Hecate,[130] who represented the *hidden* aspect of the Moon – when the Moon was sojourning <u>beneath</u> the horizon and thus hidden to day consciousness – it was Selene[131] who represented the *beauty* of the Moon's *appearance* in the night sky. Thus, it was she who was most intimately connected to the phases of the Moon and the more <u>physical</u> aspects of life – most especially the physical life of women, reflected in the female menses[132] and the sidereal rhythms of the embryonic period, conception and birth. She is the goddess who was considered important toward the growth of plants as well as health and sickness.

As the nocturnal *partner* to the Sun, **Selene** was sister and bride to **Helios**, whose chariot drove the Sun across the sky each day. Correspondingly, because Selene embodies the qualities of the Moon's nightly appearance, she appears "horned" representing the phases of the crescent Moon.

---

[129] Quoted from James Miller, *Measures of Wisdom*, p. 343.
[130] Hecate – Greek word meaning "the hidden one", see C. Kerenyi, *The Gods of the Greeks*, p. 35.
[131] Selene – "bearer of the light of the Moon", from the root Greek word *Selas*, meaning "light".
[132] Mene – feminine form of men – Greek word meaning lunar month. The Moon goddess as she appeared in the sky was also called "Mene".

Fair Artemis

Whereas Selene was celebrated for the beauty of her nightly vigil amongst the stars, it was fair Artemis who represented the quiet wonder of the rising and setting of the Moon, and thus all things "fleeting" and transitory – associated more with the soul aspects of life. We recognize her as the Greek counterpart to Diana, the Goddess of the Hunt. As mistress to the animal world, her special animal was the deer, whose gentle elusive appearance corresponds to the fleeting appearance of the rising and setting of the Moon.

It was **Artemis** who was considered the youthful, virginal guardian of children, the preserver of innocence, and thus was important to the blessing of weddings and correspondingly to the mysteries of the planting of seeds and the developing integrity of organic healing preparations.

In her aspect as guardian to the threshold of the rising and setting of the Moon, we can understand her association with all things elusive and mysterious. Relating more to the soul dimension of the Moon, she was imagined as the twin sister of **Apollo**, who was the embodiment of the "*soul aspects of the Sun in an ethical and spiritual sense*".[133]

Just as Apollo brings healing through the music of his lyre, so too Artemis was considered important to all matters of healing. In her appearance and disappearance aspect she was guardian to all travelers, paths, and even ships at sea.

Silver and the Moon[134]

"By the Light of the Silvery Moon…"

Silver is the metal corresponding to the Moon. Reflecting this correspondence, the Moon goddess Artemis was depicted in art as the "Huntress with the Silver Bow". This image points us toward the lunar aspect of silver that requires darkness for its processes to work (its salts are spoilt by exposure to light). For this reason a darkroom is a requirement for the development of film. Indeed, the entire film industry is dependent upon silver in celluloid to record light images, which are viewed in darkened movie theaters on the "silver screen". In the modern world, movie viewers who go to see the performance of the "stars" are perhaps seeking an imitation of the haunting beauty revealed by the reflection in the night sky of the stars, which, requiring darkness, have become veiled by the "light pollution" of city life.

Silver is the best reflector of visible light known, and has the highest electrical and thermal conductivity of all the metals. Silver's reflective quality is one of receptivity. Like the Moon receiving the light of the Sun, silver produces a mirroring effect that is *passive* in nature and therefore faithful to its mirrored image, whereas gold is like the Sun, which emanates its own outgoing radiance.

There is a correspondence of the faithful mirroring of the Moon within the activity of our dream life, the image-producing faculty of the human being. Our dreams occur in darkness and are illumined by the mirroring effects of the light of the Moon (the work of the angels) – offering faithful images toward the healing of the psyche and all that has been received by the light of day. Correspondingly,

---

[133] Robert Powell, *History of the Planets*, p. 25.
[134] Most of this information is a synthesis and paraphrasing of the research presented by Nick Kollerstrom from his Alchemy Web Site entitled Silver and the Moon. http://www.levity.com/alchemy/Kollerstrom_moon.html

the properties of silver used for photography create *memory* images and the silver coating of glass produces the mirroring whereby we can behold ourselves. Therapists call upon these lunar aspects of human nature for the healing of the past and a faithful mirroring of the present.

Most of the world's silver occurs dissolved in the oceans. Just as the Moon pulls upon the tides of the Earth's waters, so too silver, the Moon's metal, has a remarkably potent effect upon the water processes in nature. While it is generally known that both rainfall and tides are influenced by the lunar cycle, it is less commonly known that the dust of silver oxide is actually used to make rain. (When sprinkled on rain clouds it causes condensation.)

Ionic silver is used as a bactericide for the purification of water. We find this used in good domestic water purifying systems, which contain an ion exchange system with a silver tube serving as a bactericide. At Johns Hopkins University of Maryland, a community pool was kept clean using only a carbon-silver purifier. Researchers found no cases of ear infections or eye irritations during this time and no other disinfectants were necessary.

Water can be kept fresh by storing it in silver vessels. It has been recorded that the early American settlers purified their water while moving West by leaving a silver dollar in their water containers overnight. Following upon this practiced wisdom, a US Navy study found that ships passing through contaminated waters could make their water safe for drinking with a silver concentration of ten parts per billion (the equivalent of a homeopathic D8 concentration). This is a method commonly used by shipping companies in the modern world.

Silver's Healing Properties

Ongoing research proves silver to be a versatile and effective natural healing agent against bacteria, fungi and viruses. Viruses find it almost impossible to develop a resistance to it. Known for its antiseptic properties, it can be used to purify skin conditions, and when used in its <u>colloidal</u> form it is considered a natural antibiotic, having an antimicrobial effect.

Silver is safe for use during pregnancy and lactation, having a healing effect upon painful bouts of mastitis during the breast-feeding phase of motherhood. Silver catheters are known to prevent urinary tract infections.

In addition to silver's anti-viral qualities, silver also has an effect upon the healing of injured and damaged tissue. Following upon the success of using silver electrodes to stimulate bone-forming cells, including the healing of the skin and soft tissue,[135] silver has for many years now been used in bone healing techniques and is wisely incorporated into bandages to quicken the healing process.

Colloidal Silver and Chromatography

Process and Revelation

This modern photography technique produces a building up of images through the use of a precipitation of colloidal silver. Unlike ordinary photography, which produces the recording of light images, images produced through the process of chromatography come about not through the mirroring of light but from <u>the changing conditions of the cosmos itself</u>.

---

[135] Research pioneered by Robert O. Becker, M.D., in *The Body Electric*.

To understand this process we must call upon our imagination, the image-making faculty that is the gift of our lunar nature. For the activity of the imagination in visualizing the building up process of chromatography (which requires the use of the salt solutions of the seven planetary metals) can also serve as a revelatory means toward an understanding and imagination of the forming, building processes of healing.

The use of the seven planetary metals in chromatography was developed by Lili Kolisko as a means to explore the effect of changing cosmic conditions upon the growth of plants – for example, to discover the mirroring of the coming together or opposition of planets, the effect of solar or lunar eclipses, etc., upon the organic life of the plant kingdom.[136]

In this process a piece of filter paper is formed in a cylindrical shape and dampened with the life juices of a plant which has been cut during a significant cosmic event. This colors the paper, which is left to dry and stabilize overnight. To this is added, the following day, a metal salt solution, using the metal that corresponds to the cosmic condition appropriate to the moment.

The planetary metal salt solution serves as a catalyst, which allows the plant fluid in the paper to become visible – new forms and colors arise. The images which are produced allow one to see what is working in the life of the plant in correspondence to the changes in the cosmos.

The results are nothing short of a revelation. From the moment when the plant is picked, the plant juices are shown to follow the course of the current cosmic event. For example, the midpoint of an eclipse can be clearly seen in the changing color and form of the image.

With **chromatography** – as with the light of the silvery Moon – the Moon metal faithfully reflects the wisdom emanating from the living body of the cosmos and allows the human being to behold (as in a mirror) that all creation is of one organic whole. We can behold ourselves as created in the image and likeness of the creator. The receptive, reflective nature of the Moon's metal serves to demonstrate Sophia's wisdom through the activity of the Divine Feminine serving as vessel, to receive, hold and bear fruit. This is the faithful reflection of the creative principle.

Lunar Influences / Health

Rudolf Steiner describes how the lunar phases work upon the shaping of the human being's etheric body – the subtle body of life sustaining energy patterns which penetrates the physical body. There is an interaction between this life providing subtle body and the seven major energy centers known as the seven chakras, relating to the seven planets and inner organs of the human being. The first chakra (the root chakra) relates specifically to the Moon and is located at the base of the spine.

Steiner further describes how the full Moon works upon the outer *shaping* of this energy body (etheric/life body), whereas the new Moon influences the inner *informing* patterns of etheric life. In this way the phases of the Moon *serve* as a source of renewal for the life-sustaining energy body, which is active from the moment of conception onward throughout the whole of life and comes into dissolution only upon death.

This picture of life-sustaining nourishment relating to the lunar phases becomes even clearer when we consider the effect of the Moon on the rhythms of menstruation and ovulation, with the full

---

[136] Lili Kolisko, *The Moon and the Growth of Plants*.

Moon – symbolically speaking – activating the release of the egg from the fallopian tube. This, of course, is an archetypal image, and in practice ovulation can take place at any phase of the Moon.

According to Rudolf Steiner, knowledge concerning the soul's incarnation was particularly followed in the Mysteries of Ephesus, wherein there was an initiatory teaching revolving around the forming/informing processes of the Moon's activity within the vivifying principles of life.[137]

The Lunar Mansions: *"In my father's house there are many mansions..."* (*John* 14:2)

The Vedic system of astrology utilizes the lunar Nakshatras – a division of the zodiacal circle into 28 (equal division) "lunar mansions" – which are believed to be the bearers of 28 unique and distinguishable lunar qualities. Upon careful observation one can discover a relationship of correspondence between the lunar mansions and the formation of the human spinal column. For instance, as discussed earlier, a major star in the first lunar mansion is named **Atlas**, corresponding to the "atlas" bone which is the first of the seven cervical vertebrae which support the head of the human being. This first lunar mansion is located in the constellation of *Taurus,* which relates to the neck and throat (*"In the beginning was the Word..."*), and Atlas is the first star adjoining the seven stars comprising the *Pleiades* (the seven daughters of Atlas),[138] which are located in the neck of the Bull.

If we consider the observation of Rudolf Steiner, that the human nervous system is stimulated by the lunar phases through the activity of the fluids in the human brain and spinal column – the new Moon working upon the **brain** and the full Moon upon the *base* of the **spine** – then the correspondence of the lunar mansions with the 28 vertebrae of the spinal column becomes more and more evident. More specifically, there is a relational correspondence of the 28 Nakshatras to the seven **cervical** vertebrae followed by the twelve **thoracic** vertebrae and five **lumbar** vertebrae which are supported at the base of the spine by the **coccyx** bone, which is comprised of four vertebrae melded together in the shape of a triangle – making a total of 28 vertebrae.

Perhaps the Vedic priests who established the teaching of the Nakshatras or lunar mansions were able to attune to the Ancient Moon level of existence, when the foundation seeds for the forming of the astral body were created – the astral body coming to expression through the central nervous system that is embodied primarily in the spinal column as its "central pillar" in the physical body.

Planting by the Moon[139]

Although both the Sun and the Moon have a powerful influence upon plant life, the solar rhythm is considered too slow for use in planting schedules. However, lunar calendars are often used in agricultural practice.

---

[137] The Mysteries of Ephesus, cultivated at the great temple of Artemis of Ephesus, are described by Rudolf Steiner in his lectures *The Easter Festival in the Evolution of the Mysteries*.

[138] According to the ancient myth, the seven daughters of Atlas were awarded their place in heaven for their great piety in having wept so much on account of their father's toil in holding up the world.

[139] Information gathered from the article entitled *"Lunar Calendar for Farmers and Gardeners"* by Robert Powell reported in the *Mercury Star Journal* dated Midsummer 1977, Volume III, No. 2.

Some planting calendars indicate the Moon's highest and lowest positions in the night sky, which correspond to the Sun's summer and winter solstice points – the Sun's highest position being at midsummer and lowest at mid-winter.

With the lunar calendar we can observe that the twelve lunar months trace the rhythm of the phases of the Moon against the background of the twelve constellations with an additional month "intercalated" in years with thirteen lunar months. Each lunar month comprises four lunar weeks corresponding to the phases of the Moon.

Rainfall and weather changes appear to be correlated with the lunar weeks. In particular, new Moon and full Moon tend to precipitate rainfall, especially in the period 3-5 days after the new or full Moon. Therefore farmers often plan their planting schedules before the new or full Moon to take advantage of the anticipated rainfall.

The practice of bio-dynamic farming came about through the inspiration of Rudolf Steiner in 1924 as an honoring of the spiritual dimension which brings wisdom to the planting of crops. These ideas have spawned a body of research over the years. For example, in observing the fourfold nature of plants, Maria Thun made use of the knowledge that all plants can be classified into the four types:

Root types	potatoes, carrots, turnips, etc.
Leaf types	cabbages, lettuce, etc.
Flower types	beans, peas, tomatoes, etc.
Fruit-seed types	cauliflower, broccoli, etc.

Guenther Wachsmuth, a scientist who worked closely together with Rudolf Steiner, was the first to postulate that since one of the four elements predominates in each of the signs of zodiac, therefore the four types of plants might benefit from a planting schedule that corresponded to their most predominant element. Maria Thun set out to test this hypothesis, which proved to bear positive results. These relationships are summarized in the following Table.

Moon sign	Element	For planting crops of
Taurus, Virgo, Capricorn	Earth	Root type
Cancer, Scorpio, Pisces	Water	Leaf type
Gemini, Libra, Aquarius	Air	Flower type
Aries, Leo, Sagittarius	Fire	Fruit-seed type

In 27⅓ days the Moon passes through each of the twelve constellations of the zodiac, spending a little over two days in each zodiacal division. Hence, the influence exerted by the Moon can be readily harnessed by the farmer who wisely waits for the planting of each type of plant until the Moon is in an appropriate part of the heavens. This method of planting by the Moon, according to the Moon's constellational background (as indicated above), has been popularized by Maria Thun, who produces a yearly calendar – based on the passage of the Moon through the constellations – indicating which plants are to be sown on what dates.[140]

Independent research by Lili Kolisko tested the traditional belief that leaf crops are best sown during the waxing Moon, in contrast to root crops which are best sown under the waning Moon. She concluded that <u>all</u> vegetables have the best growth by sowing two days prior to the full Moon.[141]

---

[140] Maria and Matthias Thun, *The Biodynamic Planting and Sowing Calendar* (yearly).
[141] Lili Kolisko, *The Moon and the Growth of Plants*, p. 86.

According to Maria Thun, even the Moon's nodes bear an influence upon the growth of plants. She warns not to sow at times when the Moon is crossing its nodes, as the *"streamings from the cosmos are not helpful to plant life."*[142]

Finally, it is important to note that in the observation of the lunar calendar for successful planting, the extensive research of Nick Kollerstrom over the years reveals conclusively that the planting calendar responds most favorably to the sidereal month, relating to the actual location of the Moon against the background of the stars, rather than referring to the location of the Moon indicated in the tropical calendar in common use among astrologers.

It is important to remember that the lunar month is understood as the interval from one new Moon to the next. This is the synodic month consisting of approximately 29½ days. Quite independent of the Moon's phase is the division of the zodiac occupied by the Moon. There are, generally speaking, three ways in which this zodiacal division is defined:

1) the equal-division *tropical sign* used in contemporary astrology;
2) the unequal-division *constellation* used in astronomy;
3) the equal-division *sidereal sign* used in ancient star wisdom by the Babylonians, Egyptians, Greeks, Romans, and still used to the present day in Vedic astrology.

Kollerstrom's research shows that the results obtained by planting seeds when the Moon is in (1) are poor, in (2) are good, and in (3) are excellent.[143] In (3) the *Moon sign* is determined by the background of fixed stars against which the Moon appears, and there are twelve *sidereal signs* through which the Moon passes in approximately 27⅓ days – this being the sidereal month. (As already mentioned, in one year – actually in a period of 354⅓ days – there are twelve sidereal months.) As Kollerstrom's research findings indicate, it is in conjunction with the sidereal month, using the passage of the Moon through the twelve equal-division sidereal signs, that the best results in planting by the Moon are obtained.

The Mysteries of the Astral Body

With our exploration of the **Ancient Moon** evolution, we have come into a reflective observation of the mysteries of **movement** (*the divine breath over the face of the waters*), which serve as the birthing waters and breath for the growth processes in nature. It is through the **astral body** that creation comes into a dynamic interface with the archetypal, wisdom filled realms of cosmic space. In the process of growth the body of **time** (the etheric/life body) and the body of **space** (the astral body) unfold as an experience of the movement of creation. This is a gift which is carried by way of the brain and central nervous system in the human being. Thus, the **Moon Day** of existence bequeathed an instrument of insight for the reflection of cosmic light and breath toward the serving of divine purpose.

In the following movement of cosmic time, the solar nebula contracted further, leaving behind the planet **Mars**, whose planetary orbit defines the working realm of the **Thrones**, the Spirits of Will.

---

[142] Reported by Hazel Straker, *Astrosophy, Introduction to a Quest for a New Star Wisdom*, p. 34.
[143] Nick Kollerstrom, *Planting by the Moon* (1999), pp. 37-53.

Cosmic *Eurythmy*
"In the image and likeness…"

Mars: *"Passionate, compelling, aggressive"*[144]

Chakra: Larynx
Organ :   Gall Bladder
Gland :   Thyroid
Metal :   Iron
Color :   Red
Tones :   C and F[145]

Tuesday "Mardi" Mars Day

Now with the **fourth stage** of planetary evolution, a further contraction brings the Earth's gaseous/ watery, atmosphere into *physical manifestation*. This is the **Tuesday** of existence, Mars day, named after the Norse god, **Tiw** who was the equivalent of the Roman god **Mars**.[146]

Mars *materializes* what has been *conceptualized*, calling into creation all that is "potential" from the days of Ancient Moon – bringing it down to **Earth** and into the physical realm of worldly existence. Consciousness here becomes the material of life.

Remembering the image of the Moon as Grail Maiden and threshold for birth into earthly life, now Mars brings **force** to the contraction, pushing through the heavenly impulse, in right timing – the decisive moment for the crossing of the threshold from the spiritual into the physical.

Mars is connected with beginnings and can be seen to have a corresponding relationship to the larynx **chakra** in the human being, connected with the mysteries of the Creative Word… *"In the beginning was the Word"* … and *"the Word became flesh"* – materialized. This brings a fullness to our understanding of the words connected with Mars, *"To firmly willed existence."*[147]

In the cosmic dance of Mars we shall discover through further exploration of the planetary color, gesture and sound that the true mission of Mars is the *manifestation of spiritual will*, through **moral speech** (larynx chakra) and **right action** in the world, expressed in eurythmy by a decisive *"movement to the right"* – bringing to expression the *will* nature of the human being.

The Mars color **red** denotes **fire**, as in the "fire of divine love" associated with the work of the **Seraphim** from the realm of **Saturn**. It is the fiery force of divine love that is present in the bright red color of **blood,** which flows from the chalice and warmth of the heart, *inspired* in the days of **Ancient Sun** and imbued with the wisdom of the **Cherubim** in **Jupiter's** realm. This sacred

---

[144] Rudolf Steiner, *History and Content of the Higher Degrees of the Esoteric School*, p. 247.

[145] The correspondences are tabulated in Appendix III: *Correspondences to the Seven Classical Planets*. See also Appendix II: *Musical Tones and the Planets*.

[146] To the Greeks Mars was Ares, to the Babylonians, Nergal, to the Egyptians Mars was "The Red Star of Horus"; in the Hellenic pantheon of planetary gods worshiped in Alexandria, Mars was associated with the deeds of Hercules.

[147] "Mars in Leo" – see Rudolf Steiner, "*Twelve Moods*" in Lacquanna Paul and Robert Powell, *Cosmic Dances of the Zodiac*, p. 115.

promise which is carried in the blood has now become clear and clarified by the light of pure reflection in the days of **Ancient Moon** and is imbued with the **will** to *serve* coming from the realm of the planet **Mars** and the work of the **Thrones**, with the clear decision toward right (moral) <u>action in the world</u>.[148]

Through the *gathering* of these images which trace the first four stages of planetary evolution, we arrive at the **first half** of <u>Earth evolution</u> when the Mars force predominated. The essence of the first half of Earth evolution was a path of descent into matter – a path of involution toward the *"manifestation of spiritual will."*

Within these images we have a clear reflection and understanding of the work of the **gall bladder** within the human being, which is the organ corresponding to the planet Mars.

The gall bladder *stores* the clear (heavenly) essences, which are the pure beginnings of earthly life (the springtime of life) and sends them out in a decisive moment – directing them toward the purification of the blood (red). Here we can recognize the genesis of the Mars glyph ♂ with the circle (heavenly) from which extends an arrow, indicating a firm direction, a decided destination with clear intention, as in a military action or decision reflecting the Creative Word, *"To firmly willed existence."*

The Mars Sound "E" (pronounced "eh" in cosmic dance)

The arrow which extends from the central axis of the heavenly circle of the Mars glyph ♂ establishes the intention of holding true to the central position of morality in one's speaking and worldly deeds – neither giving over to the right with rigid, fixed attention, nor to the left with unbridled imagination. Following upon the experience of the taking hold of our astrality and the "reining in" of our emotional life in the Moon Day of existence (which was expressed with the closing of the fists and crossed arms of the Moon gesture), now with the Mars sound E, our hands *open* with fingers together, *united* and fully extended. The wrists are held straight in line with the arms so that the etheric vibration of the Mars sound may flow forth from the extended fingers.

For the expression of Mars, the eurythmy sound "E" is formed with the lower arms folded upward and crossed, gracefully forming an "X" at a natural distance from the body in the middle region between the throat chakra and the heart chakra. The forearms are held together (*united*) at the cross-over point of the "X", with the palms of the hands (facing toward the earth) and the wrists extended on a straight line in perfect *alignment* with the intention held in the forearms. This is the place of the middle, clearly defining the service of Mars toward the will of the higher "I".[149]

---

[148] As indicated in Appendix I: *Planetary Stages of Evolution*, the three previous stages of evolution – Ancient Saturn, Ancient Sun, Ancient Moon – have left their "markers" behind. These are the planets Saturn, Jupiter and Mars in our present solar system. Within our <u>present solar system</u> the Seraphim work in the Saturn sphere, the Cherubim in the Jupiter sphere, and the Thrones in the Mars sphere – see Rudolf Steiner, <u>Karmic Relationships</u>, vol. V, p. 97: *"The Beings of the higher hierarchies begin to work manifestly: first the Thrones in the Mars sphere; then the Cherubim in the Jupiter sphere; and the Seraphim in the Saturn sphere."*

[149] The eurythmy sound E (pronounced like the E in the English word "hey") can also be made with wrists crossed above the head (crown chakra) as in the eurythmy exercise with the Greek word "Evoe" signifying the "angelic greeting". Likewise, the sound E can be formed with crossed arms over the heart as in the gesture of devotion (with palms facing the heart). There is also the "big E" which can be expressed in the form of making the gesture of a cross, with arms open and extended out horizontally to the sides (palms open and facing forward).

Mars Gesture — "Above to below"

From the sound "E" arises (*like the sap rising in a tree*) the life force which moves the arms upward (*extended forward parallel to one another*) to shape the Mars gesture, taking the region of the larynx as the point of departure of the downward movement constituting the main thrust of this gesture. For this gesture the hands are <u>closed</u> into lightly-clenched fists to *contain* the force which the arms (*extended straight, but not locked*) bring down strongly and steadily (*engaging the region of the larynx, shoulders and upper arms*). When one works with this gesture in standing, firmly grounded on the Earth, allowing the genesis of the movement to come from the region of the larynx, one can experience the building of an inner fire. As with a Promethean force in the drawing down of the fire of heaven, the Mars gesture produces much energy, inspiring also the image of Hephaestus[150] stoking the fire and of ruling with an "**iron**" fist!

The Refiner's Fire — The Qualities of the Mars Gesture and Sound

The movement of the arms in the Mars **gesture** could be described as isometric. It is a <u>steady</u> downward movement, as though one is pushing down against a rising counter-force. Although forceful, the Mars gesture – like all eurythmy gestures – is also graceful and flowing. In bringing to expression an impulse which is living in the etheric realm, the force of the Mars gesture therefore undergoes a refinement, bringing to expression the tempering quality of the "refiner's fire".

Likewise the gesture for the eurythmy **sound** "E" ("eh"), while being firm, is not hard or harsh. With the "E" there is a quality of *coming to oneself* after the powerful *expenditure of will* through the Mars gesture.

The Mars Eurythmy Form

The Mars eurythmy form brings to expression the <u>rapid</u> movement of Mars as the fiery planet weaves in and out on its passage around the zodiac. The weaving pattern of the cosmic dance of Mars in eurythmy reminds us of the Moon's form in cosmic dance. However, in contrast to the dreamy quality of the cosmic dance of the Moon, the *fiery* quality of Mars brings a quickening and a clarity of intention to the movement of the Mars form. Mars, being one of the swiftest planets to complete its orbital journey, requiring approximately two years to travel around the entire zodiac, inspires fresh impulses of spiritual truth to be brought down and made manifest upon the Earth.

Here the forceful, steady movement of the arms downward (Mars gesture) actually *carries* the dancers swiftly to the right forming the outer/elongated curve of the form. Then, after the downward movement of the Mars gesture, there is an echo movement, an "up-rising" – the mirror image of the downward Mars gesture – with the arms rising up firmly and steadily, as if readying oneself for the next Mars gesture. This upward movement of the arms, which is arrested in the middle before returning all the way back to the level of the larynx, is made while completing the movement to the right, curving back in preparation for the movement to the left and the shaping of the E gesture (Mars sound). Now the movement of the form reverses direction flowing inward (toward the center) and slightly to the left – slowing the tempo a bit. On the shorter/inward curve to

---

[150] Hephaestus – Greek god of crafts, the heavenly Blacksmith. For the Romans this was Vulcan, master of sub-earthly forces, the god who forged and shaped the inspirations arising from the element of fire – the origin of the word *volcano*.

the left one forms the Mars sound "E" (in the middle region between the throat chakra and the heart chakra), completing this gesture as the curve to the left inclines back (away from the center). The "E" gesture is one of <u>defining</u> the clear boundaries (goals, intentions, destination) toward the impulse of the higher "I" consciousness.

The curve to the left is the mirror image of the one to the right and is shorter (with less gusto than the movement to the right). There *appears* to be a momentary pause at the completion of the shorter/leftward curve of the form (similar to the cosmic dance of the Moon). However, the movement of the Mars form is a <u>continuous</u> movement. The experience is one of holding in consciousness a moment for the cosmic sound "E" to gather force in the larynx, as with the gathering of a fresh impulse, which culminates in an impulse of renewal resulting in a reversal of direction once again by moving forcefully forward and further to the right for the start of the next Mars gesture.

There is a quality of reflection in the Mars form which is brought to expression with the reversal in direction of the movement from left to right changing to a movement from right to left, whereby – as mentioned above – the movement toward the left is a mirror image of the movement to the right. The elongated curve to the right (*expenditure of will*) moves first forward and then curves back. This is mirrored in the shorter curve to the left (*coming to oneself*), which also moves first forward and then curves back.

Thus the capacity for *reflection*, which is the achievement of the Moon sphere, is brought into an earthly expression in the pattern and movement of the Mars form. The words relating to the Mars form in eurythmy are, "*Movement to the right – will*".

Mars *Eurythmy* Form:

The Mars form comprises a wavelike movement (forward, then back) *continually* moving to the right and a "mirror image" wavelike movement (forward, then back) *continually* moving to the left, whereby the movement to the left is more restrained and a little less energetic than the movement to the right, so that the form in moving to the left is smaller. The whole movement, particularly the more extended movement to the right, is very dynamic – with gusto! The Mars gesture is made while moving to the right and the gesture of the Mars sound "E" (eh") is made while moving to the left – alternating with one another: Mars gesture (to the right) and Mars sound "E" (to the left).

Cosmic Dance of Mars

"Movement to the right – will"

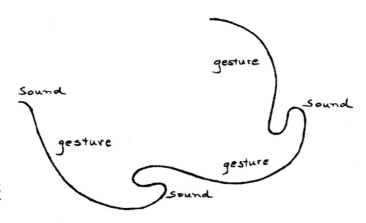

Begin: by stepping the form, coming into connection with the music and surging force of the form, which is an energetic sweeping movement **forward**, curving around and **back** toward the **right** and then <u>reversing</u> – curving **forward** and **back** toward the **left** – taking hold of one's forces once again, readying for the next "surging" impulse of the music.

Movement: an energetic, fast-paced movement **forward** and then **back** to the **right**, while forming the Mars gesture.

Bringing divine will down into material reality. Allow the sweeping movement to energize the gesture. Movement is always orientated toward the center, although this downward gesture seems *slightly* diagonally orientated toward the left.

On the curving **back** toward the **right**, slow the pace of the movement readying to reverse, bringing the Mars gesture to completion by drawing the arms up into the horizontal, ready to form the Mars sound "E". *Readying for a fresh impulse of change toward the future.*

Mars Gesture: "*above to below.*" On the long sweeping curve **forward** to the **right**, raise arms up parallel to level of larynx, hands lightly clenched.

Then on the part of the curve moving **back** to the **right**… press arms down forcefully but steadily. This is not a chopping gesture but rather as though pushing against resistance from below. Head may follow gesture, gazing down toward the Earth, or gaze is directed straight ahead.

Mars Sound "E": On the curve **forward** to the **left**, bring the arms to the cross "X" position between the larynx and heart – lower arms touching and hands opened out, fingers extended, wrists in alignment with crossed arms. The completion of this gesture is "crisp" and clearly defined.

Mars — "The Red Star of Horus"

How are we to resolve the eurythmy expression of the qualities of Mars in cosmic dance with the planet's reputation as the **god of war**? The question alone evokes the promise of a lively conversation.

In ancient times the watchers of the night sky beheld the <u>swift</u> and <u>erratic</u> passage of the fiery planet as malefic, and thus they associated Mars with the underworld and believed it to be responsible for the stirring up of war.

Indeed, Mars completes its orbital dance around the Sun in just 22½ months (on average). The pattern of its movement back and forth across the ecliptic displays marked variations both in time and in space *"to a degree not found in any other planet"*. The distance from the Earth when the orbit of Mars swings out beyond the path of the Sun is sometimes seven times that of his nearest approach inside the Sun's orbit. In addition, the timings of Mars' conjunctions and oppositions with the other planets also vary, by sometimes as much as 50 days.[151]

The one Mars rhythm which can be counted on – and which was known also to the Babylonians – is the 79-year rhythm of the conjunction of Mars with the Sun, occurring almost exactly in the same position of the zodiac again after 79 years. This rhythm applies, of course, not just to conjunctions between the Sun and Mars, but to any aspect or phase between the two planets.

Perhaps variation and speed reveal the key to the understanding of the paradoxical nature of the red planet's reputation as a "necessary poison". For Mars brings a stirring and compelling force to the rhythms of life with the fresh breath that ushers in the healing agent of *change* toward the progress of the future.

The sounding of Mars in the depths of the soul calls for <u>resolution</u> – moving and stirring the soul toward actions reflecting a moral dignity and a speaking out of the truth toward a realignment with spiritual values.

Expressed in the language of music: all harmonies require the stirrings of disharmonies, for within the dissonance the listening heart longs for the *promise* of resolving (re-<u>solving</u>) the disharmony in reaching toward a higher octave.

In this way we can begin to understand the perspective of the ancient Egyptian culture toward Mars as the "**Red Star of Horus**". To the Egyptians Horus was the son of Isis (wisdom). Thus, Mars was beheld simply as the red star of **Horus**, representing the wisdom of time's unfolding. In other words it is implicit that there is an *inherent* intelligence in the speed and variation of the planetary dance of Mars.

Trusting the red planet with the ability to resolve all in the unfolding of time, Mars could be understood as a force which *divides* – consider the image of the Mars glyph ♂ with the arrow which splits the endless round of heavenly time. Mars parts the waters, marking a clear path toward destiny decisions and decisive actions in the material world, sometimes requiring a "parting of the ways".

According to Marsilio Ficino, *"Mars warms the coldest things and energizes the sluggish"*.[152] We see this in human biography with the seven-year period ruled by Mars coming between the age of 42 and 49, when life experience and the constancy of patterns preordained by the past suddenly breaks free into *widened* vistas of possibility.[153]

---

[151] Hazel Straker, *Astrosophy, Introduction to a Quest for a New Star Wisdom*, p. 49.
[152] Thomas Moore, *The Planets Within*, p. 187.
[153] See the *"Seven Year Periods"* discussion in the Moon section of this study material.

By analogy we can consider that Mars is the first of the so-called "outer planets" – signifying the planets which revolve *beyond* the orbit of the Sun, bringing a widened perspective to the human psyche. In the unfolding of human destiny the karmic patterns and responsibility (response-ability) which were woven into the etheric body during the seventh lunar sidereal month of the embryonic period – this being related to the Mars sphere – begin to unfold around the age of 42 when the influence of Mars bears down upon the human psyche, stirring up feelings of unrest and discomfort with the sameness of the past, bringing the <u>strength</u> of new resolve to break through barriers and blockages that have hidden the truth or broken the integrity of alignment with the spiritual morality of one's higher calling.

"Manifestation of Spiritual Will"

> *The united personality will never quite lose the painful sense of innate discord.*
>
> (Carl Gustav Jung, *Psychology and the Transference)*[154]

Through the tensions which arise during the Mars years (age 42-49), the soul acquires the *will power* to fulfill its destiny. In his book *The Planets Within* Thomas Moore describes the arousal of Martian fire as a strength, which *"splits the psyche like a diamond into its glittering parts – bringing <u>potency</u> to <u>sustain</u> their creative conflict."*

The goal is to *contain* the lively geyser of vital force that streams from above. This brings understanding to the significance of the "from above to below" planetary gesture of Mars in eurythmy, wherein the response to the natural rising of life from the depths of unresolved conflict is to close the hands in a gesture of *containment* and to impress and inform (with Mars force) the matters of life with the inspiring patterns of cosmic order in time – *"From above to below", "Thy kingdom come, thy will be done", "Not my will, but thy will be done."*

Mars / Ares — The God of War

> *Mars, the ruler of Ares, inflames the fervent spirit.* (Marsilio Ficino)[155]

These words speak for the inner battle – the inner rage that ensues when the *well-armed* Super-Ego torments the mundane concerns of the lower self. Thomas Moore describes this as an *essential* human and transhuman force of conflict.[156]

Following upon the Sun years (age 21-42),[157] when the strivings of the human personality and individuality generally have begun to bear fruit, the Mars impulse in the following seven-year period (42-49) forces a passage into the unsuspecting psyche – presenting the full force and *promise* of the future. The events of these times can seem to arise as a "sneak attack" from an uninvited guest and sometimes there appears to be a shattering of the vessel. However it might seem, one is not alone in the shattering, for it is during the Sun years of life that the lower self is able to make the crucial connection with the higher Self. This is the time when the seeds of spiritual potential are planted and the soul ripens into a readiness for the harvest of life's possibilities.

---

[154] Quoted from Thomas Moore, *The Planets Within*, p. 191.
[155] Ibid. p. 187.
[156] In Christian esoteric tradition this is called the *"Carrying of the Cross"*. Valentin Tomberg describes this in his *New Testament Studies* as a process inherent in Christian initiation.
[157] See the discussion on the seven-year periods in the Moon section of this study material.

During the Mars years from 42 to 49, when the soul quickens with the pulse of the spiritual will, the heart must be ready to say "yes." Only then can the sense of spiritual *purpose* be born.

The heart, like clay, requires fire to achieve the integrity of its form and shape. The birth of purpose then signifies that the heart has accepted something. The sense of purpose arises from the fiery alchemy of Mars. If the heart accepts, the willing acceptance of <u>holding</u> the <u>tension</u> produces <u>will power</u>. Only then can the sense of true purpose become fixed and hold a direction.

Again, we are reminded of the significance of the Mars glyph, with the arrow held firm and pointed in a distinct direction. Also, we can appreciate the gesture for the Mars sounding of "E" with the lower arms crossed in the middle, in the region of the heart – or even a little higher, between the larynx and the heart – setting a firm boundary and taking a firm stand for <u>strength</u> so that the heart can express itself without being wounded.[158]

The good news is that the Mars sense of urgency brings enthusiasm, courage, and initiative toward future undertakings that require *sacrifice* – and thus heralds the birth of true spiritual purpose.

The Birth of Harmony

The Resolution of the Octave

In the Mars years the soul longs for the harmony of love, which promises to bring resolution to the two opposing forces – the call of success in the material world and the impulse of morality and higher truth which resounds in the chalice of the heart. Now the soul longs for a passionate and meaningful purpose in the world, and the Mars impulse seeks to clear the way toward the fulfillment of the higher will forces.

This sense of urgency in the soul comes to expression in the myth of Ares and Aphrodite, wherein Ares longs with a passionate heart for Aphrodite, the embodiment of true archetypal beauty. Their marriage produces a child, which they name "Harmony". However, Harmony turns out to be not a *pleasant* blend of the two, but rather "the *tension* between the two poles *created* out of their opposing force" – "*like the taut string of the lyre*" in Rilke's "*Sonnets to Orpheus*".[159]

Now we can begin to approach the idea of Mars as a "necessary poison" – the *tension* which bears the potential to *create* the birth of higher purpose, giving expression to the higher will which is born of sacrifice.

Mars thus brings new understanding to our notion of *harmony*, which is no longer a blending of sounds but rather the clear distinct sounding of two tones working together toward a higher purpose.

Mars — Relationship to the Constellations

Rulership of Scorpio – the Alchemy of Transformation

<u>Scorpio</u> is said to be the birthplace of the planet Mars. In ancient times, Scorpio was envisaged not as the Scorpion as seen in today's time, but rather as an Eagle. These two opposing perspectives seem to hold the paradoxical nature of the qualities of Mars – both the threat of the sting of death (to the lower ego forces) and the promise of transcendent perspectives, with the Eagle representing the perspective of the higher will forces. Perhaps from these shared perspectives Mars is said to rule Scorpio,

---

[158] The crossing of the lower arms can be in the region of the wrists, so that the pulse points for the meridians from the two currents of life energy, the active (right) and the receptive (left) come into union.
[159] Quoted from Thomas Moore, <u>The Planets Within</u>, p. 188.

meaning that the qualities of this region of the heavens have a particularly Martian tone. Also, the qualities of Mars seem to be enhanced in Scorpio – this signifies the designation of rulership.

The challenge inherent in Scorpio is to hold back the sting of the wounding tongue and to *still* the emotional waters in order to hear and perceive the call of the higher perspective (the Eagle). John, the author of *The Revelation to John*, is said to represent the Eagle, whereas Judas manifested the Scorpion's sting of death.

Antares, the main star of Scorpio, which is called the "Heart of the Scorpion" (located at 15° Scorpio), actually means *"rival to Mars"* – rivaling Mars on account of its bright red color.[160] Antares bears the imagination of the alchemy of the fiery furnace of the heart to transform the will and give direction for higher purpose. The alchemists of ancient times believed that **iron,** the metal associated with Mars, could only be transformed into gold when the Sun was in Scorpio. How are we to understand this mystery?

We know that Mars appears the most brilliant and powerful when located opposite the Sun. When the Sun is in Scorpio, Mars shines with the most fullness when standing opposite in the constellation of Taurus, the Bull. Since "the sting of death" bears the *promise* of resurrection,[161] correspondingly within the powerful forward charge of the Bull lies the *potency* of the "*Creative Word.*"[162]

Both Mars and Taurus have a correspondence to the throat region in the human being – Taurus more to the form of the neck and throat, and Mars to the function of the larynx chakra. The challenge of Mars is toward the moral speaking out of truth.

The **Nathan Jesus**[163] and **Mahatma Gandhi**[164] were both born with *Mars* in conjunction with *Venus*, a conjunction which bears an image of the alchemical wedding of fire and water.

Both Jesus and Gandhi were supreme examples of the power of the *octave* with the purpose to bring the fire of the Creative Word down into manifestation on the Earth.

Mars' Rulership of Aries

Impulse toward Sacrifice

Mars brings the courage toward moral deeds requiring great sacrifice as well as the strength to endure change and the promise of new beginnings. These are qualities, which are mirrored in the constellation of **Aries** the Ram, whose heart (15° Aries/central decan) remembers the Mystery of Golgotha,[165] the ultimate *sacrifice* of Christ in a deed of devotion toward the future *promise* of humanity. In the service of this promise came the birth of the *Solomon* Jesus on the evening of the 5th of March in the year 6 BC[166] with the conjunction of *Jupiter* and *Mars* at 5° Aries, in the first decan of Aries, where the Mars forces are particularly strong, since this decan is ruled by Mars.[167]

---

[160] Antares was one of the four Royal Stars – see Robert Powell, *Christian Hermetic Astrology*, pp. 16-20.
[161] The Moon was in Scorpio at Christ's resurrection – see Robert Powell, *Chronicle of the Living Christ*, p. 176.
[162] See Hazel Straker, *Astrosophy, An Introduction to a New Star Wisdom*, p. 53.
[163] Robert Powell, *Chronicle of the Living Christ*, p. 149, indicates that there was a conjunction of Mars and Venus at the birth of Jesus of Nazareth (also known as the Nathan Jesus), and that this Mars/Venus conjunction occurred in the first decan of Scorpio (2°/3°), which is ruled by Mars.
[164] See Peter Treadgold, "*Astrofire*" Computer Program – database of historical personalities, available from the Sophia Foundation of North America, www.sophiafoundation.org.
[165] Robert Powell, *Chronicle of the Living Christ*, p. 175.
[166] Ibid. p. 146.
[167] Lacquanna Paul and Robert Powell, *Cosmic Dances of the Zodiac*, p. 18.

Rudolf Steiner was born with the Sun in the heart of Aquarius with the clear purpose to serve the future. On the night of his birth, **Mars** stood like a beacon of light in <u>conjunction</u> with the main star, **Hamel**, of the Ram, close to the heart of **Aries**, in the region where the Sun was located on the day of the **Crucifixion**, bringing the fiery promise of moral speech to *serve* the memory of the Mystery of Golgotha.

One could draw upon the analogy of Mars in Aries – as bearing the potential toward transformation through the "alchemy of fire" – to describe the burning of the Goetheanum, which represented the embodiment of Rudolf Steiner's life's work, as a *sacrifice* of fire.[168]

By way of correspondence, Mars in Aries bears the potential of transformation through the "*spiritualization of the blood*". It is noteworthy that the sacrifice of the blood of Christ, called the "Lamb of God", took place in the Age of Aries, when the Sun stood in the middle of the sign of Aries. The Mystery of Golgotha was a blood sacrifice toward the spiritualization of the Earth and all her creatures.

Mars — Exaltation in Capricorn

Mars is said to be exalted at 28°**Capricorn**, implying that this is the zodiacal location where the fiery red planet reaches its greatest intensity of influence.[169] This is the region of the heavens which is marked by the stars forming the tail of the **Goat** – and because this region of the heavens is known as the "watery region", the ancient star watchers beheld the constellation of Capricorn as a Goat*fish* – a goat with the tail of a fish.

Why does Mars appear as his most brilliant, powerful self at 28°Capricorn? At this position Mars is in conjunction with the star **Deneb Algedi** marking the tail of the Goat (or Goatfish) and it is possible that Mars is exalted here on account of some special affinity with this star – rather like the Moon, which is exalted in the Pleiades, with which the Moon has a special connection.

The present orbit of Mars reminds us of the extent of the sphere of the Ancient Moon. The impulse for the shaping of the Ancient Moon came from the region of the constellation of Aquarius. Aquarius was then the starting point for the whole development of the Ancient Moon – and together with Aquarius, the two constellations flanking the Water Bearer on either side: Capricorn and Pisces.[170] If we consider Capricorn as the Goatfish, as the Babylonians did, it is clear from the symbolism of the images of these three zodiacal signs that they all have to do with water, the substance of the Ancient Moon, and so – even though the central impulse for the Ancient Moon came from Aquarius – this impulse was also supported by the constellations Capricorn and Pisces on either side of Aquarius.

> *The present Mars is a repetition of the Ancient Moon. The Ancient Moon reached as far up as the present position of Mars ...An impulse had been given at a certain place. The Ancient Moon revolved around in a circle and returned to the point from which it had begun. This happened in the region of the zodiac known as the Water Bearer. The human being received consciousness on the Ancient Moon (or Old Mars) in the sign of the Water Bearer after one revolution had been completed...*[171]

---

[168] Rudolf Steiner built the Goetheanum as an extraordinary work of art in the period 1914-1922. Made of wood, it unfortunately burnt down on New Year's Eve 1922/1923.
[169] Robert Powell, *Hermetic Astrology*, vol. I, p. 230.
[170] Rudolf Steiner, *The Spiritual Hierarchies*, pp. 51-52.
[171] Ibid. pp. 106-107.

This receiving of consciousness was the gift of the astral body that was bestowed upon human beings at that time during the Ancient Moon evolution. Perhaps the conjunction of Mars with Deneb Algedi reminded the Babylonians of this gift – connected with Mars – coming from that region of the zodiac? The sight of Mars on the tail of the Goatfish – about to enter Aquarius – was perhaps *telling* of that gift of consciousness emanating from the grace-filled waters of Aquarius, the constellation which is said to bear the promise of the future.

In this way Mars serves as a beacon toward the challenge that is inherent in the region of Capricorn, which requires the *sacrifice* of the head forces, representing the *overcoming* of the hardened, fixed thinking of the past to the thinking *with* the fluidity of the circulation and warmth of the heart – making ready for the impending change which gives birth to the future.

Thus the exaltation of Mars at 28° Capricorn brings the culmination of Mars' compelling <u>force</u> and <u>courage</u> as a surge of <u>strength</u> to "swim upstream" in order to reach the *source* of the Creative Word, inspiring moral deeds which serve the future unfolding of Earth evolution.

Human Physiology — "The Measure of War and Peace"

The Gall Bladder Organ

The themes of alchemy, blood and sacrifice, as described in the relationship of Mars to the constellations, are also present in the human physiological processes of **circulation**, **metabolism** and the <u>pathologies</u> which develop when our lives fall out of alignment with cosmic wisdom.

We see this wisdom expressed in the world conception of Platonism in this way:

> *Unless the creative energy (Creative Word) of the Ox (Bull) is restored to the head, it is illumined only by the pale light of the intellect.*[172]

After purification, which is the work of the gall bladder, the power of the metabolism (Ox) restores the royal strength of the head, endowing it with the power of <u>concentration</u> (made possible through the metabolism of the *concentration* of the pure essences stored in the gall bladder) and <u>courage</u> – the will of the heart inspired by Mars.

In Plato's *Timaeus*, metabolism is called the "manger" in the Ox's stall. Without purification the "ox-like" qualities dull the head. Purification in the thought life as well as in the realm of nourishment is mirrored in the strength of the metabolism.[173]

These teachings are calling for a transformation in the process of thinking – a sacrifice requiring that the intellect become infused with the warmth and life of the heart – wherein the mental faculties resound with the life and vigor of spring.

The French word for "fret" means to "make bad blood". Worries and concerns, dead thinking of the past – without the circulation and warming of the living thoughts born of spiritual reflection in the present – *freeze the will*. This results in poor *circulation* and thus the *inability* to sustain and rebuild the living cells of the organism.

---

[172] Ormond Edwards, *The Time of Christ, a Chronology of the Incarnation*, p. 32.
[173] Ibid.

The necessary condition for the circulation of all the physiological aspects of life is that the mind be free. This requires a coming back to one's own center of sovereignty, allowing a return to the *resounding* constancy of the true unfolding of destiny.

Good distribution of the blood reflects the ability to digest one's life and correspondingly results in the alchemy of good digestion and circulation. Essences can be transformed into building the body, but not if there is a disturbance to the ability to follow one's own nature. The resulting agitation brings a spiritual emptiness to the blood in the heart – leading to an inability to feel peaceful.

The unrest can lead to insomnia and all the mental and emotional inner life can become disturbed.

If the disturbance comes too strongly upward, anger persists. If the fiery force flows to the mouth, it is possible that the bitterness will be expressed verbally.

Here we can remember the challenge of Scorpio, which is ruled by Mars, to hold back the biting tongue. For if the tension is held – as with an arrow held taut in the bow – a great anger has the power to *create* a decision…

However, if the disturbance pushes downward, fear develops and paralysis of the will ensues – fear pervades the heart when one cannot properly digest one's life experiences. Over time the heart becomes injured and there is a loss of the sense of self, destiny and inner sovereignty.

The work of the gall bladder is decisive toward maintaining the equilibrium for life within human physiology. Life itself, because it is in movement, is always presenting a state of disequilibrium, which must be brought to equilibrium. The center of power in the movement toward equilibrium is the *silence* in the heart. When one finds oneself unable to make a decision, it is due to a spiritual emptiness in the gall bladder. Symptoms in the ear are often due to gall bladder emptiness.

> *Symptoms of pathology* – *if the heart is unable to master good thinking, it is because of a misalignment of relationships between the heart and the spirits of purpose and will.*
>
> (Ancient Classical Medical Text)[174]

The will is different from thinking and purpose. The will is moving – purpose is fixed, and in turn brings stability. Moral action and speech come from the universe; the heavenly position of the kingdom is symbolized by the circle in the Mars glyph ♂. The arrow coming from this center means acting toward what is appropriate according to circumstances and ability. This means not being paralyzed, for it is unnatural not to act.

How does it all work and what role does Mars bring to life's unfolding?

The Iron Will of Mars

> *He who knows what iron is knows the attributes of Mars. He who knows Mars knows the qualities of iron.* (Paracelsus)[175]

The red planet Mars is high in iron content with a surface soil of 15% iron, which is three times the average level on Earth. Iron amounts to 5% of the Earth's crust, compared with the 0.01% total of all the other classical metals present on Earth – leading Rudolf Steiner to describe the others as visitors!

---

[174] Claude Larre and Elisabeth Rochat de la Vallée, *The Seven Emotions*, pp. 162-163, concerning the ancient Chinese medical text *Su Wen* regarding "*thought weighed down with preoccupation*".

[175] Quoted from the research of Nick Kollerstrom from his Alchemy Web Site entitled: *The Iron Will of Mars*. *http://www.levity.com/alchemy/Kollerstrom_mars.html* – much of the following information on iron is a synthesis and paraphrasing of the information in this research.

One could say that of the seven classical metals iron is the earthly one – having a stronger connection with Earth than the others, as iron is the only one which aligns with the Earth's *magnetic* field.

The iron on Mars is red because it is highly oxidized (ferric). When there is reddish soil it means that iron is present – so Mars is red!

Blood is red because of the iron in it. Blood becomes red as the iron-containing molecule (hemoglobin) carries oxygen throughout the body. Copper and iron are found *bound* together in the Earth and likewise interact in the blood – copper catalyzes the iron *metabolism.* Thus the attraction of the iron will of **Mars** to **Venus,** whose metal correspondence is copper, brings *harmony* to the metabolic process. Of the seven metals iron is the only one that *burns.* Correspondingly, iron is the key to the combustion processes within the tissues. In this way food is turned to energy.

Iron is present not only in the circulation of our blood and metabolic systems but also with our **breathing process.**

It is the same hemoglobin – iron-containing molecule – which turns the blood red in the carrying of oxygen that *also absorbs* the product of combustion (carbon dioxide), so that the blood becomes blue and carries the carbon dioxide back to the lungs. Breathing is an **iron** process – within the circulation of the blood which rhythmically alternates between *red* and *blue* – from "oxygen carrying" (spiritualization of the blood) to "CO_2 carrying" (alchemy by fire) away from the lungs then back again.

However, it is the lemniscatory movement of the Sun forces in the heart which rules the day. This is the pivotal point of balance and equilibrium for life, which the gall bladder "field martials" with decisive action toward the purification of the blood. Anemia – the lack of iron in the blood – could well indicate a lack of Mars in the character, as the Mars impulse brings courage and will, which strengthen and call forth the higher qualities of one's true individuality. In turn, this has a strengthening effect in the building up of forces within the blood.

Mars — A Close Encounter

Summer 2003 has been characterized as "the summer of Mars" – accompanied by severe heat experienced in many regions around the Earth – when the fiery planet made its closest approach to the Earth in human history. On August 27, 2003 Mars appeared 85 times brighter than when its orbital odyssey began, and its encounter with the Earth was the closest it has come in approximately 60,000 years. That is an interval ten times longer than recorded history – taking us back to Neanderthal times.

This close encounter, which has playfully been called a "cosmic kiss", occurred approximately 35 million miles from the Earth. On August 29, 2287 Mars will come even closer (by 43,248 miles) than in 2003. The apparent new cycle of 284 years reflects the scientific observation that during recent millennia the orbit of Mars has become more elongated, due to the gravitational pull of the other planets. Because of this, Mars has been approaching closer to the Sun at the perihelion point of its orbit. On August 27, 2003 Mars aligned with the Earth *inside* the orbit of the Sun, in opposition to the Sun from the perspective of the Earth (Mars–Earth–Sun).

Close Encounters of a *Third Kind*

Mars is approximately one-half the size of the Earth. Due to its 25° axis tilt (similar to the 23½° axis tilt of the Earth), the red planet has seasons ranging from extreme cold in the winter to moderate temperatures in the summer. The atmosphere is mostly carbon dioxide (CO_2) with less then 1% of the oxygen (O_2) density that exists on the Earth. The gravity on Mars is 38% of that on the Earth at sea level. Whereas there is a 24.37-hour day on Mars, due to the planet's size and speed of rotation (roughly comparable to the Earth), Mars has a 687-day year. The extended period of Mars' orbit around the zodiac is due to the planet's exotic orbital pattern.

Accompanying Mars are two small natural moons, Phobos and Deimos, which have now been joined by two *reflective* envoys sent by NASA in January 2004 – the working rover robots named "Spirit" and "Opportunity". As for life on Mars, the data from the rover findings suggest that this may have been possible in the past. Life and water go together, and the findings indicate that there has been enough liquid water present at the red planet's surface for significant periods of time that there might once have been life. There is water at or near the surface in many areas today, and water in the past extensive enough to alter rock formations. Specific rock deposits have been found which preserve a record of a past environment that could have been favorable for life.

Pictures of the Martian topography have revealed some rather curious anomalies – monumental structures resembling a sphinx-like face, an enormous five-sided pyramid, a complex of over twelve smaller pyramids, and a mound a mile wide and 500 feet high, complete with a peripheral ditch and central spiral groove, which has been likened to Silbury Hill in Wiltshire, England. Of course, there has been speculation about the meaning and origins of these sites. However, *The Scientific American* maintains that they are mere formations rendered by the tremendous power of the Martian atmosphere and solar wind conditions.

The Aggressive Approach

In ancient times the Babylonian stargazers beheld the erratic movement of Mars with such awe that they named him Nergal, the **god of war**, and believed that they must enact ways to appease him, lest he incite war.

The approach of Mars' close encounter with the Earth in 2003 occasioned the reenactment of this ancient custom in relationship to the reputation of Mars for inciting war, as millions of people around the world were inspired to march and speak out for peace in an effort to ward off the U.S. War with Iraq, which has erupted a tinderbox of hostility throughout the Middle East – an indisputable call for change and realignment with the higher spiritual *sounding of Mars* toward right moral action in the world.

Cosmic *Eurythmy*

"In the image and likeness…"

Mercury: *"The joy of communal existence…"*

Chakra:	Solar Plexus
Organ:	Lungs / Large intestine
Gland:	Adrenals (affecting circulation and muscular action)
Metal:	Mercury (Quicksilver)
Color:	Yellow
Tone:	D[176]

Wednesday "Mercredi": Mercury Day

Following upon the first half of Earth evolution, with the powerful influence of Mars toward involution – *bringing the spiritual down into material manifestation* – we have come to the **Wednesday** of existence reflecting the second half of Earth evolution, with the influence of the planet *Mercury* toward *change and transformation*. Now the force of evolution becomes the theme of the day. This is *our* day – the life and times we are living in – a time of transition from the hardening results of a purely materialistic world into a *movement*, a "quickening pulse", which beckons us toward transformation and the higher octave of Love.

Of the seven planets, **Saturn, Jupiter, Mars** came into being during the three prior stages of planetary evolution: Ancient Saturn, Ancient Sun, Ancient Moon. Then with the continued contraction of the solar nebula over millions of years during the Mars phase of Earth evolution **Mercury, Venus,** the **Moon**, and the **Earth** have come into existence, bringing together their unique qualities and tones to the *communal* planetary dance around the heart of our solar system, our glorious Sun. Correspondingly, the resounding tones of the seven planets live *within* the *inner* life of the human being, making possible *our* communal connection with the cosmos.

The birth of the Moon, having emerged or separated itself from the Earth (in the region of the Pacific Ocean) brought the gift of inner reflection to the soul consciousness of the human being. Likewise, the Sun has given birth to the planets **Mercury** and **Venus**, bringing significance to the words relating to the Mercury form in eurythmy, *"the joy of communal existence"*. It is the theme of *movement*, however, which best describes the unique qualities and tone of Mercury.

---

[176] The correspondences are tabulated in Appendix III: *Correspondences to the Seven Classical Planets*. See also Appendix II: *Musical Tones and the Planets*.

As we shall discover, Mercury plays a significant role toward the *communal* ideal of the "Harmony of the Spheres". For if we consider the Sun (sounding the tone C) as the prime mover in the first *movement* in the musical score of resounding/unfolding cosmic harmonies and sound, then Mercury (sounding D) is surely the second.[177]

Mercury is the planet whose orbit is closest to the Sun and was therefore imagined by the ancient stargazers as the "*messenger of the gods*", serving as *intermediary* between the Sun and the other planets. The Greeks imagined Mercury as **Hermes**, the fleet-footed, winged messenger whose orbit visits the entire zodiac in just under a year, moving alternately in the region between the Sun and the Earth/Moon and then in the realm away from the Earth beyond the Sun, weaving the pattern of a 6-pointed star (Seal of Solomon). We see the path of the Mercury orbit mirrored in the planetary glyph ☿, which depicts the *connection* of the Sun and the Moon to the cross representing the Earth.[178]

Similarly the human **lung system**, which is the organ corresponding to Mercury, in its function as master of the respiratory system, serves as the closest companion to the heart, which is the *inner Sun* of the human being. Adding to this picture the function of the **adrenals**, which are the corresponding Mercury glands, and their significant effect upon *circulation* as well as on muscular action – our ability to move – we have then a physiological imagination of the *inner* movement of Mercury within the human being *resounding* as a mirroring of the outer planetary dance.

The Mercury Sound "I"

With the Mercury sound "I" – spoken "ee" in cosmic dance – we add our human sounding to the "*joy of communal existence*" with an opening *movement* of the arms <u>out</u> away from the heart reaching <u>up</u> with the left arm (heart) toward the cosmic realm and <u>down</u> toward the Earth with the right arm (will) – so that the outstretched arms form a diagonal line of *connection* between the cosmic realm and the Earth, with the listening heart of the human being serving as the intermediary and connecting link.

The Mercury Gesture

With the Mercury gesture the arms reverse – now reaching <u>up</u> with the <u>right arm</u> (will) and rotating the arm (hand open with fingers together and extended in alignment with the arm) in a *quickened* clockwise movement (gathering the wisdom of the cosmic realm), while the <u>left arm</u> (heart) extends <u>down</u> in connection to the Earth. The left arm remains *still* to provide a ground of stability, an anchoring, for the "lightening" activity from above. Again the arms form a diagonal line of *connection* with the heart as the intermediary link between the *gathering* of cosmic knowledge and *service* to the Earth.

---

[177] See Appendix II: *Musical Tones and the Planets*.
[178] It is also possible to see in this symbol a representation of the head of Hermes/Mercury with winged hat on top of the caduceus (staff of Mercury).

Mercury Cosmic Dance Form

Now just as Mercury has a close relationship with the Sun, so too **Hermes** has a close relationship with **Apollo,** who according to ancient myth taught Hermes the art of music after Hermes the "**god of thieves**" playfully stole Apollo's *cows* – representing the Divine Feminine expression of the Creative Word in Apollo's realm, Apollo being the spiritual soul of the Sun.[179]

The form for the cosmic dance of Mercury brings expression to these ideas by tracing the image of a musical clef. The imagination of the movement of "fleet-footed" Hermes, who carries the "**caduceus**" – the symbol of medicine and healing with the upright staff and intertwined serpents – is *revealed* in the *spirit* of liveliness which lives in dancing the form.

The dancers begin with their arms forming the *communal* sound "I" (many "I"s together form "we") as they move joyfully in toward the center of the circle – the tracing of the straight line mirrors the upright staff of the caduceus. Then the movement *quickens* as the dancers sweep backwards forming a double curve, a backward "S" movement.

While the arms celebrate the Mercury gesture of *"gathering cosmic thought"*, the sweeping backward double curve traces the serpentine movement of the circulating life force within the human being. Then the dancers travel on with a joyful "fleet-footed" movement to the right, while simultaneously continuing the Mercury gesture of *"gathering cosmic thought"*.

The Mercury dance gives expression to the ideal of working together in brotherhood in a communal spirit of co-creating with the divine world – in co-operation with higher wisdom in the service of a better world – expressing the words relating to the Mercury form in eurythmy, *"The joy of communal existence"*.

---

[179] See the Mercury verse in Appendix IV: *Music and Planetary Verses for the Seven Classical Planets.*

Mercury *Eurythmy* Form

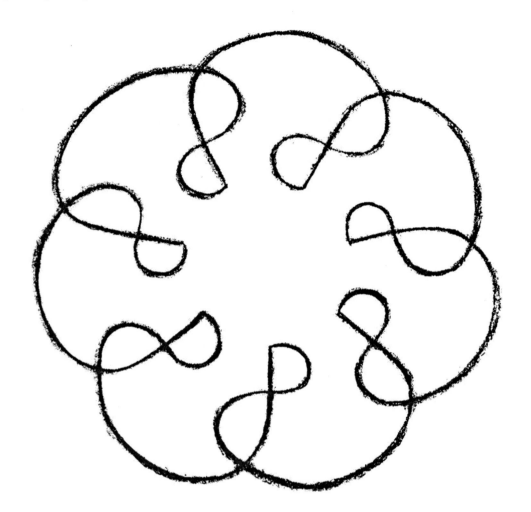

The Mercury form is very similar in appearance to the shape of the treble clef (G clef) used in musical notation – placed at the beginning of the stave to indicate the absolute pitch. The Mercury form represents the *caduceus* ("staff of Mercury") but with only the backward "S curve" (without the forward "S curve") curving around the central staff of the caduceus. (Normally the caduceus is made up of the central staff around which are entwined two "S curves" – one forward and one backward, the backward one being a mirror image of the forward one.)

The gesture for the Mercury <u>sound</u> "I" ("ee") is formed gradually (beginning with both hands in the region of the heart) while moving on the straight line ("staff") toward the center of the circle, so that it is complete – with arms fully extended – when one reaches the center. Then follows the Mercury <u>gesture</u>, which is formed while moving back around the backward "S curve".

94

Cosmic Dance of Mercury

"Joy of communal existence…"

Begin by stepping the form, becoming familiar with the musical motif.

The **Mercury** *form* is danced with the light-footed joyful exuberance of youth.

Mercury Movement:
Begin with a straight movement in toward the center of the circle (tracing the upright staff of the caduceus) while forming the Mercury sound.

Mercury Sound "I" ("ee"):
Arms form a diagonal line, opening from the heart, *left* arm <u>up</u> (diagonally forward) and *right* arm <u>down</u> diagonally back). Hands are open (fingers together) in alignment with extended arms.

The *Caduceus*:
Move back, curving first to the right, then a larger curve to the left, while forming the Mercury gesture…

Mercury Gesture:
Reverse the arms, raising the *right* arm <u>up</u> (diagonally forward), the *left* arm <u>down</u> (diagonally back). The right arm circles in a "quickened" clockwise gesture, the left arm remains still.

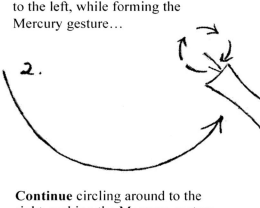

Continue circling around to the right, making the Mercury gesture until the musical motif indicates the next movement in toward the center with the Mercury sound "I".

"Gathering cosmic thought"
While circling around to the right, continue the clockwise circling of the upraised right arm, forming a diagonal line with the lowered left arm, which remains still.

Mercury and the Crescent Moon

"Mediating, conciliating…"[180]

If we are to stay with our *experience* of the expression of the planetary gesture and sound of Mercury as an accurate "telling" of the qualities and essential nature of the effect or mirroring of Mercury's movement within the human being, then correspondingly we can also come to an understanding of Mercury's *relationship* within the family of the planets and the constellations of fixed stars which exist beyond the orbit of our Sun.

Remembering and reflecting upon the significance of the upturned crescent Moon which is the *crowning* sign of connection within the Mercury glyph ☿, we remember that it is in *movement* that we find the key to the essential nature of Mercury. We can experience in the *movement* of the planetary dance form the "*quickened*" path of the planet known as the "**messenger of the gods**", which serves as *intermediary* and connecting link between the Earth and the Sun and the greater family of the galaxy beyond.[181]

Moving in toward the Earth, Mercury *serves* as herald and provides a connecting link of vitality and renewal drawing upon the life-sustaining forces of the galaxy. Here Mercury, also known as the "**god of thieves**", can be seen as the "Robin Hood" of the family of planets, for it is through the constancy of Mercury's planetary dance that the human being partakes of the fruits of the harvest of cosmic life.

With the Mercury sound "I" ("ee" as in "meet"), there is a *meeting* with the Earth and a sounding forth of "it is I", while at the same time there is a *listening* through the extended raising of the <u>left</u> hand – relating to the human heart and feeling nature. Thus, the Mercury sound "I" seeks a *feeling for* the quality and breath of earthly life.

This feeling, listening, sounding of the Mercury sound "I" is an *activity* of constancy that is also mirrored in the functioning of the human lungs in the breathing process, which *responds* to the conditions of our emotional life and environment. Correspondingly, we can experience in the gesture of the sound "I" the constancy of connection between the cosmic realm and the Earth through the mediating listening heart of the human being.

This meeting, this listening, is experienced as a burst of exhilaration, as the *movement* of the planetary dance *circulates* back toward the cosmic realm of the fixed stars of the constellations. We experience in this *movement* the very pulse of life, which breathes between the cosmic realm and life on Earth – mirrored in the *receiving* capacity of the human being of vitality and renewal, which is *given* with the taking in of each fresh breath.

---

[180] Rudolf Steiner, *History and Content of the Higher Degrees of the Esoteric School*, p. 247.
[181] Due to Mercury's proximity to the Sun, the planetary orbit of Mercury is the swiftest of all the planets. As seen from the perspective of the Sun, Mercury completes its orbit around the entire zodiac in **88 days**.

The Staff of Life — The Caduceus

The "given" which is the staff of life, the promise of life on Earth – represented by the caduceus "staff of Mercury" – now comes into *movement*, into solution, becoming the living waters of life. The intertwined movements of the serpents, which are conjoined to the staff of life, represent the *movement* of the spinal fluids, which are "quickened" by the breathing process.

There is in the brain stem (relating to the Moon) the knowledge or command to breathe. According to the fieriness of Mars (the command of Mars in relation to the lungs can be thought of as, "*Fire, ignite now…*"),[182] the lungs are *called* into *movement*, like a bellows fanning the flames of earthly life. The lungs function toward the drawing in of fresh oxygen to refresh and purify the blood and to exhale the old stale breath containing the "burn-off", the carbon dioxide of the circulatory blood.

Mercury — The Herald's Wand — The Sun

The miraculous working of the lungs, this great orchestration of the stirring of cosmic forces within the human being (brought to expression with the planetary gesture of Mercury), is in *concert* with the entire galaxy. For the normal pattern of human breath is 18 times per minute – maintaining a constancy of rhythm in a 1 to 4 ratio with the rhythm of the heart, which beats 72 times per minute. Thus the mediating rhythm of the human heart mirrors the rhythm of the progression of the vernal point, which moves backward 1° through the zodiac in a period of 72 years.

Now we can draw nearer to an understanding of the significance of the Mercury planetary glyph ☿ with the upturned crescent Moon above the life-sustaining fullness of the Sun connected to the cross, the crossover point of cosmic and earthly life.

The herald's wand of the caduceus thus represents the current of vital force, which the two serpents carry as negative and positive polarities throughout the human body through the circulation of the blood. We can experience this crossing over of the activity of change and transformation in the serpentine movement of the Mercury planetary dance form, which flows out first to the right toward the positive, active charged force of life generated by the forces of the Sun in relation to the Galactic Center – the Great Central Sun of our galaxy[183] – and then to the left toward the receiving, magnetic currents of the Earth forces, which *receive* the life of the Sun.

The Sun, as we know, regulates the life of the human heart. By analogy we might say the heart is the "prime mover" in the orchestration of cosmic sound within the human physiology and that after the heart, which is the Sun organ within the human being, *then* comes the *movement* of Mercury in the functioning of the lungs. Out of the one comes the two – for out of the organic forming of the human lung system comes the functioning of the two lobes, which serve as *minister* and *chancellor* to the heart, toward the regulation of life-giving forces within the human being.

---

[182] See the Mars verse in Appendix IV: *Music and Planetary Verses for the Seven Classical Planets.*
[183] See Appendix V: *The Galactic Center.*

The Lungs

The organ of the lung system can be likened to an inverted tree with the *trunk* of the tree forming itself as the main bronchial tube, which *branches* out forming the two lobes of the lungs with interior branchings that divide further into a multiplicity of tiny capillary fibers or twigs extending out toward the *leaves* of the tree – which form in approximately three million luminescent bubbles and serve as membranes to absorb life-bringing oxygen in the process of inhalation and in the releasing of carbon dioxide with each exhalation. This process is reversed in the life of the plant kingdom, wherein the leaves of the trees and plants absorb carbon dioxide and exhale oxygen.

There lives within the lungs a force which instinctively knows how to govern life. In this way the lungs govern and serve as master of the vital forces, which comprise the reaping of the harvest of cosmic life toward the maintaining of health and healing for the entire human body.

Perhaps it is out of this knowledge that the ancients connected with Mercury in order to learn ways to heal others. We can recognize in the image of the caduceus, the symbol of medicine and healing – with the herald's wand surrounded by two serpents, intertwined and *topped* with *two* wings – a remembrance that these currents of life can be controlled by our thoughts, which are ultimately carried back to the cosmic realm through the exhalation of the two wings of the lungs.

Something of this cosmic mystery informed the imagination in the myth of Hermes' theft from Apollo of the Sun god's cow herd (representing cosmic thought) – as Hermes, having just been born (representing the taking in of the first breath), magically enticed Apollo's cows to walk backwards away from Apollo's realm, leaving a clear imprint of their imagined return back to the Sun.

Mercury — The Great Cosmic Educator

Hermes, the winged "messenger of the gods", can be seen depicted with wings on his feet, indicating swiftness in *movement*, and with wings on his helmet, indicating swiftness of thought in his capacity as "herald of the gods".

This imagination of the twofold nature of the herald's wings is mirrored in the alternating currents of the spinal fluids – flowing up to stimulate the brain toward the activity of *thinking* and down for the stimulation of muscular activity required for *movement*.

In his function as **herald of the gods**, Mercury is most often associated with the faculty of intelligence. This can be experienced in the planetary dance of Mercury, when the serpentine movement back toward the cosmic realm is accompanied by the Mercury *gesture* with the *"gathering of cosmic thought"*. Just as with the reversal of the spinal fluids, there is a reversal of the arms – as the right arm and open hand (relating to the activation of the will) now extends up toward the cosmic realm and circles around rapidly collecting cosmic thought, while the left arm and open hand extend down toward the Earth and remain still, serving as an anchoring and listening agent toward *service* in the world.

The clockwise rotation of the raised right arm represents the taking in of the weaving cosmic intelligence by way of associative, combinatorial thinking. This mode of thinking, used all the time in daily life, is not on the same level as the wisdom-filled philosophical thinking of Jupiter – although, as indicated in the next section (Jupiter), Mercury leads toward Jupiter, and thus human intelligence leads toward wisdom.

Mercury — Intellectualism

> *It is the opposite of the Venus gesture. It is the opposite of the loving, devoted manner, the loving wisdom. It is egoistic being.* (Rudolf Steiner)[184]

The anchoring of the listening, feeling capacity of the human being, brought to stillness by the left arm and hand extended down toward the Earth, serves as antidote and healing agent toward the balancing of the challenging aspect of Mercury – *pure intellectualism.* Hermes, in his youthful exuberance, is well known for his cleverness and cunning. However, wisdom tells us that the intellect used for purely self-serving purposes can become cold and ruthless if not mediated by the caring forces of the heart.

The words of Rudolf Steiner – regarding Mercury's impulse toward intellectualism, inevitably resulting in egoism (*"egoistic being"*) – suggest that the task toward mastery of the Mercury forces within us, as well as in our relationship to the activity of Mercury in the world, *lives* in the learning to discern the true meaning of the terms ego, egoism, and the "I" in relation to the thinking capacity of our intellect. The following definitions can serve toward clarity in this direction.

Ego — (written with a capital "E" to distinguish it from "ego") is the Latin for "I", relating to the *conscious* thinking subject.
Self — the unique spiritual essence of the individuality.
egoism — *self-interest* as the foundation of attitude and behavior signifies *systematic selfishness.*
ego — also means "I", but when written with a small "e" it relates to the lower self or egotistical nature of the human being. *"By giving the ego full rein the "I" is put to death."*[185]

Mercury — The Human Being — "I"

> *Becoming a space of central <u>vitality</u> – light, life, love.* (Jacques Lusseyran)[186]

The movement of Mercury within the human being activates a vital universal force. This sheds light on the purpose of Hermes' magical powers – *"to accomplish the miracles of one thing".*[187] The Mercury sound "I" informs us of the essential essence of Mercury, which is toward *the forming of the "I"* – *enlivening* the body vessel in order to *receive.*

Becoming conscious of the *activity* of Mercury within us thus requires *"...the intention to experience our body as a <u>living activity</u>...for consciousness is full-bodied; the more numb our body, the harder it is to alter our actions <u>and</u> the less aware of our effect upon the world."*[188]

The Mercury gesture and sound describe an *activity* of receptivity – a listening, feeling receptivity that is mediated by the heart, wherein the purpose of one's *attention becomes* an *activity* of pure receptivity. *"Active receptivity becomes an experience that unfolds the self."*[189]

---

[184] Rudolf Steiner, *Eurythmy as Visible Speech*, pp. 117-118.
[185] Jacques Lusseyran, *Against the Pollution of the I*, p. 114.
[186] Ibid. p. 21.
[187] *Meditations on the Tarot* – historical note concerning the Emerald Table (*Tabula Smaragdina*), p. 22.
[188] Robert Sardello, *Freeing the Soul from Fear*, pp. 67, 169.
[189] Jacques Lusseyran, *Against The Pollution of the I*, pp. 18-19.

Cognitive Intelligence

Within the Mercury activity of *receptivity* there is the aspect of *cognition*, wherein the human being is called to recognize *feeling* as a *way of knowing*. Cognitive feeling differs from sensation in that it requires inner reflection. Here we are reminded of the gift of inner reflection represented by the crescent Moon as the *crowning* of the Mercury planetary glyph, ☿.

The "*gathering of cosmic thought*" can be characterized as the *activity* of *spiritual touch* in that there is a quality of reaching toward a meeting point which resonates as a *feeling* of inspiration – having also a subtle bodily effect and thereby necessarily requiring the activity of the human heart in listening/feeling/thinking toward cognitive discernment.

Quicksilver Intelligence

> *Alas, the nimble quicksilver intelligence can end up as the 'mad hatter' and is jumping all over the place.*[190]

The exhilarating qualities of Mercury's stimulation in the brain bear the challenge of learning to harness the mercurial "flightiness" which is quickened by this planet that wants to know everything and has many interests.

We might say that by analogy, Mercury is the *Regent* of our time. For in this second half of Earth evolution we have through the inventions of technology opened ourselves to a true "information highway" which – if not wisely used and mastered – can be devastating to the soul. For the *vitality* of the human soul requires that we savor, taste and endure the living qualities of life. However we might encounter this time of media overload, it is important to remember that the term "artificial intelligence" is a telling sign that the true faculties of human intelligence are being challenged.

Large Intestine — Secondary Organ of the Lungs

We see this also in human physiology with the lungs falling prey to "manic" states masking as elation and joy, brimming over with ideas ungrounded in reality – causing a loss both of reason and of sense of purpose. Manic conditions injure the soul and can result in a loss of awareness and caring for others.

In human physiology the **large intestine** *serves* as the secondary organ of the lung – bearing witness to the wisdom of the body. The wisdom that lives within the functioning of the lungs instinctively knows that what has been taken in (received) must be <u>digested</u>. In the language of the soul, it is through the digestion of life's intake that the soul comes into a state of integrated wholeness.

This is the true sounding note of Mercury's planetary dance, which offers a multiplicity of perspectives – a true beholding of the "other", a meeting, a listening for "who am I amongst them?" and, ultimately, "how can I serve?". In this way Mercury's stirring of intelligence leads us ever onward joyfully toward wisdom, in the service of Sophia.

> *The "I" nourishes itself exclusively on its activity.*   (Jacques Lusseyran)[191]

---

[190] Nick Kollerstrom, "*The Metal-Planet Affinities – Mercury*" – www.levity.com/alchemy/Kollerstrom_mercury.html.
[191] Jacques Lusseyran, <u>*Against the Pollution of the I*</u>, p. 120.

Mercury — Second Half of Earth Evolution

In Relation to Human Biography

In our discussion of the seven-year periods which are mirrored in the unfolding of human biography, the Mercury period is the second phase of destiny unfoldment relating to the ages between 7 and 14. This is the period of time when the child awakens from the dreamy lunar orbit around the mother and enters into a time of expanded awareness – off to school, the first encounter with peers, and the inevitable jockeying for position in the childhood hierarchy. The exhilaration and exuberance of learning and discovering are accompanied by acts of power and bravado, which require the active protection of the child's *Guardian Angel*. Although the child has not awakened to a conscious awareness of this invisible guiding hand of providence, it is nevertheless a "*given*".

The Realm of the Archangels

Correspondingly, the Mercury realm is that of the regency of the **Archangels,** who serve as guiding forces in the development of culture and language. They steer the course of the evolution of nations and peoples through the shaping of culture.

In this *second* half of Earth evolution, when Mercury quickens our souls and motivations, may our "listening" hearts serve as mediators toward change and transformation under the wise guidance of the Archangels who serve communities, nations and peoples. For true to the impulse of Mercury, we live in a time of global expansion, economy and trade among nations – a true meeting of the "other", bringing us to understand the reputation of **Hermes** as the **"god of commerce and trade"**.

Mercurial Reflections in Modern Life

The Resolution of Eros and Harmonia

Following upon the first half of Earth evolution, which reached its culmination with the Mystery of Golgotha,[192] we find ourselves deeply embedded in *materialism* and painfully separated from the awareness of "*spirit become matter*", which was the spiritual purpose of the Mars force. Correspondingly, the "iron will" of Mars has resulted in the coming of the Iron Age and the Age of Industrialization giving birth to Hephaestus' fiery forge now used for the shaping of weapons and the towering skyscrapers of banking and trade. The weaponry of war has become big business and expanding global trade has become the business of the day.

The tale of the *Merchant of Venice*, set on the sunlit isle where the golden image of the goddess Fortuna dances in the wind overlooking the sea,[193] is a true mercurial tale for our time, a telling portrayal of the "pound of flesh" required of "greed". On this island formed entirely through the conscious design of man's cunning and intelligence, peoples from around the world come to celebrate the carnival or communal dance of masked delight and "shape-shifting" inspired by the "trickery" of Hermes, the master of shape-shifting often referred to as the "**trickster**".

---

[192] In the Foundation Stone Meditation, Rudolf Steiner referred to the Mystery of Golgotha as the "*turning point of time.*"

[193] The sculpture of Fortuna, the goddess of good fortune, overlooks the Basin of San Marco in Venice.

Moreover, the city of Venice is inextricably wedded to the enchantment of Venus, the goddess of beauty and love. According to one legend **Hermes**, the delight of the gods, born of a lively childhood and bursting with vitality, grew to manhood and married **Aphrodite** – a marriage which gave birth to yet another enchanting "trickster" – named **Eros**, the herald of romantic love.[194] And true to our time, the mercurial pulse lives at the heart of our present-day obsession with beauty and eternal youth, and also our preoccupation with sexual expression.

Now here we have a paradox. For we can recall that in mythology the god **Mars** also wedded **Venus**. And the child of their union was **Harmonia**, who we remember is the *living tension* of her parent's polarities…"*Martian fervor engenders strength, Venus tames*" (Marsilio Ficino).[195]

If we consider that **Aphrodite**, the goddess of love also married **Hephaestus**, the heavenly blacksmith (although we are told she was unfaithful), then we have all the elements of alchemy: the *marriage of opposites* (Mars and Venus), the *burning fire of transformation* (Aphrodite/Hephaestus), and the *coming into resolution*, a movement and a re-forming state in the marriage of Hermes and Aphrodite – offering a plausible cause and spiritual purpose for the goal of the fourth stage of planetary evolution and bringing about an ***evolution*** in the consciousness of humanity toward the understanding of **Eros**, the *spiritualization* of sensuality and the development of wisdom in the service of Love.

Are these not *tensions* that live in our time? Might there be a *reversal* taking place, brought about by the mercurial pulse toward change – Women's Liberation, Women's Emancipation, Women's Rights, women gaining strength and stay-at-home dads, gender confusion, same-sex marriages?

Is this "Harmonia" seeking re-solution, the root cause for the word hermaphrodite – signifying the marriage of Hermes and Aphrodite?

Perhaps Marsilio Ficino, the astro-musicologist of the Renaissance, a time when the spirit of Venice flourished, offers a way through to an understanding of this labyrinth of possibilities. Ficino observes that the approach of Venus never impedes the strength of greatness, but rather represses the strength of anger. For this reason Mars always follows Venus, she is always in the lead, for "*love never follows audacity*".[196]

Toward this cause Mercury offers a *solution* – as illustrated in Botticelli's beautiful painting of the "*Primavera*" in Florence.[197] The painting reveals Venus resplendent in the verdant gardens of spring, new life, and a *greening* of possibility – with Mercury pointing upwards and *beyond* the garden of the senses. "*Mercury can lift the soul out of the limitations of a material view of things*", writes Thomas Moore in *The Planets Within*.[198] In this way Mercury becomes the regent of "possibility becoming".[199] With his lively imagination he lifts the soul out of the literal – "*interprets without killing*" – this is mercurial magic for the intelligence.

---

[194] Carl Kerényi, *The Gods of the Greeks*, pp. 171-172. Another legend speaks of Eros as the son of Ares and Aphrodite, ibid. p. 71.

[195] Quoted from Thomas Moore, *The Planets Within*, p. 187.

[196] Ibid. p. 187.

[197] See reproduction of Botticelli's "*Primavera*" on p. 146.

[198] Quoted from Thomas Moore, *The Planets Within*, p. 148.

[199] "Possibility becoming" expresses the unlimited potential for that which is seeking to come to expression through manifestation.

Mercury — God of Communication

Artfulness in expression, eloquence in speaking and writing, cleverness, clarity and wit – all are Mercury virtues, acknowledged and revered as cosmic gifts by the ancient cultures.

The Egyptians associated Mercury with **Thoth**, the "*god of secret wisdom*", and for the Babylonians Mercury was **Nebo**, the "*god of writing*". Then, of course there is the Egyptian teacher of mystery wisdom, **Hermes Trismegistus** ("*Thrice Greatest Hermes*") – the very expression of the threefold nature of wisdom… mysticism, gnosis and magic (or astrology, cabbala and alchemy). All are endeavors of the "hermetic tradition" offering gateways of connection to the spiritual, astral and etheric realms.

Bringing the concrete into solution, into *movement* – Mercury informing our intelligence – keeps the soul in motion in the seeking of truth and significance.

Telecommunications, computer chat rooms, virtual reality, cyberspace – all are present-day inventions of the Mercury influence in the second half of Earth Evolution. Uncannily proclaiming himself with "E" mails, "E" tickets[200] and the "yellow" pages – for yellow is the planet's color – Mercury inspires a *meeting* place for "possibility becoming". In our day the hermetic practice of drawing upon *correspondences* – applying the hermetic maxim "*as above, so below*" – has given way to an abundance of correspondence!

Toward the Development of the Ego

Following the lead of mercurial, associative thinking, there is an interesting correspondence of Mercury's intuitive *informing* of change in the historical understanding of Mercury within the tradition of the northern Germanic tribes of central Europe. In these traditions the naming of our day **Wednesday** was inspired by the Norse god **Wotan**, who was the spiritual head of all the Anglo-Saxon chiefs. The Norwegian counterpart was **Odin**, the spirit of wisdom and the discoverer of *runes*. Wotan was the Norse god of the wind, as was also Odin. Among the Anglo-Saxons Wotan was the highest of the gods. He *ruled* over victory and wars; he was the victor of cultures; and through *mantric verses* was a magical healer. Cunning and powerful, he was the ideal for kings of the Germanic tribes.

Wotan was an outstanding hero. However, much like the image of the Greek god Hermes, he was not perfect, but rather *leading* toward the future. The remarkable correspondence here is that Wotan was the god who *gradually replaced* Tiw (the Norse god, corresponding to Mars, that inspired the naming of our Tuesday) within ancient Germanic consciousness. Tiw had formerly been the chief god of the ancient Germanic tribes. It is interesting to follow this change in the consciousness of the Germanic peoples, as Rudolf Steiner has characterized the Germanic culture as mirroring the development of the "Ego" or "I" (German "Ich"). As evidenced in the painful history of Germany during World War II, this culture has been presented with the task of discernment, having been seduced by Hitler's inversion of Mercury's magical influence.

---

[200] The English pronunciation of "E" is precisely the eurythmy sound "I" (pronounced "ee") for Mercury.

Hermes — The God of Thieves

The 10 Petal Lotus Flower

Where might the "organ of discernment" be within the human being? The planet Mercury bears an influence upon the **solar plexus region**, which is generally considered the *movement center* within the human being.[201] In the Hindu tradition of the naming of the seven life-energy vortices called chakras, the solar plexus is referred to as the "**10 petal lotus flower**".

In relation to the solar plexus as the movement center in the human being, we can understand how by association, imaginatively speaking, for the Greeks – as well as being the "*god of healing*" – Hermes could also be thought of as the "*patron of thieves*", when the faculty of *movement* is allowed to act without the guidance of the higher Self.

The 10 petal lotus flower, located at the solar plexus center, is the *central focus* of the **astral body** – just as the Moon chakra, the 4 petal lotus (the root center) is the *focal* reference for the physical body, and correspondingly the Venus chakra, the 6 petal lotus, located between the solar plexus and the root chakra, is the mediating center for the etheric body (the mediator between the astral and physical bodies). Lastly, the heart chakra, the 12 petal lotus, is the *focal* reference for the Ego.

It is the <u>astral</u> body which is considered the "*soul*" body – just as the <u>etheric</u> body relates to the "*life*" body. The astral body is gradually transformed through our spiritual and moral progress on the path of development. Yet it also retains the patterned soul memory of all the untransformed deeds of the past. Imaginatively speaking, it bears our "shadow nature" – the side of human nature which does not consider the rights of others, is entirely self-serving and grasping. The virtue of **temperance** is its antidote, and paradoxically the virtues of Mercury can serve the human being in the exercise of **right judgment** – formed independently of sympathies and antipathies – so that our actions and movements in the world are carried out in the light of reason and conscience, deciding on right judgment and holding to it.[202]

Here again it is remarkable that the Mercury glyph ☿ mirrors this wisdom, for it is the <u>Moon</u> realm of the Guardian Angels which *remembers* our soul karma, while the <u>Sun</u> realm is the region of our "Ego" or "I", our essential spiritual essence. The Mercury movement within the human being works toward the *bringing together* of these two realms, as a point of reference in a myriad of opportunities.

> *I have allowed two apparently conflicting influences full freedom to react upon one another deep within me.*
> (Pierre Teilhard de Chardin)

The healing mantram for the Mercury solar plexus chakra (our center of movement) are the words of Christ, "*I am the door*".[203] They are an antidote to the "archetypal trespass" of the "*taking of the apple*" (an act of theft), i.e. the temptation to eat from the fruit of the Tree of Knowledge of Good and Evil. To guard against "trespassing", no deed should proceed without concurrence of the faculties of the higher self in the human being – the Christ "*I AM*" being the perfected archetype of the human being whose actions are motivated by sacrifice and service in the name of Love.

---

[201] Robert Powell, *Hermetic Astrology*, vol. I, pp. 136-138 discusses the relationship of the seven chakras to the seven classical planets, based on Rudolf Steiner's indications. See also Appendix III.
[202] Ibid. pp. 136, 196.
[203] Robert Powell, *Christian Hermetic Astrology*, pp. 133-135, 163-165.

Also related to the Mercury chakra, the fifth petition of the Lord's Prayer ("*Forgive us our trespasses as we forgive those who trespass against us*") is a knowing prelude to the awareness in the spiritual world of what might proceed from an astral remembrance of conscience calling for *resolution* in the solar plexus of each incarnating soul… "*Father forgive them, for they know not what they do.*"

The Healing of the Paralyzed Man at the Pool of Bethesda was the healing miracle of Christ toward the healing of the past in the Mercury center of the human being. In this miracle a man lay paralyzed beside the healing waters of the pool of Bethesda for 38 years. Angels were said to appear at this pool from time to time and stir the waters with healing vibrations. However, not one person in 38 years had helped the man to enter into the healing waters when this took place. So he had waited there until the coming of Christ, the Divine "I", who knew that the karmic background to the man's paralysis lay in a prior lifetime, when his *movement* faculties had been used destructively. Christ's moral words of truth healed the man – "*Arise, take up thy bed and sin no more*" – restoring to him the mercurial gift of movement.

In line with the tradition of the Cabbala – one aspect of which is the spiritual essence and wisdom of numbers – it is important to note that 38 years reflects the wisdom of the **Metonic** cycle, named after the Greek astronomer Meton (fifth century BC). 38 years indicates a period of *twice* 19 years – 19 years being the Metonic cycle which measures the time it takes for the Sun, Moon and the Earth to come into cosmic alignment again, presenting an archetypal image of coming back into alignment with the higher "I". Twice this period indicates the principle of divine grace, where one is given a "second chance" if one misses the first opportunity for encountering – through Christ – the higher "I".

The call of Mercury is to stimulate the impulse of "striving toward perfection" – the coming into alignment with the higher "I" ("*not I, but Christ in me*") as the spiritual goal of every incarnation – which is depicted symbolically in the Sun, Moon, Earth alignment of the Mercury glyph ☿.

"*Community above us, the Christ within us*" – these words of Rudolf Steiner are mirrored in the planetary gesture of Mercury. With the gathering of cosmic thought from the community of our "brother stars", we connect with life on Earth through our *deeds* – expressed through movement – mediated by the human heart, the solar organ through which comes our connection to the spiritual essence of our Sun. The vast realm of the Sun and the stars, which reflect the life of the Galactic Center, the Great Central Sun of our galaxy,[204] is the realm of the Christ which lives within the human heart.

The Adrenal Glands — the Astrality of Movement

The astral body relates through the chakras to the etheric body by way of the corresponding glands. The glands affect the activity of the etheric body through the stimulation of the internal organs (heart, lungs, kidneys, etc.).[205] The **adrenal glands** within the human being function in cooperation with the Mercury organs: the lungs and large intestines.

The adrenals look like little huts perched atop the kidneys. This brings an imagination of the marriage of Mercury/Hermes, relating to the adrenal glands, in association with Venus/Aphrodite, relating to the kidneys. The adrenals work with the minerals to regulate blood pressure (the volume of blood which carries the circulation) and toward the conducting of nerve impulses for the

---

[204] See Appendix V: *The Galactic Center.*
[205] See the tabulation in Appendix III: *Correspondences with the Seven Classical Planets.*

contraction of the muscles. The adrenal glands produce the adrenalin hormone which is known for its "fight or flight" readying action, speeding up the heart in order for the necessary blood to flow into the muscular system. The male hormone androgen is also produced in small quantities toward this end, quick defensive action – again serving the twofoldness of Mercury: stimulating thinking and/or movement.

Mercury — Cosmic Harmonies

Staying with the Mercury theme of the impulse toward *movement*, let us observe the planet's movement within the greater body of the solar system. Assuming that the planetary orbits are set in *harmony* with the wisdom of cosmic order, we can observe Mercury's movement in its orbit, which is closer to the Sun than that of all the other planets. So too the human lungs, the Mercury organ within the human being, are set correspondingly closest to the heart, the Sun organ. The wisdom of the cosmos is mirrored in the human being in that the lungs are nearer to the heart than all the other organs.

The Sun is the source of cosmic light, warmth, and sound, which is received by Mercury and then metamorphosed, to be radiated out as vitality and intelligence from Mercury, resounding in the musical tone "**D**" and the color **yellow**. Is it coincidence that it is vitamin **D** which is the nutrient of vitality that is absorbed from exposure to the Sun? The color yellow, the Mercury color, lifts the spirits and stimulates the faculty of attention necessary for concentration and learning.

The word *Hemera* (Greek for "day"), derived from the same root as the word *Hermes*, refers to the brightness of day and day consciousness. Yellow, the color of Hermes/Mercury, is thought to be excellent for classrooms to stimulate learning – brightening the day and bringing the element of warmth.

Mercury — Morning and Evening Star

Further evidence of the twofold nature of Mercury is revealed in the observation of Mercury's dance between the Earth and the Sun.

From the perspective of the Earth, Mercury's movement around the zodiac is never far from the Sun – sometimes lagging behind and thus from the Earth can be viewed as **morning star** rising ahead of the Sun shortly before sunrise, or moving ahead of the Sun in the zodiac appearing as **evening star** in the early twilight hours after the Sun has set. It is unfortunate for eager star gazers, particularly in more northern climes, that appearances of Mercury as morning or evening star are relatively elusive, as they depend upon degree and latitude in relation to the Sun and the horizon, and Mercury's distance (elongation) from the Sun never exceeds 28°.

The Seal of Solomon

Mercury transited across the face of the Sun on May 7, 2003, as it does usually 12 or 13 times a century.[206] Transits of Mercury, when the planet is aligned exactly between Earth and Sun, are relatively rare.

---

[206] *National Geographic* (July 2004), p. 10.

There is a remarkable vitality to Mercury's dance in concert with the Sun – coming into conjunction (meeting) with the Sun either behind the Sun (superior conjunction) or between the Earth and the Sun (inferior conjunction). Transits of Mercury across the face of the Sun can only occur when there is an <u>exact alignment</u> of the Earth–Mercury–Sun at the inferior conjunction. In addition Mercury appears alternately as morning and evening star in relation to its distance in longitude (elongation) from the Sun, whereby the planet's latitude also plays a role in determining its visibility as morning or evening star.

Although the pattern of these meetings *changes* from year to year, within a year's time the alternating pattern of inferior and superior Mercury/Sun conjunctions forms a 6-pointed star, which can be imagined by joining or connecting the positions of the three inner and three outer conjunctions – revealing the alternating patterns of two triangles – the one nearer to the Earth enveloped and embraced by a more cosmically orientated one, relating to Mercury's movement beyond the orbit of the Sun.[207]

    Set me as a seal upon your heart.   (*Song of Songs* 8:6-7)

The 6-pointed star, which is formed by the two interpenetrating triangles, is referred to as the Seal of Solomon. It is the symbol of Sophia, as the representation of cosmic wisdom. In the interplay of the two triangles of the Seal of Solomon – with the lower triangle pointing upwards, representing the striving of the human soul toward a connection with the spiritual world, and the upper triangle pointing down, representing the movement of the spiritual world within the human being – lives the work of the World Soul, which holds the two in balance. Mother (Earth), the Daughter (Sophia), and the Holy Soul, comprising the Divine Feminine Trinity, can be represented symbolically by the downward-pointing triangle, which interpenetrates the upward-pointing triangle representing the Trinity (Father, Son, Holy Spirit).[208] In this way wisdom has built her temple within the human being.

    So now I have come out to meet you, to seek you eagerly, and I have found you.

                                          (*Proverbs* 8:13-15)

In his journals, Goethe confessed that within his breast there lived two souls – both the longing for heaven and the impulse to plunge himself into earthly experience. He described these alternating mysteries drawing upon the genius of hermetic images and symbols in the fairy tale of *The Green Snake and the Beautiful Lily*. In nature the lily mirrors the shape of a 6-pointed star. In Goethe's fairy tale the beautiful lily represents Sophia. Moreover, the lily's 6 petal form is associated with universal language – the language of light formed from the flames of pure love.

Hazel Straker, in her delightful book on astrosophy,[209] points out that the 6-pointed star appears particularly in the flowers of the lily family as well as in the snowdrop and iris,[210] comprising three small petals encompassed by three larger ones. This is the form arising from the rhythmic movements of Mercury's conjunctions with the Sun. We can discover the imprint of Mercury also in the crystalline structure of the snowflake and the hexagonal form of the delicate cell membranes of the honeycomb of the beehive.

---

[207] Robert Powell, *Hermetic Astrology*, vol. I, p. 135 indicates the 6-pointed star formed by Mercury's conjunctions with the Sun.
[208] Robert Powell, *Divine Sophia, Holy Wisdom*, pp. 14-15.
[209] Hazel Straker, *Astrosophy – Introduction to a Quest for a New Star Wisdom*.
[210] In Japan the iris is the symbol of *marriage* and *fidelity*.

The Seal of Solomon — The 10 Petal Lotus Flower (Mercury Chakra)

Let us now proceed from the macrocosmic form (Seal of Solomon) traced out by Mercury in the heavens to a consideration of the microcosmic correspondence (Mercury chakra) in the human being.

If we envision the interpenetration of the two triangles forming the Seal of Solomon[211] coming together in the region of the abdomen, below the umbilical center of the human being, then by way of analogy we can also come to the significance of the true meaning of the 10 petal lotus flower. The lotus flowers or chakras are spiritual organs in the astral (soul) body, which penetrate into the etheric (life) and physical bodies through the function of the glandular system.

Mirroring the 5-pointed star, the form of the **physical body** reveals a fivefoldness with the four limbs and the head (the *willing* limb of the heart). The etheric (life) body bears the pattern of the cosmic archetype which *enlivens* man, and has the form of a 5-pointed star, which mirrors the fivefold forming of the human being. An *interpenetration* of the etheric/life body with the physical body (established through coming into incarnation between conception and birth) is apparent in the region of the umbilical center as the place where life sustenance streams into the embryo through the umbilical cord. Just above the navel is the solar plexus, where the *movement center* – emanating living vitality – is seen clairvoyantly as a **10 petal lotus flower**, the bearer of manifold soul influences from the memory patterns of the astral body. The form in which the 10 petal lotus flower is seen is that of two interpenetrating 5-pointed stars, one with the point up (relating to thought) and one with the point down (relating to movement).[212]

In the relationship of the threefoldness of the Seal of Solomon and the fivefoldness of the 10 petal lotus flower, we recognize the Fibonacci sequence of the unfolding cosmic spiral that we see evidenced in the growth of plants – for example, in the arrangement of leaves on a stem or in the branching of trees.

The Marriage of Heaven and Earth

Toward the Growth of the Soul ...Where the transcendent Self accomplishes union with the personal self.[213]

Within the 6-pointed star pattern of Mercury's orbital dance, there lives the imagination of the planet's movement within the human being as a fulfillment of the promise during the second half of Earth evolution, evolving from the Mars impulse toward bringing the spiritual into physical manifestation which guided the first half of Earth evolution.

It does penetrate every solid substance ...   (Emerald Table)

The _Emerald Table_ (_Tabula Smaragdina_) of Hermes describes the *unity* of heaven and earth as a *"fundamental will"* (Mars/will) – the *Thelema... "doth ascend from earth to heaven; again it doth descend to earth (Mercury/movement) and united in itself* (Holy Soul) *the force from things superior and things inferior"* (_Tabula Smaragdina_, 8).[214]

---

[211] The Seal of Solomon is often interpreted as the marriage of masculine (spirit) and feminine (soul) or, alchemically speaking, the marriage of fire (masculine) and water (feminine). As indicated in the chapter on Venus, the Seal of Solomon is the symbol of the Venus chakra in the region of the abdomen.

[212] Robert Powell, _Hermetic Astrology_, vol. I, pp. 244-245.

[213] _Meditations on the Tarot_, p. 289.

[214] Ibid. p. 282.

Clearly the movement of Mercury within the human being is vital to the work of the Holy Soul *"wherein cerebral intellectuality will bow before wisdom (Sophia) and will unite with her"*.[215]

When made conscious, the work of the Holy Soul becomes a path toward the overcoming of "egoism", which is the challenge of Mercury's stimulation of the intellect toward intellectualism. The danger is that the intellect becomes purely self-absorbed. This opens the way to the temptation of doubting the guidance of the higher faculties and, consequently, the temptation to "take" or "grasp" without care or attention to others, i.e. the acting out of *astrality*, whereby unbridled impulses govern all actions – this being the very opposite of prudence and action based on knowledge and discretion.

> *I, Wisdom, dwell in prudence, and I possess knowledge and discretion …*
>
> (*Proverbs* 8:12-17)

Mercury — Relationship to the Constellations

Ruler of Gemini and Virgo

The regions of the heavens where the Mercury forces are most strong are in the constellations of Gemini, the *Twins*, and Virgo, the *Virgin*.

Mercury in **Gemini** enhances the youthful, energetic aspects of Mercury – sharing correspondences with the brightness of day in the Gemini color yellow, representing "clarity of thought", and with the sounding tone of the Mercury D *resounding* in the Gemini key of D major.

The Mercury theme of *"the joy of communal existence"* finds home ground and a resounding resonance in the region of Gemini, which stirs the impulse toward community and the ideal of brotherhood/sisterhood, as well as encouraging true relationship between people. Following on from the region of Taurus (the forming of the larynx, providing a "home" for the impulse of Mars toward *moral speech*), Mercury in Gemini *quickens* the *intellect* and thus stimulates the gift of *communication*, which is central to the purpose of the *meeting* with the "other".

2° Gemini lies directly opposite from the Galactic Center (2° Sagittarius), which is the direction of the heart of the galaxy. This creates an axis of "dynamic tension" which is of central importance in the relationship of our solar system to the Central Sun at the heart of the galaxy.[216] Thus, for example, the Sun was at 2° Gemini at the event of Pentecost, when the divine fire of love streaming from the Central Sun poured down upon the disciples gathered on Mt. Zion.[217] It is noticeable that, in general, a "quickening" occurs as planets enter into this region of Gemini. Given, moreover, that Mercury is the "ruler" of Gemini, when Mercury is in this region there is a resounding tone of quickening strength, as a *homecoming* and clarion call for Mercury, the fleet-footed, winged messenger of the gods.

Gemini awakens the *feeling* nature and also bears the gift of *movement*, particularly in the arms, which in eurythmy are referred to as the "wings of the heart". The gesture and sound of Mercury, brought to expression in the "gathering of cosmic thought" and feeling for the nature of things – the striving to understand through the activity of "making a connection" – are thus supported by the constellation of Gemini.

---

[215] Ibid. p. 283.
[216] See Appendix V: *The Galactic Center*.
[217] Robert Powell, *Chronicle of the Living Christ*, p. 178.

The major stars of the Gemini realm serve as guiding lights toward the service of *wisdom*. Beautiful **Sirius**, some 40 degrees south of the ecliptic and thus not usually thought of in connection with the constellation of Gemini, has a longitude of 19½° Gemini. Thus 19½° Gemini is the longitudinal degree through which the influence of Sirius flows into our solar system.[218] Known to the Egyptians as the *Star of Isis,* also known in ancient times simply as the "*radiant one*", this star is the brightest star in the heavens and, according to Rudolf Steiner, is the "*heart of Jesus-Zarathustra*",[219] who incarnated as the *Solomon* Jesus, whose birth is described in the *Gospel of St. Matthew*. Sirius, with a luminosity 24 times brighter than our Sun, *brilliantly* marks the *mouth* of the constellation of Canis Major, the Greater Dog, in the central region (middle decan) of Gemini, which is ruled by **Mars**, the planet that governs *speech*. Here there is a cosmic impulse that clearly serves the purpose of Mercury in his role as the "*great cosmic educator*" – known to the ancient Egyptians as the *god of communication*.

At a latitude of 76° south, and thus 36° further to the south than Sirius, the second-brightest star in the heavens, **Canopus**, is more or less directly beneath Sirius, and has a longitude of 20° Gemini, which is the zodiacal degree where its influence flows into our solar system. Known to the Egyptians as the *Star of Osiris*, it marks the oar of the constellation of **Argo**, the *Great Ship of Redemption,* whose stars reside primarily in the last decan of Gemini. In antiquity Canopus – from *Kahi Nub* meaning "Golden Earth" in Egyptian – was also called the "*Star of Egypt*" and the Arabic title was "*Suhail*", which among the Persians was a synonym for wisdom.[220]

The bright stars marking the heads of the Twins, **Castor** and **Pollux,** are thought to represent the duality of the human being and are associated with the left and right shoulders. The cosmic twin, Castor, corresponds to *Apollo*, and the earthly twin, Pollux, corresponds to *Hercules,* one of whose twelve labors entailed substituting for Atlas by temporarily holding up the weight of the world. This deed calls attention to the atlas bone which is the point of *connection* at the base of the brain which *orders* the function of the lungs – Gemini being associated with the shoulders and arms and also with the lungs and the element of Air.

The mystery of the "two becoming one" – symbolized in the coming together of the two triangles which form the 6-pointed star of the **Seal of Solomon** – indicates the challenge inherent in the form traced in the heavens by Mercury, and mirrored in the human being. This challenge begins in the constellation of the Twins, the main impulse of which works toward the marriage of the lower nature and the intentions of the higher will coming to expression through the "I" (Ego) – the divine nature of the individuality.

Mercury in Virgo

Having traveled through Gemini meeting the challenges inherent in this constellation associated with the element of Air, then through the resounding *cradle* of cosmic sound in the constellation of Cancer, associated with the element of Water, and further on through the constellation of Leo, associated with the element of Fire and the forming of the heart – and having overcome the Leo challenge of "ego inflation" – **Mercury** arrives in **Virgo**, *wisened* by cosmic sound and *warmed* by the forces of the heart. Virgo is associated with the element of Earth, stability, and the perfection of

---

[218] Lacquanna Paul and Robert Powell, *Cosmic Dances of the Zodiac*, p. 24 describes how stars far above or below the ecliptic exert an influence upon our solar system through their stellar meridians, which are specified by their longitudes in the sidereal zodiac – 19½° Gemini in the case of Sirius, as indicated in the star catalog of *Astrofire*.
[219] Johanna Keyserlingk, *The Birth of a New Agriculture*, p. 89.
[220] Richard Hinckley Allen, *Star Names*, p. 67-72.

form. Hence, Mercury in Virgo is mature and grounded, fulfilling the goal of Mars in coming down to a *meeting* with earthly life.

Virgo is associated with the great work of *digestion*, reaping the harvest of the *intellect's clarion call* in Gemini, which has been deeply felt in Cancer and warmed by the heart in Leo.

Mercury's Exaltation[221]

15°Virgo, the heart region of Virgo, marks the *exaltation* of Mercury,[222] becoming his most radiant self in this region of Virgo that *remembers* the Sun's location for the birth of the Solomon Mary.[223] Here Mercury fulfills his mission as *herald* for the constellation of Virgo, revered by the ancient star watchers as "Queen of Heaven", the heavenly representative of Isis-Sophia *serving* as gateway for the birth of Mary-Sophia's *incarnation* into earthly life, becoming the vessel for the *fulfillment* of "bringing the spiritual into physical manifestation".

Not far from this region, 11°Virgo remembers the bestowing of the *gift of healing* upon the disciples,[224] again marking a celebration of Mercury's work toward healing symbolized by the caduceus, the symbol of medicine and the herald's wand of Hermes, the fleet-footed winged messenger of the gods.

Mercury — Quick Silver — Alchemy

Correspon*dances*

The Indian word for alchemy, *Rassayona*, literally translated means "the *way* of Mercury". Reflecting with the nimble *intelligence* of Mercury, we recall that hermetic thinking *unites* the three worlds – spiritual, soul and physical – because the Greek god Hermes could travel between the three worlds. According to legend, Hermes was able to travel down into the underworld and to unite the physical realm and the heavens in the *activity* of *connection.* He was able to bring things into *movement*, dissolving that which is solid, therefore effecting change and transformation through *solution* and bringing *clarity* to light by exposure to Air (the activity of thinking) and warmth of heart (the *feeling* for thought). We can also call upon the Egyptian teacher of the mysteries, Hermes Trismegistus, *"Thrice Greatest Hermes"*, as the patron of alchemy to understand how central the role of the Mercury metal *quicksilver* is to the fiery art of transformation in the service of alchemy.[225]

In alchemy the Mercury metal is obtained through the heating of the *red* ore cinnabar. The sweat globules of the ore produce the liquid called *quicksilver,* which is thought to be the *starting point* toward the making of gold, the metal of the Sun. We recognize the shining liquid in the transparent

---

[221] Robert Powell, *Hermetic Astrology*, vol. I, p. 230.

[222] Ibid. p. 227.

[223] Robert Powell, *Chronicle of the Living Christ*, p. 155 indicates that the Sun was at 16° Virgo at the birth of the Virgin Mary.

[224] Robert Powell, *Christian Hermetic Astrology,* p.108 – on this occasion the gift of healing was bestowed upon Andrew, John, and Judas Barsabbas, who then were empowered to help Christ in his healing work.

[225] Hermes Trismegistus, the great teacher of the Egyptian mysteries, including alchemy, brought to earthly manifestation many aspects associated with the *planet* Mercury, associated by the Greeks with the god Hermes. Bearing in mind that the Greek Hermes refers to a god and the Egyptian Hermes Trismegistus refers to a human being, there are nevertheless interesting correspondences between the Egyptian Hermes and the Greek Hermes in terms of their respective spheres of interest and activities.

tubes of the modern-day thermometer – having an interesting correlation to the "mercurial movement" of the spinal fluid within the human being.

In concor*dance* with the hermetic representation of the planet Mercury, quicksilver resists the solid state – a quality which alchemists characterize as "having a very special *inner* mobility and vitality".[226]

Perhaps it is in *response* to mercury's *resistance* to the solid state that we now request mercury amalgams (tooth fillings) to be removed in dentistry – that, out of our *feeling* for the truth, we are resisting mercury in a *solid* state as having a cumulative effect upon our health. Likewise, it is with mercurial insight that we "*resist*" the accumulation of mercury pollution in our air and water supplies.

Just as Hermes, the *messenger* of the gods, *serves* by bringing into *connection*, the **Mercury metal** *amalgamates,* i.e. different metals can be brought together by dissolving them in mercury. In modern times this term is used in commerce, a reflection of Hermes as the god of commerce, wherein different businesses *amalgamate* into one entity – consider, for example, the mergers of major corporations.

Correspondingly, the tendency of mercury to form unique and unusually complex compounds mirrors the influence of Mercury toward associative and innovative thinking. Thus organometalic mercury compounds *catalyze* the *synthesis* of an ever-evolving range of medicinal and organic products – also showing up in the destructive image of fire through the combining of mercury iodide in explosives.

Mercury — Companion to the Sun

How might life be, being so close to the Sun? The relatively small but *mighty* Mercury is 40% smaller than the Earth and yet extremely dense, only slightly less dense than the Earth, with an iron and "heavy metal" core equal to the size of the Moon, comprising 70% to 80% or approximately three-fourths of the planetary diameter, and a thin silicate covering or crust. The heavy metal core creates a gravity twice that of the Moon, and the highly reflective silicate crust renders a surface terrain that is entirely lunar in appearance. Although 40% larger than the Moon, Mercury is nevertheless relatively small, smaller than Jupiter's moon Ganymede or Saturn's Titan. The heavy metal core yields a magnetic field 1% that of the Earth, indicating that the iron core is at least partially molten, which through the swift rotation of the planet would create a "dynamo" effect.

As discussed earlier, in terms of naked-eye observation Mercury might be considered the most *elusive* of all the seven classical planets, due to its planetary orbit circumnavigating so close to the Sun. At greatest elongation Mercury is but 28° from the Sun. There is a story that even Copernicus, the great astronomer who lived in *misty* northern Poland, lamented on his deathbed as to never having seen the elusive planet.[227] Mercury can only be observed in the twilight hours of dawn or dusk or, under *ideal* viewing conditions, in the darkness immediately preceding dawn or immediately following dusk, since it is always relatively close to the horizon. Although difficult to penetrate through to a closer observation due to the planet's close proximity to the Sun, the spacecraft Mariner 10 has recovered some rather interesting mercurial eccentricities. For instance,

---

[226] Nick Kollerstrom, "*The Metal-Planet Affinities – Mercury*", www.levity.com/alchemy/Kollerstrom_mercury.html.
[227] *The Solar System, A Scientific American Book*, p. 37.

that of Mercury's 3:2 rotational/orbital *dance*, with Mercury rotating 3 times on its axis for each two orbits around the Sun. True to the Greek association of Mercury with Hermes, the fleet-footed messenger of the gods, who was taught the art of music by the Sun god Apollo, this 3:2 rotational/orbital rhythm has its equivalent in music to the *interval* of the "fifth".[228] Even though Mercury speeds around the Sun in 88 days, because of the 3:2 resonance with its 58.7-day planetary rotation, one day *on* Mercury is 176 Earth days long! (3 x 58.7 = 176 and 2 x 88 = 176).

In alignment with Mercury's reputation for inspiring cosmic communication, it was in contemplating the eccentricity of Mercury's orbital pattern that Einstein conceived of his *General Theory of Relativity*. The correct prediction of the motions of Mercury, whereas Newton's Laws had failed, was an important factor in the early acceptance of the Theory of Relativity.[229]

Now because we associate Mercury with everything that has to do with our thinking, the obvious question that arises is, "What about the perspective from the Mercury sphere?" BRIGHT and HOT, right? Hot, Yes. As it receives 10 times as much solar energy per unit of surface area as the Moon, Mercury has the harshest surface environment of any planet. As for heat, temperature variations are the most extreme of all the planets, 900°F (482°C) on the day side and -300°F (-184°C) on the night side.

But bright, it is not … for Mercury has little or no atmosphere to scatter the light frequencies from the Sun and therefore, if one were standing on the surface of Mercury, one would see that the sky is always black! As observers gazing out into space, our closest planetary companion would be the Sun, appearing 2½ times larger than from the perspective of the Earth, and our neighboring planets, Venus and the Earth would appear as two bright stars, Venus creamy-colored and our beautiful blue-colored Earth.

One would imagine – with little or no atmosphere and such severe heat – that water would not be an element to be found on Mercury. However, the observations recovered from the Mariner 10 spacecraft revealed that there are glaciers hidden in deep craters at the northerly pole – hidden like a holy grail – protected from the Sun's rays due to Mercury's approximately 0° tilt on its axis. The constancy of this unique *upright* standing yields for Mercury a perfectly circular sphere for *mercurial* contemplation.

---

[228] The octave is produced by halving the length of the string, and the fifth by shortening the string to ⅔ of its length.
[229] http:www.crystalinks.com/mercury.html

Cosmic *Eurythmy*

"In the image and likeness..."

Jupiter: *"The inner has triumphed..."*

Chakra:	Third Eye
Organ:	Liver
Gland:	Pituitary
Metal:	Tin
Color:	Orange
Tones:	E and G[230]

Thursday "Jeudi": Jupiter Day — *"Streams of flowing wisdom"*[231]

Thursday, the day of **Jupiter**, is "**Thor's** day" – named after **Thor,** the Norse "**god of thunder**". Thor, who was considered the god of the planet Jupiter, was known to the Greeks as Zeus. It was the Romans who called this planetary god by the name Jupiter. The planet Jupiter corresponds to the stage of planetary evolution that follows the second half of Earth evolution, the Mercury stage in which we are presently living. "**Future Jupiter**", the fifth stage of planetary evolution, takes up the great work of the Earth becoming a Sun.

Rudolf Steiner's words for the eurythmy form "*the inner has triumphed...*"[232] reveal the work of social and cultural moral development that has been stirred by the *mercurial* influences of our day. The *work* of *becoming* fully incarnated on the Earth presupposes the spiritualization of the human body vessel and the intoning of moral values from the cosmic realm which engender progress in the human being's creative endeavors toward becoming a harmonious world community. This requires the *inner work* and discipline of the *refiner's* fire to develop and master the marriage of the cosmic and earthly forces within the living body of humanity.

The planetary glyph for Jupiter ♃ provides a "telling" symbol to understand the role of Jupiter toward this great work. We see that the Jupiter glyph reveals the crescent Moon *balanced* on the *horizontal*/earthly arm of the cross, the *connecting* point of cosmic and earthly life, representing a progression of cosmic influence within the human being. No longer is the Moon *below* the cross as with the Saturn glyph ♄ relating to the crown chakra, or as the crowning element *above* the circle and the cross with Mercury ☿, the messenger of the gods, who serves as a connecting emissary between heaven and earth– but rather with Jupiter ♃ the reflective powers of the Moon sphere "*open*" onto the plane of earthly life.

What does this tell us about Jupiter as a creative influence in our life? It is precisely through the **Jupiter center** in the human being, relating to the **Third Eye chakra** that the lunar gift of *inner reflection* becomes possible for the human being.

---

[230] The correspondences are tabulated in Appendix III: *Correspondences to the Seven Classical Planets*. See also Appendix II: *Musical Tones and the Planets*.

[231] See the Jupiter verse in Appendix IV: *Music and Verses for the Seven Classical Planets*.

[232] This is the eurythmy form adopted for the cosmic dance of Jupiter.

To the ancient astrologers Jupiter was known as the "**great cosmic thinker**". Serving as the regent of cosmic wisdom, Jupiter *fathered* creation through the inspiration of cosmic thought.

In mythology the planet Jupiter is associated with the Greek god **Zeus**, who was the son of Chronos, the god of Saturn – the reaper of the harvest of time. Zeus, in turn, was the father of Hermes/Mercury, the messenger of the gods. If we think in terms of honoring the cosmic hierarchy, we come to understand that the role of Jupiter is to *serve* Chronos, the creator of cosmic order and time, which is reflected in the dance of the seven planets through the constellations. Correspondingly, the role of Hermes/Mercury as the son of Zeus is to serve Jupiter in interpreting cosmic thought to the human being.

Jupiter — "The Great Cosmic Thinker"[233]

Jupiter, as the leader of the pantheon of planetary gods, is known as the "great cosmic thinker" – bringing wisdom to bear upon the thinking realm, so that the *inner light* of wisdom *triumphs* in one's *outer activity* in the world.

Just as in cosmic space the orbit of Mars and the Sun *hold* the central axis between the streaming of cosmic wisdom from Jupiter to his cosmic emissary, Mercury, the messenger of the gods, so too the Mars chakra (concerning *moral* speech) and the heart chakra (corresponding to the Sun and the *warmth* of love which encompasses the whole) must seek an inner accord of *tempering* and harmony in order for wisdom to be born in the world – *fathered,* so to speak, by Jupiter/Zeus. *Moral logic* then informs and inspires outer activities in the world.

The Jupiter color **orange** reflects the aura of mediation – as the Jupiter center *serves* to *harmonize* the fiery red of the Creative Word (relating to Mars) with the enlightening warmth of the Mercury yellow in the activity of *movement* in cultural affairs.

Jupiter Gesture — "The inner has triumphed..."

The Jupiter gesture is a "telling" symbol or sign toward the understanding of Jupiter's essential role of "tempering" or attuning the body vessel to receive cosmic thought.

The left hand (reflecting the *feeling* nature) is closed softly and held facing the heart chakra, while the right hand – <u>beginning</u> as an interface *between* the closed left hand and the heart chakra – remains open (reflecting *will* activity) and tenderly circles <u>up</u> and around the closed fist of the left hand, receiving the warmth and wisdom of the heart, bringing it up and circulating it out into daily life. With the Jupiter gesture, there is an uplifting, outpouring quality, radiating from the open palm of the circling hand around the closed fist which remains steady and constant before the majesty of the heart.

In this way the feeling nature is *held* back by the closed fist of the left hand while the activity of the will nature *opens* to receive the warmth of cosmic wisdom which has been "stepped down" or *tempered* in the crucible of the heart – the work of the *inner Sun* (heart chakra), which is attuned in rhythm and pulse to the harmony of the universe.

---

[233] Robert Powell, *History of the Planets*, p. 23. Jupiter was the leader of the pantheon of planetary gods – not only for the Babylonians, but also for the Greeks – and in that capacity Jupiter was the "great cosmic thinker."

Beginning as an <u>interface</u> between the heart chakra and the feeling nature (held in check by the closed left hand) – the *open* right hand rises up between the heart chakra and the closed left hand and moves out into the world bringing the inner light of wisdom out into the activities of daily life. "All things in right timing" is *Jupiter <u>thinking</u>* in the "tempering" of activities in public and private life.

Jupiter sound "O" — "Streams of flowing wisdom"

With the Jupiter sound "O" – pronounced "oh" in cosmic dance – the arms and hands open *out* from the heart and form an open circle at heart level, palms facing the heart. The fingertips of the left and right hands reach out to one another creating an *embracing* circuit of warm heart forces streaming through the arms and hands, while the open palms face inward toward the heart, receiving from it, and also raying out an appreciation for the whole of creation. The "O" gesture is like a great Sun at heart level, circumscribed by the arms and hands, full of light and warmth.

Jupiter Form — "The inner has triumphed"

The rhythm and form of the Jupiter planetary dance reflects the balanced steady nature of Jupiter's orbit in cosmic space, requiring approximately twelve years to travel around the zodiac, spending approximately one year in each of the twelve constellations. As with all of the planetary dances, the planetary <u>gesture</u> is formed in a <u>movement back</u> or away from the center of the circle, while conversely the <u>sounding</u> of the planet ("O") is formed in a <u>movement *inward*</u>, moving toward the center, representing the Earth.

The Jupiter form mirrors the Jupiter gesture in the steady forming of inner and outer semi-circles. First there is a subtle <u>backward curve</u> to the left – allowing the shoulders to lead the movement into a gentle semi-circular curve <u>back</u> and around to the right while forming the Jupiter <u>gesture</u> with the open right hand revolving upward and out and around the closed left hand held in front of the heart chakra. This movement is then *mirrored* with a <u>movement in</u> toward the center, beginning with a subtle forward <u>curve,</u> first the shoulders inclining to the left, with a slight movement forward to the left, and then circling inward to the right, making a gentle semi-circular form while forming the "O" sound, embracing creation with the full warmth and appreciation of the heart.

And so the form continues repeating inner and outer semi-circles, always to the right, reflecting the direction of the movement of the planets through the twelve constellations. One can *experience* in the dancing of the measured cadence of the Jupiter eurythmy form the nobility and kingly nature of the planet Jupiter.

Jupiter *Eurythmy* Form

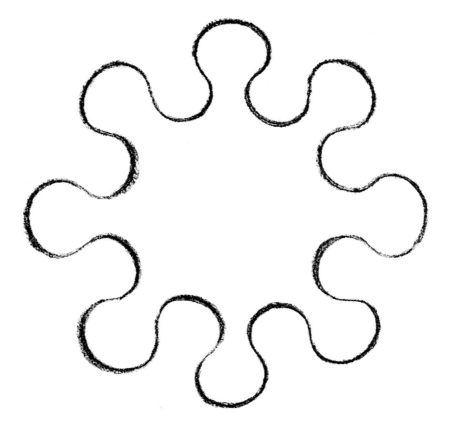

The Jupiter form contrasts with the choreography for Saturn. The latter is a crystalline, star-like form entitled "the outer has triumphed", since it is an expression of the outer shaping forces of existence that work all the way down to matter, shaping even the human skeleton. The Saturn forces are architectural in nature.

In contrast, the Jupiter forces are sculptural in nature. Thus, the Jupiter form has no straight lines. It is rounded, comprising an outer curve and an inner curve, whereby – as with all the planetary forms – the overall movement is to the right. The Jupiter form, entitled "the inner has triumphed", refers to the inner shaping forces that guide the human being from within and which find their expression in the human muscular system. The Jupiter form is a sculptural masterpiece of wisdom-filled harmony and symmetry inwardly related to the rounded quality of the Jupiter sound "O" ("oh"), whereas the Saturn form is an architectural "crystal structure" inwardly connected to the elongated quality of the Saturn sound "U" ("oo").

Like the Saturn form and the Sun form, the Jupiter form is often stepped in a measured way to the music. As in the case of the Sun form, with the Jupiter form there are, depending on the music, a total of either 12 or 16 steps – 6 (or 8) steps for the curve back (outer curve, beginning with the left foot stepping back) and 6 (or 8) steps for the curve forward (inner curve, again beginning with the left foot stepping forward).

Cosmic Dance of Jupiter

"The inner has triumphed"

Begin by stepping the form, coming into an *inner* harmony with the music.

1. Outer Semi-Circle:
Moving *back*, sensing the flowing curve, step back to the left and **around** to the *right*, forming a semi-circular curve – continuing **forward** *curving* to the *right*.

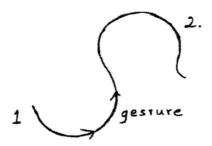

2. Inner Semi-Circle:
Moving forward with a slight curve to the left, then continuing forward to the right forming an inward semi-circular curve, continuing around and then curving back to complete the semi-circular form.

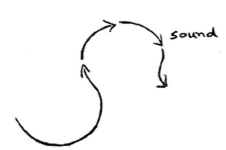

Continue the form: overall movement to the right. Continue forming first the *outer*, then the *inner* semi-circular curves of the form. *(Embracing creation with the warmth of the heart).*

Allow your *shoulders* to lead you into the *gentle* curves of the form.

Jupiter Gesture:
Left hand remains stationary (lightly closed) in front of the heart chakra. Right hand (open palm) is first held *behind* the closed fist of the left hand, then begins slowly rotating *up*, *out* and *around* the left fist, during the outer semi-circular curve of the form.

Jupiter Sound: "O"
Begin forming the "O" on the slight curve to the left. Arms open to form an open "O". Complete the "O" in the center of the forward semi-circular form, hands at heart level.

Alternate: Forming the Jupiter *gesture* during the outer semi-circular curve, then opening the arms to form the **sound** "O" on the **inner** semi-circular curve of the form.

Jupiter — "2 Petal Lotus Flower"

The Pituitary Gland – Master Gland of the Glandular System

The Jupiter center in the human being – most commonly referred to as the "Third Eye" chakra – is the center (astral organ) related to the **pituitary gland**, which is the "master gland" of the glandular system.

In the Hindu tradition the Third Eye chakra is called the "2 petal lotus flower", referring to the astral organ of <u>thought</u> and <u>intuition</u> which is located above the bridge of the nose, centered in the forehead between the brows.

Seen clairvoyantly, the two petals of this center appear in the beginning like outstretched wings, following the curve of the brows. However, when this center has been awakened and activated, the two petals appear uplifted in a more vertical orientation – like horns.[234] Michelangelo's dynamic sculpture of Moses in the church of *San Pietro in Vincoli* in Rome depicts Moses with two protruding horns in the region of the forehead.[235] In the case of Moses, the 2 petal lotus flower was fully developed and activated, making it possible for Moses to receive and translate cosmic thought for the people of Israel. He was the great initiate of the Age of Aries, when the vernal point was located at about 20° Aries.

The two petals could be imagined as antennae or "feelers" reaching toward a cosmic connection. According to Rudolf Steiner, the ability to hold or to ask profound questions helps to develop this organ of perception.

This center is considered the "seat of ego consciousness" relating to the sense of "I AM" belonging to the personality – "I am me". The aim of the hermetic path is to *link* the Jupiter-centered consciousness of the ego/personality with the Sun-centered consciousness of the true Ego/higher Self/individuality, bringing Jupiter's cosmic wisdom into the daily walk of life on Earth – becoming a force of moral logic.

Jupiter / Venus — "As above, so below"

Traditionally the "2 petal lotus flower" or "Third Eye" is associated with the *faculty* of "philosophical thinking" and is *schooled* through the practice of "right thought".[236] This practice is one of the exercises belonging to the "eightfold path", which entails the practice of "right speech" in relation to the Mars/larynx center, "right endeavor" in relation to the Sun/heart center, "right judgment" in relation to the Mercury/solar plexus center, "right standpoint" in relation to the Venus/abdomen center, etc. Contemplating "right thought" (Jupiter) together with "right standpoint" (Venus), we can come into an understanding of the Third Eye chakra's relationship with the Venus center, the life center – the latter being the "receiver" in the human being that responds sensitively to impulses coming from the other chakras, and thus responds to the level of spiritual thought active in the Jupiter center. If the "I AM" sayings corresponding to the chakras are also taken into account – *I am the light of the world* (Jupiter chakra) and *I am the way, the truth, and the life* (Venus chakra) – the interrelationship between these two chakras opens to a deeper

---

[234] Robert Powell, *Hermetic Astrology*, vol. I, pp. 133-134. See also Appendix III.
[235] Ibid. "San Pietro in Vincoli" means "St. Peter in chains".
[236] Philosophical thinking is of an existential nature, concerned with the great questions of existence, and is to be distinguished from the mercurial, associative thinking on the level of practical thinking in daily life. Concerning the practice of "right thought", "right speech", etc., see Robert Powell, *Hermetic Astrology*, vol. I, pp. 195-197.

understanding..[237] Clearly the Venus center ("below") requires the harmonizing of the higher faculties – especially from the Jupiter center ("above") – in order to *seed* life with wisdom and truth ("as above, so below").

Jupiter / Mercury — Mercury / Venus

In this way it is also possible to come to a deeper understanding of the working together of the Jupiter and Mercury centers within the human being. Here the two interpenetrating pentagrams of the **10 petal lotus flower** of the Mercury/solar plexus chakra need to be considered: the upward-pointing pentagram having to do with mercurial associative thinking, and the downward-pointing pentagram relating to the mercurial impulse toward movement. The upward pentagram receives thought from the Jupiter chakra (2 petal lotus flower) and the *downward* pentagram translates thought into action, becoming an activity or activating principle for the <u>will</u> in the carrying over of thought into movement. This impulse descending from the Mercury chakra impacts also the Venus chakra, calling for the principle of *"right standing"* to be carried by the Venus center, providing guidance for "the way" to live.

The Liver — Corresponding Physical Organ for Jupiter

The liver functions as the Jupiter organ within the physical body of the human being. By way of analogy: if the heart is the seat of sovereign power within the "body kingdom", then the liver is the chief of staff and commander of defense in service to the heart – in the cleansing of the blood and the release of vital nutrients into the body. In traditional Chinese medicine the liver is associated with the season of spring, the fresh green of new creation, and the element of wood, being completely vulnerable to the fire of the heart, which communicates to the liver through the activity of the small intestines in the receiving and sending of food stores to the liver for detoxification, the sorting of waste material, and the redistribution of nutrients.[238]

Thus an inner alchemy occurs, which in turn provides a streaming of warmth throughout the human body. Now an interesting picture emerges: the processing centers in the liver are made up of thousands of lobes containing millions of layered cells around a central vein. These liver lobes are hexagonal in shape,[239] creating a picture of correspondence with the cellular shaping of the membranes in a honeycomb, wherein the taking in of flower essences condensed in the flower pollen is transformed into the golden elixir of honey.

Correspondingly, the hexagonal lobes of the liver filter the life-bringing blood supplies through the "gateway" arteries which exit from each corner of the hexagon. The elixir produced from the work of the liver is the rich green liquid called *gall*, embodying the wisdom of Jupiter to sort the waste products from the nutrients, which are then further refined in the gallbladder that carries out the orders of the liver.

On the physical level the liver, as the Jupiter organ, reflects this planet's work in the heavens, calling us to carefully order life – inwardly and outwardly – in the light of wisdom.

---

[237] Robert Powell, *Morning Meditation in Eurythmy*, pp. 3-5, 12 gives the correspondence of the seven "I AM" sayings to the chakras, in turn related to the seven classical planets. See also *Meditations on the Tarot*, p. 228.
[238] As discussed in the Sun section of this study material, the small intestines are the secondary organ of the heart.
[239] Thomas O. McCracken and Richard Walker, *Der 3D Anatomie Atlas*, p. 97.

The Hidden Wisdom of Myth

A Bee's Tale[240]

Perhaps something of these mysterious inner workings lives in the legends of Jupiter-Zeus' birth and of his being *suckled* by bees. According to one of the ancient myths, it was in a sacred cave of bees that Rhea (Mother Earth) gave birth to Zeus (signifying the earthly incarnation of Jupiter). The cave was inhabited by sacred bees who served as nurses for Zeus. The gigantic bees would attack intruders who sought to steal the sacred honey, the source of vitality for the new-born Zeus. It was said that Zeus gave the bees their golden bronze color and remarkable vigor. We can observe a correspondence in these images to the warding off of harmful toxins evidenced in the jaundiced golden bronze coloring of a newborn's skin when the liver is functioning toward the safe return of the internal vigor of new life – a sign of Jupiter-Zeus wisely ruling his kingdom.

Another story tells of Zeus being suckled by the daughters of the Cretan King Melisseus. His daughters were called "Melissae" – meaning bees.

The *Melissae* were the virgin attendants of Artemis in the ancient initiation temple at Ephesus, where the initiates were trained to hold in consciousness the mysteries of creation – an early training toward the development of the awakened capacity of the Jupiter center (Third Eye) to behold the wisdom of creation.

The cave of Jupiter's birth thus signifies the mysteries of life which are *hidden* and yet suckled by sacred attendants (Melissae/bees) who wisely *serve* in the well-being of the kingdom.

The Inner Alchemy of Thinking

Jupiter and the Liver

The ancient astrologers beheld Jupiter as the "great benefic" – the bearer of *good fortune,* which is the natural unfolding of the wisdom of creation and thus the birthright of the human being.

When these heavenly influences become knotted, blocked or congested, this is an indication that something is wrong in the thinking. When there is a blockage, the generative flow of wisdom from the Jupiter center, resulting in the natural flow of life through the meridians, experiences a deviation and can no longer nourish the muscular forces. In this way an excess of worry and fear interrupts the natural flow of gifts from above.

Anger, however, is the natural *movement* of the wood element of the liver seeking *resolution.* This creates an upward force which, when subjugated or held in check, enables the *thinking* to pass on to the following stage of *reflection* – often bringing the promise and fortune of new life and serving to *kindle* the decision-making process. In this way the wood element of the liver gives a healthy dynamic to the thought process – calling forth strength of thought which is able to turn toward the contemplation of higher truth. At this level life is already on the way to organizing itself.

---

[240] Carl Kerenyi, *The Gods of the Greeks*, p. 94.

The physiological functions of life are interconnected. The liver can be characterized as the *general* in the center. However, the general relies on information from the organic integrity and wise counsel of all the inner planetary organs of the body kingdom.

> *Serving as the chief of defense for the physical body, the liver's function is to defend against attack ... "fighting against the measurement in our mind to liberate the thing that has been measured."*[241]

This requires by necessity the *expansive* quality of **Jupiter thinking** which is holistic and neutral, offering new perspectives and insights to bring one back into alignment with the flow of life.

Living thought or real thinking through the gnosis/knowing of the heart can analyze a situation and take charge – serving to dominate irresolvable fear and thereby re-establish the balance of working harmony within the inner planetary organs of the physical body. This return to harmony is reflected in a *springtime* of redistribution of one's priorities and movement/activities in daily life. In this way pathology can be seen as a *symptom* that thinking has deviated from the central motivation of purpose.

The function of the liver as the "*general* of the *armed forces*" is to spread the influences of *living* thinking throughout the kingdom – serving the sovereignty of the higher will of the heart in the maintaining of balance in the blood and in the unblocking of passages due to stagnation caused by *impoverished* thinking.

In this way the practice of right thinking serves Jupiter's role as the bearer of "good fortune" toward the vitality of life.

The Case of Obsession

If the heart is unable to master good thinking, something is out of alignment between the heart and the spirits of *will* and *purpose*. In today's fast-paced world a plethora of images and stimulations enter the heart as impressions from the outside which cannot be properly processed, sifted through and digested. The soul requires *lived experience* of life qualities that are endured over time. When the time required for *reflection* and inner dialogue with the higher will of the heart is bypassed, then real *living* thinking cannot be built up through the activity of the Jupiter chakra, which otherwise would have an enlivening effect upon the blood. Instead of living thinking, desire is transmitted to the blood – reflecting that the "spirit of vitality" has been malnourished.

Desire becomes the byproduct – the desire to *possess* that which cannot be processed. In this way *purpose* is scattered uncontrollably in the outer life. However, if the desire is stilled and the will is allowed to follow the natural currents – the higher will is served through the harmonization or inner alchemy of the Jupiter streamings.

> *It is the faculty of the "lower self" to **reproduce** the experience and knowledge of the "higher Self" or if you like, the faculty of the "higher Self" to imprint its experience and knowledge upon the consciousness of the "lower self". It is the **link** between the "higher eye" and the "lower eye", which renders us authentically religious and **wise**, and **immune** to the assaults of scepticism, materialism and determinism.*[242]

---

[241] Claude Larre and Elisabeth Rochat de la Vallée, *The Secret Treatise of the Spiritual Orchid*, p. 58.
[242] *Meditations on the Tarot*, p. 346.

The Cave — Thinking and Cosmic Sound

Two Jupitarian Tales

The image of a cave is often found in the legends of Jupiter-Zeus – perhaps making reference to the bony structure of the human head or cranium, which is itself a rounded, hollowed-out cavity and is the seat of the Jupiter influence in the human being associated with the thinking process.

Earlier we explored the legend of Zeus being born in a *sacred* cave and of being suckled by *bees*. However the *cave* image occurs again in the stories of Zeus' early manhood – this time accompanied by eagles.

In one such legend Jupiter-Zeus is confined to a cave by his father Chronos, who had become angered by Zeus' zestful, expansive nature – a tendency toward excessive behaviors and the good-natured jovial side of life. Chronos, aware of the destiny of his son, sought to restrict Zeus' rapacious activities in order that his true cosmic purpose might be born. It is said that during his confinement, Zeus was nourished by *eagles* bringing the nectar of higher thinking – making possible the fulfillment of his destiny as the "great cosmic thinker".

This legend seems to suggest that when the outer activities of Zeus were restricted, an inner capacity was developed. One could say that an inner *"sounding"* occurred.

We find an uncanny echoing of this cosmic mystery within the life biography of the great classical composer Ludwig van Beethoven, whose early death was found to be a result of acute cirrhosis of the liver. Although Beethoven himself was not a heavy drinker, his liver had evidently been stressed beyond its natural capacity.

Beethoven has been likened to **Prometheus**, who stole the creative fire of heaven (from the realm of Zeus), bringing it down into the realm of human experience, which brought about the birth of the individualized will activity that – particularly since the Renaissance – is evident in the drive for the expression of religious freedom, in the process of scientific discovery, in new art forms, and which we now, as modern human beings, take for granted.

Echoing the intentions of the previous tale, **Zeus** became angered by **Prometheus'** theft of the divine fire from his own fiery realm and consequently <u>chained</u> Prometheus to a *rock*, allowing an eagle (higher thinking) to peck away at his liver by night.

The inner ear, we are told, is embedded in one of the hardest bones of the body, which in German is called the "rock-bone". This produces the *resonance* of sounding within the inner realm.

We recall how Beethoven, who was of a choleric, fiery temperament, tragically became deaf – an event which he himself described as a result of a rageful acting-out of anger at having been disturbed while composing – "*…and jumping up in a rage I threw myself on the floor as actors do…and when I arose I found myself deaf and have been so ever since.*"[243]

---

[243] Eugen Kolisko, "*Beethoven's Destiny,*" *Starlight* vol. 5 (Fall 2005), pp. 14-18 (Sophia Foundation of North America: Palo Alto/CA, 2005). See page 18: "*I heard from a well-known musician that in a personal conversation that he had with Rudolf Steiner the latter said, 'Beethoven is Prometheus'.*"

Ear, liver and limbs have an inner connection through sound. The sounding of the movement of the muscles can be perceived through a stethoscope. This is the sounding of our will activity made manifest in the movement of our limbs which respond to the vibrational movement of sound.

In listening, however, the stream of movement is turned *inwards* and thus the response to sound is reversed. The principle in the inner ear is that the vibrational movement of sound is stopped – stilled – so that *sound* rather than *movement* occurs. The liver is the mediator of this polarity.

The liver stores the *nectar* – sugars – which are transported to the muscles for willed activity. Beethoven's *movements* were confined to his music. In his outer life he was scarcely able to come to a decision – a telling sign of the compromised functioning of the gall bladder in responding to the liver.

Beethoven's ears had become sclerotic and hardened, and his liver diminished. However, through the intensity of his individuality, like the bound Prometheus before him, Beethoven again stole the fire of heaven and brought its sounding to his music. This was the result of an intense inner listening which was heightened as the *outer* soundings of his earthly existence were restricted. It was the nectar of heavenly sound which devoured Beethoven's liver and at the same time fed the soulful fiery quality of his music.

This is the wood element of the liver sacrificed entirely to the fires of the listening heart in the seeking of *resolution.*[244]

The role of Jupiter is to inspire the inner will impulse toward acts of free thinking due to grace – leaving human beings free to think, to act, and to create independently out of their own unique individuality. Beethoven's triumphant music leaves a legacy of cosmic sounding, bearing witness to divine grace finding its fulfillment through the individuality of the human being, as a listening, resounding vessel for the good.

Soul Work — "Tuning Up" With Jupiter

The Peacock's Tale

How do we *attune* ourselves so that our lives have resonance and harmony? Harmony by necessity requires the practice of good habits and virtues. However, the *music* of the soul, according to Thomas Moore in <u>The Planets Within</u>, requires keeping the *tones* distinct and not lost in the blend. This requires a tempering and tuning of the planetary tonal centers – honoring and *remembering* the importance of the *intervals*, the distance between two tones.

The tale of the peacock's tail can help toward the understanding of cosmic tempering. The **peacock** is the animal which is sacred to the realm of Jupiter. Thus the spreading of the peacock's tail can be

---

[244] It is interesting to note that Jupiter is referred to as the "Wood Star" in the Korean and Japanese cultures – as indicated in the teaching of the Five Elements: Metal, Water, Wood, Fire, Earth, of traditional Chinese medicine. The Five Elements – corresponding on the one hand to the five visible planets: Venus, Mercury, Jupiter, Mars, Saturn, and on the other hand to the five inner organs: lungs, kidneys, liver, heart, spleen – differ somewhat from the Four Elements of the Greek medical tradition. The teaching of the Five Elements can be traced back to <u>The Annals of Lu Buwei</u> (239 BC), but is probably much older. In Japanese and Korean the names of the days of the week are directly linked with the Five Elements teaching as follows: Tuesday (Mars) is the "day of the planet of fire", Wednesday (Mercury) is the "day of the planet of water", Thursday (Jupiter) is the "day of the planet of wood", Friday (Venus) is the "day of the planet of metal", and Saturday (Saturn) is the "day of the planet of earth".

likened to the *revelation* of *multiplicity* from the Jupiter sphere of influence – calling for the tempering of the human capacity to remain sovereign within the multiplicities of life experience. Jung likens the peacock's tail to the alchemical image of springtime and the foretelling of the arrival of new life. He describes how the *eyes* of the sky are reflected in the colored eyes of the peacock's tail, representing the seven planetary spheres.

In *The Planets Within* Thomas Moore relates how Jupiter's influence tempers the soul so that the lower *"ego loses its senex (desire for control) becoming more imaginal and flexible – able to tolerate ambiguity, contradiction and movement, because these are processes of temperament"*.[245] This is listening to the inner streaming of life – thinking and creating in response to the inner music which *"tempers by constellating"* and thus must paradoxically endure the *"contradiction of dissonance"* which results from a tolerance for the holding of a multiplicity of perspectives.

Thus a well-tuned soul/body vessel – like a fine-tuned instrument – will necessarily *feel* dissonance more profoundly and thereby (as with good music) *respond* appropriately, taking measures to seek resolution. This is the work of soul *inherent* in the intervals of cosmic harmony in time.

Remaining constant to the activity of tempering requires that we understand that the influence flowing from the Jupiter center of our being is "seminal" – capable of bringing "seed-like" intentions of profound spiritual potency ("fathering" creation). *Seed* thoughts are fructifying for the birth and renewal of culture and for sustaining it. The example of Moses receiving the Ten Commandments is an example of a seed-like matrix of such spiritual potency as to *sustain* the growth of the Hebrew people.

Following upon this understanding we can appreciate the healing potential of "seed matrices", which have remained pure in their pattern and wholeness, serving as healing agents toward restoring the integrity and wholeness of the individual. Sacred icons, prayers, flower or star essences, homeopathy – all are examples of "tuning" instruments bearing seed potential for the body, soul, and spirit.

Jupiter Soundings in the Ancient World

The wisdom of the *seed*-bearing potential of Jupiter was known to the ancient world.

The ancient city of Babylon was known as the holy city of the god Marduk, whose star Jupiter was called "the great star", "the planet of the king" or "the royal planet".[246]

The ancient Babylonians celebrated the New Year on the first New Moon following after the vernal equinox.[247] The New Year's festival was dedicated to the god Marduk with prayers and the enactment of the Babylonian *epic of creation* in which Marduk overcame the dragon by instituting order rather than chaos, peace instead of war.

According to the Babylonian epic of creation, Marduk ordered the cosmos by setting up "three stars apiece" – relating each month to one of the twelve signs of the zodiac. Thereby Marduk ordered the

---

[245] Thomas Moore, *The Planets Within*, p. 200.
[246] Robert Powell, *History of the Planets*, pp. 7-9.
[247] The Iraq War was declared on March 20, 2003, right at the time of the vernal equinox, and brought chaos rather than peace to the region of ancient Babylon (considering the proximity of Baghdad to the site of ancient Babylon).

cycle of the year. In addition he preordained the course of human destiny and the history of humanity.

In the guiding of fate and evolution the ancients believed Marduk was the god associated with Jupiter, the great star which met in council with the other planets.

In this way there was an understanding in the Babylonian mind of the "stepping down" of wisdom from the cosmic realm to humanity, with Jupiter serving as mediator between the cosmic seed matrix and the gods. The king's role was to mediate between the gods and the human realm, and his guidance was revealed through images received in dreams or through clairvoyance.

Just as the Babylonians received knowledge by way of dreams or clairvoyance, now the work of receiving cosmic revelation requires the active participation of the "will to know" in the formulating of questions toward the development of the Jupiter center (Third Eye) in the capacity to receive answers. In this way human destiny has progressed into the realm of individual freedom.

The Babylonians, according to Rudolf Steiner, had the task of taking the lead in the progression from clairvoyant knowledge to knowledge based on *measure, weight and number*.[248] Marduk-Jupiter led the way in this development.

Throughout the ancient world Jupiter was associated with wisdom. To the Greeks Marduk became Zeus, the king of the gods who ruled from the heights of Mt. Olympus. Jupiter was the star of Zeus, astronomically known as Phaethon, "the radiant one".

To the Egyptians Jupiter was referred to by various names, including "the star of Osiris" and "Horus of the secret". Osiris, "lord of the Duat" and "judge over the dead", who passed through death and resurrection, was an Egyptian prefiguring of Christ. Horus, the son conceived through the marriage of Isis and Osiris, is perhaps a foretelling of the marriage of Christ and Sophia, the marriage of the creative *source* of life with *holy* wisdom.

Although Osiris is essentially a Sun god, it is interesting that the Egyptians also associated this god with Jupiter. According to Valentin Tomberg, the seven petitions of the Lord's Prayer relate to the seven chakras in a descending sequence, with the first petition ("*Hallowed be thy name*") relating to the crown chakra, the second petition ("*Thy kingdom come*") relating to the Third Eye, etc.[249] The Lord's Prayer was therefore given by Christ as a "tuning instrument" toward the development of the seven lotus flowers – the seven chakras in the human being's "soul body" – relating to the astral world. Since the Egyptian Duat corresponds to the "kingdom of heaven", and since Osiris was the lord of this kingdom (Duat), the Egyptian association of Osiris with Jupiter was perhaps a premonition having to do with that which is experienced in present-day consciousness as the "kingdom within" – relating to the petition "*Thy kingdom come*".

With the Egyptian association of Jupiter with Osiris we have an imagination of wisdom *flowing* from the *capacity* to "gather" the pieces in order to bring into wholeness. We recall that in the Egyptian teaching of Isis and Osiris (who were both brother and sister and husband and wife), it is Isis (holy wisdom) that gathers the fragments of her beloved Osiris who has been cut into pieces by his jealous brother. The fragments of Osiris' body were cast into the river, in other words brought into *solution* – able to flow – as with the fluidity of *living* thought.

---

[248] For an expanded understanding of the spiritual significance of measure, weight and number, see Valentin Tomberg, *Christ and Sophia*, pp. 316-327: "Weight, Measure, and Number in the Spiritual History of Humanity."

[249] Valentin Tomberg, *Lord's Prayer Course* (Sophia Foundation of North America: Palo Alto/CA, 1996).

Jupiter for the Egyptians had to do with *creative* intelligence and was a *vivifying* source, a benefactor to help solve problems by inspiring a *rounded* perspective – taking one out of the personal, thereby *serving* the whole.

Perhaps it was this association of Jupiter as a sustaining source of wholeness which lived as an intuition in the ancient world as concern for moderation in the government of the peoples and for the fructification of social and civic life – inspiring an intelligence of stability, unchanging in its capacity to create and sustain a social environment that was psychologically nourishing.

This sense of Jupiter as a guiding spiritual source for community and culture lives in the Greek legend of Athena, the goddess who sprang into life from the forehead of her creator father, Zeus – as the intelligence of *polis* – the genius of the city and state. Through the intelligence of Athena, Zeus became the helping *father* of all people. As preserver and bestower, Jupiter brings equilibrium to everyday life.

Jupiter's Relationship within the Constellations

Jupiter's Rulership of Sagittarius

We remember that the *aim* and central purpose of **Sagittarius** is to *know* the truth.[250] By way of analogy, we could imagine that the *tension* of the **Archer's** bow represents an *inner* seeking of understanding (gnosis), which can be felt inwardly as a *longing* toward the future.

Thus the rulership of Jupiter over this region of the heavens can be understood as a *potent* and telling sign of the "collaboration" of the heavens toward cosmic evolution – coming to expression with the words describing the Jupiter eurythmy form, "the *inner* has triumphed".

Just as the Jupiter glyph ♃ reveals the gift of the Moon's reflective nature *lifted* up and *supported* by the horizontal axis of the cross (representing the daily walk of life) – recalling Jupiter-Zeus as the father of all people, in all walks of life – so too the image of the Archer as a **Centaur** reveals the upright horseman *supported* by the strength and power of the horizontal plane of existence. There lives in the *tension* of the image an imagination of the human being striving to overcome and to transform the lower instinctual nature which is inherent to incarnation.

We find an echo of these themes in the myth of Jupiter-Zeus, wherein Zeus' father, Chronos, having full knowledge of Jupiter's destiny to become the "great cosmic thinker", constrains Jupiter to a cave (representing the human cranium) in order to curtail the youthful Jupiter's expansive, exuberant nature.

In the service of this theme the liver, the corresponding organ of Jupiter in the human physiology, functions as the "general of defense" for the human heart which – like the wisdom of Chronos – is attuned to the *inner* rhythms of the universe and bears the imprint of the individual destiny.

Here Sagittarius shares the same challenges that are inherent in the qualities of Jupiter. For when the *"joie de vivre"* inspired by Jupiter is not tamed or tempered, the human being can be subject to pathologies of over-indulgence. Perhaps the presence of the heavenly **Lyre** in the region of the final decan of Sagittarius, above the hindquarters of the Centaur, represents the antidote to instinctual

---

[250] Lacquanna Paul and Robert Powell, *Cosmic Dances of the Zodiac*, pp. 77-78.

temptation. We may recall that the *Lyre* was the instrument of **Orpheus**, whose heavenly music was said to tame even the wild animals.

Like the rounded eurythmy gesture for the Jupiter sound "O", Jupiter's full rounded expansive nature is known to *seed* the great cultural impulses of history. Also known as the "great benefic", Jupiter is the bearer of good fortune and is thought to bring prosperity, believed by some to be an indicator in stock market expansion or decline. Correspondingly, the function of the 2 petal lotus flower is to spread the wealth of the *harvest* of well-nourished *thought life* (Jupiter) throughout the *kingdom* of the human soul, which in turn has an effect upon the function of the liver to direct the distribution of fluids in the human physiology, thus ensuring a sense of well-being (or lack thereof).

The stars which form the arrow of Sagittarius in the heavens bear yet another *telling* image. For the arrow of the Archer's bow can be seen to point toward the tail of the Scorpion. Scorpio shares the challenge of Sagittarius to hold back the "sting" of the tongue in order to gain the clarity of a higher perspective. The "sting" which a biting tongue can deliver may be likened to the wounding of an arrow.

This challenge is mirrored in human physiology when the liver discerns a misalignment with the heart's most sacred intentions and comes to the defense of the *kingdom* in fiery anger, sending currents of heat upward which can embitter the speech. However, when the anger is contained, the heat can rise up and stimulate the Jupiter center (Third Eye), inspiring thoughts toward right decision in the walk of daily life.

Here it is interesting to note that recent astronomical research has revealed that the stars which form the arrow of Sagittarius point directly toward the Galactic Center, which was discovered to be located at 2° Sagittarius. This discovery strengthens the imagination of the *tension* of the Archer's arrow drawing forth from the fiery source of creation with an *aim* to know the "Heart of God" or Central Sun located at the Galactic Center, around which all the stars/Suns of our galaxy revolve.[251]

Jupiter's Rulership of Pisces

The pull or *tension* toward the spiritual realm of cosmic thought is also imaged in the region of the constellation of **Pisces**, the *Fishes*, with the _two fish_ – one swimming up toward heaven, the other swimming horizontally toward the constellation of Aquarius, expressing a movement and a *longing* toward the future, a foretelling of the Age of Aquarius.

Again there is a *tension* inherent in the image of the *Two Fish*. They reveal a constancy of activity in maintaining a balance between the spiritual and earthly dimension of existence. Here Jupiter's rulership of Pisces serves to *ground* the mystical inclinations inspired in the region of Pisces, which if not tempered can lead to a loss of grounding in the daily walk of life – making one subject to illusions and/or delusions.

Jupiter's *seeding* impulse serves to stimulate the creative imagination represented by the celestial horse **Pegasus**, whose body of stars stretches over the first decan of Pisces. The constellations residing in the decans of Pisces can provide a *telling* background for the strength of Jupiter in Pisces. Jupiter's thinking *serves* toward the freeing of **Andromeda** (third decan), the *Enchained Woman*, representing the soul challenge of the Divine Feminine not to drown or be swallowed by the great celestial whale **Cetus**, representing a repository of the instinctual unconscious life.

---

[251] See Appendix V: *The Galactic Center*.

Likewise **Cepheus,** the *Crowned King* (second decan of Pisces), brings a *telling* image to the understanding of the *noble* influence of Jupiter in Pisces as the *kingship* which results from the *crowning* of cosmic thought.

Exaltation of Jupiter

15° **Cancer** marks the point of exaltation for the *radiance* of Jupiter in full magnitude. 15° Cancer lies just beyond the **Praesepe** cluster (12½° Cancer) of stars imagined as the *Beehive* center of Cancer. The ancient star gazers believed the *Beehive* to be the *portal* or gateway for the birth of incarnating souls for the purpose of gathering the nectar of earthly experience to take back to the Queen of Heaven, the heavenly Sophia (Cosmic Wisdom).

Sounds like Jupiter's theme song – as well as recalling the myth of the new-born Jupiter being suckled by bees!

The Healing Miracle of the Man Born Blind

The <u>Healing of the Man Born Blind</u> was the gift of Christ toward the healing of the 2 petal lotus flower for humanity.[252] This brought about an evolution from the clairvoyant way of seeing and knowing common to the ancient world to the birth of the human being's individual capacity to think and converse *with* the cosmic world. In relation to this healing miracle Christ spoke the words, *"I am the light of the world"*, which is the "I AM" saying corresponding to the 2 petal lotus flower.

Through the event of the Golgotha Mystery lives the *seed* matrix or archetype for the modern human being's task in upholding the rightful use of the Third Eye center (2 petal lotus flower). Like the seven "I AM" sayings, the seven sayings from the Cross are mantra given by Christ for the seven lotus flowers (chakras). The **"I AM" sayings** bring **divine light** into the seven chakras, as took place at the transfiguration of Christ on Mt. Tabor, whereas the **Sayings from the Cross** mediate **divine warmth** to the seven lotus flowers, as took place archetypally at the Crucifixion with the outpouring of divine love through Christ's sacrifice. As mentioned above, the "I AM" saying for the 2 petal lotus flower is *"I am the light of the world"*. Likewise the Saying from the Cross for the 2 petal lotus flower is *"Eli, Eli, lama sabachthani"*, usually translated as *"My God, my God, why hast thou forsaken me"*.[253] Through these words of Christ spoken from the Cross we are given the *freedom* to connect with the cosmic realm. However, the human being who is left completely free, feeling no support whatsoever from heaven or earth, feels forsaken. Then, out of a completely free decision to unite with the Divine, the words *"Eli, Eli, lama sabachthani"* may be experienced on a new level as *"My God, my God, how thou hast glorified me"* – signifying the inner birth of the divine "I AM".

With the "I AM" saying of Christ, *"I am the light of the world"*, the "light of the world" that was sacrificed on Golgotha on behalf of all beings gave birth to the *inner* light of truth for all humanity. This archetypal deed of sacrifice brings new *light* to our understanding of the *central* focus and divine purpose of Jupiter expressed in the words "the *inner* has triumphed". For with this deed, the two-sighted vision of worldly seeing, i.e. the tendency toward illusion with the left eye, and the godless seeing of materiality with the right eye, became wedded to the sacred.

---

[252] Robert Powell, *Morning Meditation in Eurythmy*, p. 4.
[253] In the Hebrew language in which these words were spoken (*"Eli, Eli, lama sabachthani"*), they can also be translated *"My God, my God, how thou hast glorified me"* – see Robert Powell, *Morning Meditation in Eurythmy*, pp. 9-10.

Thus was born the capacity to behold with spiritual sight – or through higher insight – by way of the faculty of the Third Eye to receive answers in response to the posing of questions to the cosmic world. This is the fulfillment of the petition *"Thy kingdom come"* of the Lord's Prayer.

As mentioned above, in the Hebrew language the words from the Cross, *"My God, my God, why hast thou forsaken me?"* can also be translated *"My God, my God, how thou hast **glorified** me."*[254] With this expanded understanding of the words from the Cross related to the healing and attunement of the Jupiter center (Third Eye), we come into the fullness of the words of Christ spoken to the *beggar* who had been "blind since birth" – *"Neither did this man sin or his parents, but that the works of God should be made <u>manifest</u> in him"* (<u>John</u> 9:3). It was the *spittle (life-imbued* water) of Christ's *saliva* <u>mixed</u> with the *clay* of earthly life that through the *light* of *truth* brought the gift of seeing to the blind man.

Beholding the Given — Jove Has More Children!

Jupiter in Cosmic Space

True to the legend of the Jupiter god **Zeus** as the "creator god" who spawned many children, the planet Jupiter has more *children* than all the other planets. In scientific language the children of Jupiter are called <u>satellites</u>, comprising <u>moons</u> and <u>asteroids</u>.

In addition, it has now been discovered that Jupiter has a ring system comprising a main ring and two encircling gossamer rings – all in the region of the four inner Moons. Jupiter's four largest **Moons** (Ganymede, Callisto, Io and Europa), were originally observed by Galileo on January 7, 1610. **Ganymede** is the largest moon in the solar system and is larger than the planets Mercury and Pluto. **Callisto** is the third largest moon (Saturn's Titan is the second) in the solar system and is almost the size of Mercury.

As of April 2005, 63 moons of Jupiter have been observed[255] – 23 of them were discovered in 2003 alone! Four of these 63 moons (Metis, Adrastea, Amalthea, and Thebe) lie within the orbit of the large moon Io, which is thus the fifth of Jupiter's moons. The other three "Galilean moons" – Europa, Ganymede, and Callisto – follow as numbers six, seven, and eight.

The orbits of the inner moons tend – true to Jupiter's nature – to be *rounded* and *fairly circular* in pattern.[256] They lie in the plane of Jupiter's equator, giving a living picture of Jupiter's reputation toward upholding equilibrium in the circulation of the life forces.

Then there are the **Trojan asteroids**, which number 1,891 as of January 2006. The Trojans move along the same orbit as Jupiter around the Sun and are 60° ahead or behind Jupiter.

True to the Babylonian name, "the great star", Jupiter is the most massive of the other planets – comprising about 2½ times the total mass of all the other planets put together. With a volume 1300 times that of the Earth, Jupiter is 318 times more massive than the Earth, with a diameter almost twelve times that of the Earth.

---

[254] Ibid. Normally, since Christ spoke in Aramaic, his sayings are in Aramaic. In this instance, however, he was quoting the words of David's lament from <u>Psalm</u> 22:1 and thus he spoke in Hebrew.

[255] The Asteroid Belt between Mars and Jupiter contains millions of asteroids. Some of Jupiter's moons are believed to be former asteroids captured by Jupiter's gravitational pull.

[256] The tidal force of Jupiter works to circularize the orbits of the moons closest to it, and this holds true for the first four Moons: Metis, Adrastea, Almathea, and Thebe. Yet the larger moons whose orbits are farther away from Jupiter: Io, Europa and Ganymede form a resonance with one another which causes the gravitational effects of the three moons to distort their orbits into elliptical shapes, since each moon receives an extra tug from its neighbors at the same point in every orbit it makes.

Difficult though it is to imagine, Jupiter is a gaseous planet with a rocky core surrounded by liquid hydrogen. Jupiter's density is one-quarter that of the Earth. Quite beautiful to behold, both through a telescope or natural viewing, Jupiter appears as a regal steadying light in the night sky.

With a telescope one can behold the famous "great red spot" of Jupiter[257] reminding one of the red dot depicting the Third Eye which is painted on the foreheads of Hindu believers, who revere the wisdom of Jupiter as sacred.

Among the planets, Jupiter, Mercury and Venus are the most graceful and upright in their orbital patterns. Mercury's tilt is 0°, whereas Jupiter and Venus each have only a 3° tilt of their axis.[258] Thus there is an "as above, so below" mirroring, so to speak. Correspondingly, in the relationship between the Jupiter, Mercury, and Venus chakras in the human being, the Jupiter chakra serves as a guiding principle of life to the intelligence and will (movement) forces of the Mercury chakra and also to the life-bestowing Venus chakra within the physiology of human life.[259]

On the evening of December 21 in the year 2020 it will be possible to behold a truly noble sight: a conjunction of Jupiter and Saturn – a so-called *great conjunction*. This is called a *great conjunction* as it is a relatively uncommon event which occurs only every twenty years. The coming together of Jupiter and Saturn is thought to bear an *informing* gift that appears to *seed* new change for the cultural and artistic life, which can be seen to come into full flower when the two planets are opposite one another approximately ten years later, followed by a waning stage of the new cultural impulse, leading up to the next conjunction of the two planets, again some ten years later.[260]

Yet another interesting correspondence is the celebration in India every twelve years when Jupiter arrives in the constellation of Aquarius. Millions of Hindus honor this event by gathering at the source of the River Ganges. "OM" is the sacred, holy sound of the Hindus, used as a "tuning" sound to connect with the cosmic world. In eurythmy the "O" sound corresponds to Jupiter and the "M" sound to Aquarius, representing the pouring forth of the waters of grace for all humanity. It is noteworthy that the baptism of Jesus in the River Jordan took place when Jupiter stood in Aquarius – sounding "OM" as the Christ descended to unite with Jesus.[261]

Astrologers associate Jupiter with rain and thunder weather conditions, giving credence to Jupiter-Zeus' reputation as the "god of thunder". Indeed today's high-powered telescopes reveal that Jupiter's richly-colored fluorescence is the result of continuous lightning activity in its atmosphere – an activity which creates huge thunderstorms which reverberate throughout the solar system. Thus the mighty sounding ("O") of Jupiter's cosmic wisdom embraces the whole of our solar system.

---

[257] The giant red spot is an oval-shaped, counter-clockwise moving storm which is about four times larger than the planet Earth. This storm, visible just south of Jupiter's equator, has been raging for several centuries.

[258] The tilt of Jupiter's axis is 3.13° and that of Venus is 177.4° (tilted at 3° upside down!).

[259] Appendix III – the first Table shows the reciprocal relationship between the Jupiter chakra related to the hypothalamus (pituitary gland) and the Venus chakra related to the pancreas and the region of health, harmony and balance in the human being. Likewise, the reciprocal relationship between Jupiter/Zeus and Mercury/Hermes is evident, with the latter – as the "messenger of the gods" – acting in service of the higher wisdom and directives of Zeus.

[260] This rhythm of the Jupiter/Saturn conjunctions – waxing for ten years, then waning for ten years – can be grasped by way of analogy with the Sun/Moon rhythm of the two-week waxing phase, leading to the opposition of Sun and Moon (Full Moon), followed by the two-week waning phase leading to the next conjunction (New Moon).

[261] Robert Powell, *Chronicle of the Living Christ*, p. 161.

Jupiter's Metal — Tin[262]

Tin is the Jupiter metal, and true to Jupiter's reputation for star quality and big events, the Oscar awards are said to be made of tin and covered with gold – accompanied with the exuberance of *thunderous* applause.

The association of tin with the planet Jupiter was expressed in the naming of the Etruscan sky god Tinia, who coincided with the Roman deity Jupiter and the Greek god Zeus, and was depicted with lightning bolts, a spear and a scepter – a true image of Jupiter ruling over his kingdom.

Like Jupiter, tin has an *expansive* nature, is easily shaped and malleable, and is known as a preserver for various aspects of nourishment, principally food, as well as being useful for the sealing of wine bottles – in line with Jupiter's jovial nature and reputation toward conviviality!

Bronze is an alloy of copper and tin – an imagination of the marriage of Venus (copper) and Jupiter (tin), coming to expression in the Bronze Age (inspired by Jupiter) and the preservation of beauty and form in the expression of bronze sculpture (inspired by Venus). British pewter is a marriage of Cornish tin (Jupiter) with Welsh lead (Saturn) and is revered for its non-tarnish quality, remaining ever youthful in its appearance.

Keeping pace with the times, the flickering light of the modern liquid computer screens have a tin oxide film for their panels. Jupiter's presence in making wisdom accessible has been harnessed unwittingly to the modern fast-paced "information highway" of today's culture and life.

May the protective spirit of Jupiter guide us in *right thinking* toward the advancement of culture in this technological age.

The Transformation of the Astral Body

The fulfillment of the Jupiter stage of evolution will be the transformation of the astral body. The human being's task will be to evolve into a state of *manas,* wherein the astral body is completely cleansed and purified, so that what is received through the streamings which flow from the memory held in the astral world becomes pure *manas,* pure substance or *bread from heaven.*

Perhaps the account in the book of <u>Genesis</u> is a foretelling of what is to come with the understanding of certain themes repeated in octaves. In the book of <u>Genesis</u>, we are told that in the beginning the human being was surrounded by four *streams* of life-bearing substance, represented by the four rivers which flowed out of the Garden of Eden, and that the human being was to live by the *seed*-bearing fruits of the spiritual garden. However, when the human being fell out of connection with the spiritual world, the source of the "divine seed" (*manas*) dissolved in a flood of destruction, requiring that the human being begin once again to come back into connection with this divine stream, resolving all transgressions from the past.

---

[262] Nick Kollerstrom, "*The Metal-Planet Affinities – Tin*", <u>The Alchemy Web Site</u> <u>http://www.levity.com/alchemy/kollerstrom_tin.html</u>. The commentary on Jupiter and tin is a synthesis of information provided from this site.

Cosmic *Eurythmy*

"In the image and likeness…"

Venus: *"Loving, mild, gentle…"*[263]

Chakra:	Sacral (abdomen)
Organ:	Kidneys
Gland:	Pancreas
Metal:	Copper
Color:	Green
Tones:	F and E[264]

Friday "Vendredi": Venus Day — *"In praise of the gods"*

Friday, Venus Day, celebrates the <u>sixth stage of planetary evolution</u> – **Future Venus**. Humanity at this future time, having undergone a further step on its journey toward becoming united with the Sun, will be participating in the process of the metamorphosis of our solar system, and thus will dwell upon a future planet orbiting around the Sun in the same orbit as present-day Mercury. Following upon the Jupiter stage of planetary evolution, the Future Venus stage will be one in which the <u>atmosphere</u> of that future planet will become permeated with *moral warmth*.[265] This will develop and evolve from the *wisdom-filled, light-filled* evolution of Future Jupiter. Thus, for Future Venus, the gifts of Future Jupiter evolution will *father* the expansive perspectives that *seed* the love of community in the future.

The sixth stage of planetary evolution (Future Venus) begins the work of the <u>transformation of the etheric body</u>, wherein the human being becomes love-filled, permeated with the substance known as *buddhi* (life spirit). The planet called **Venus** in our present-day solar system points the way toward this future evolutionary stage. In this way Venus bears the promise of a true **springtime** of life, verdant with "possibility becoming", which is the *pregnant* promise of the Venus color **green**. Life lived in harmony with the highest nature of Venus becomes more and more an act of *devotion* dedicated to the good, the true and the beautiful.

Friday, Freitag (in German), is named after the Norse goddess, **Freya**, who was the equivalent of the Greek goddess of *love* and *beauty* – **Aphrodite**.[266] Venus *"the shining one"* was the star of Aphrodite and was believed to be her dwelling place. The brilliant radiance of Venus was regarded as a manifestation of her divine beauty.

---

[263] Rudolf Steiner, <u>*History and Content of the Higher Degrees of the Esoteric School*</u>, p. 247.

[264] The correspondences are tabulated in Appendix III: <u>*Correspondences to the Seven Classical Planets*</u>. See also Appendix II: <u>*Musical Tones and the Planets*</u>.

[265] Future Jupiter's goal is the *transfiguration* of the astral body into living wisdom. As the human being takes up the spiritual life, the astral body gradually becomes purified and impressed with the archetypal pattern of our spiritual heritage – *living* the transfiguration of Christ, becoming *light-filled*. At this stage of Future Jupiter, humanity's dwelling place will coincide with the current orbit of the planet <u>Venus</u>, i.e. humanity will then no longer dwell upon the third planet (Earth) from the Sun, but on the second planet (Venus) at the Future Jupiter stage. Following this, humanity will then dwell upon the first planet (Mercury) from the Sun during the Future Venus stage, which will focus on the transformation of the etheric/life body of the human being into the substance of love – becoming *love-filled* – hence the name *Venus* for this future stage.

[266] To the Egyptians Venus was the planet of <u>Isis</u>, whereas the Babylonians knew the goddess associated with Venus as <u>Ishtar</u> – see Robert Powell, <u>*History of the Planets*</u>, pp. 12, 16, 23.

As a goddess, Aphrodite/Venus was considered to have both a heavenly and an earthly dominion. Her qualities were especially associated with the season of **spring** and the elements of both **Air** and **Water**.[267] Above all she was the personification of womanhood, a sacred vessel with the capacity to sustain generation and growth – a divine dominion to hold and to contain life.

Like Mercury, Venus appears both as morning and as evening star. In ancient times these appearances were believed to be two separate stars and were referred to as the *"twin sisters"*.[268] This is a twinship which is mirrored in the form and function of the kidney organism of the human being.

The Kidney Organ (House of Venus)

Botticelli's exquisite painting of the *"Birth of Venus"* in Florence depicts the beautiful Venus emerging in full womanhood from the sea. The **kidneys,** which are the corresponding organ associated with Venus, mirror the *purity* of this lovely goddess born from the sea – in *serving* to purify and draw toxins from the *water element* in the human physiology. The kidneys are considered the *mother* of the organs having dominion over the functioning of liquids everywhere in the human body vessel with the capacity to hold and to contain.

Here in the human physiology we see the "partnering aspect" of Venus as a twofold goddess, relating both to air and water, heaven and earth. The astral body, related to the element of air (just as the etheric body is related to the element of water), rays into the kidneys, so that the kidneys become the bearer of the astral body in the metabolism, regulating the detoxification of the flow of nutrients in the digestive process.

---

[267] Botticelli's painting *"The Birth of Venus"* depicts her standing as mediatrix *between* the elements of Water and Air.

[268] According to ancient Akkadian texts written in cuneiform, Venus' appearance as morning or evening star originally was conceived as *two* planets, a pair of *"twin sisters"*, only later appearing as *"Inanna"* in her temple at Nineveh, which was called "the *house of the twins"* – see Robert Powell, *History of the Planets*, pp. 11-12.

The Pancreas Gland

The pancreas is the corresponding gland associated with Venus and is located in the region of the **abdomen** (life center), the Venus center of the human being.

The ancient astrologers believed Venus to be the consort of Jupiter calling the two planets the "two benefics" – Jupiter "the greater benefic", and Venus "the lesser benefic".

We can observe this pairing also in the human physiology, wherein the Jupiter center (Third Eye), which governs the function of the pituitary gland, the "master gland" of the glandular system, maintains an "*as above, so below*" relationship with the Venus center, which governs the **pancreas.**[269]

The Venus center *listens* attentively for the comfort derived from the higher perspectives of spiritual thought received through the activity of the Third Eye – in response to the questions which inevitably *arise* in the taking in of the daily bread of existence. This in turn effects a balancing current within the metabolism (coming to expression through the pituitary gland's communication within the glandular system, affecting the pancreas). The TRUTH of proper nourishment *depends* upon a *benevolent* thought life.

Cosmic Dance of Venus

The cosmic dance of Venus celebrates this *partnering*, as a metamorphosis of the *sounding* gesture of Jupiter's "O" becomes a full-bodied, grace-filled walk of the "Circle of All", and a *circling* in toward the Earth in an offering of gratitude, with the Venus sound "A" ("ah") – "*in praise of the gods*", which is the name for the Venus form in cosmic dance. Jupiter's gesture of *inner* force and containment (with the right hand moving around the left, circling in the region of the heart chakra, expressing wisdom) is metamorphosed into a full-bodied circling in toward the Earth, as the arms and hands *open out* and are *lifted up* into the Venus gesture "A", expressing wonder and openness permeated with love.

"Handmaiden"

In the cosmic dance of Venus the dancers pay special attention to the feeling capacity of the hands, allowing them to soften into a quality of *gentleness*, emanating care and love.

It is said that of all the planets Venus has a special caring for all that transpires upon the Earth. She listens attentively. "*Venus receives into herself everything that comes from the Earth.*"[270] In the dance of Venus, we listen with our hands.

Venus Gesture – "Devotion"

Beginning with a slow-paced, *steady* walk proceeding counter-clockwise around the circle, the dancers form the Venus gesture, which is oriented toward the center of the circle (representing the Earth). The left arm and hand (relating to the heart and feeling life) extend down and back (oriented

---

[269] See Appendix III, first Table.
[270] Rudolf Steiner, "*The Spiritual Individualities of the Planets*", <u>The Golden Blade</u>, vol. 40 (1988), p. 48.

toward the subconscious soul life) and rotate slowly <u>counter-clockwise</u>, stirring the depths of the subconscious. The left hand is open, fingers together, aligned with the extension of the arm; the palm is soft in an attitude of care and listening. This is the capacity of the Divine Feminine, the Holy Soul of the community, to sense the mystery of life with benevolence.

Simultaneously, the right arm (relating to the activity of the Ego) extends down from the shoulder and *bends forward* at the elbow at an angle of 90°, with the palm gently opened, facing up – in an attitude of **devotion** – *beholding* the content of the stirred subconscious, which is the "given" of daily life, and *offering it up* in order to receive the higher streaming down from the spiritual world.

The Venus gesture brings to fulfillment the promise of the *horizontal* axis of the Venus glyph ♀ through the *activity* of the Ego, expressing itself in the gesture of the *right* arm, which becomes the horizontal axis of the cross, offering *up* the concerns of daily life for the *reflection* of higher perspectives.

Correspondingly, the caring forces of the heart are brought to the stirring of the subconscious by the streaming of the heart into the *left* arm, which brings to fulfillment the promise of the radiance of the Sun, bringing light to enlighten the darkness of the subconscious realm.

Venus Sound "A"

Responding to the rhythm and motif of the music, at the *appropriate* time the dancers move in unison (expressing the sense of community), circling in toward the center of the circle (a movement *toward* the Earth). Moving around in a counter-clockwise direction, the dancers simultaneously form the Venus sound "A" – spoken "ah" in cosmic dance – allowing the arms to flow *out* and *up*, forming a "V" shape, which opens out from the heart. In an attitude of *praise* and *gratitude*, the dancers become a Grail vessel to receive divine love, the living substance of grace.

Although the dance will vary in tempo and pace according to the music, imitating earthly existence, the gestures of *grace* and *devotion* remain constant in a mood of *charity* toward one's earthly life. The word "charity" is derived from the Greek word *charis* connected with the verb *chairein*, meaning "to rejoice". In Greek mythology the **Charites** represented the threefold nature of Aphrodite. The Romans needed two words to translate "charis": *venus* meaning "beauty", which was their name for the love goddess, and *gratia,* a word which for them contained the qualities of "thankfulness" *and* "favor" – describing the heavenly *reciprocity* of true gratitude. Thus the Roman name for the three goddesses was the **Gratiae** ("Graces"). The three were the personification of grace, beauty, and charm, and they danced together by the light of the Moon.[271]

---

[271] Carl Kerényi, *The Gods of the Greeks*, pp. 99-101.

Venus *Eurythmy* Form

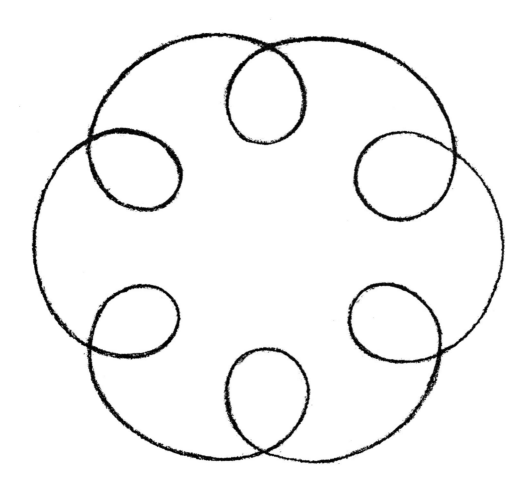

The Venus form expresses the movement of Venus as seen from the Earth. The movement to the right, around the circle, is precisely the movement of Venus when moving *direct* (forward) through the zodiac. The movement tracing out a circle is that of Venus moving *retrograde* (backward), forming a near-circular "loop" in toward the Earth at the center of the circle. The Venus form, in all its simplicity, is an expression of beauty and harmony, mirroring the almost perfect form traced out by Venus in the heavens. (Of all the elliptical forms of the planets in their orbits around the Sun, that of Venus comes closest to being circular.)

As with the forms for Saturn, Jupiter and the Sun, depending on the music, it is sometimes appropriate to step the Venus form: generally a total of either 12 or 16 steps – 6 (or 8) steps for the curve around the circle to the right (commencing with the right foot stepping to the right), and 6 (or 8) steps for the circle forward (starting with the right foot stepping forward to begin the counter-clockwise circle).

Cosmic Dance of Venus

"In Praise of the Gods"

Venus has to do with the depths of our emotional life and an offering up in devotion to higher wisdom. Carry yourself gracefully, as Venus has to do with everything beautiful and harmonious.

Begin by stepping the form, then add the gestures:

Movement: A slow, graceful movement to the right. On the long curves to the right, the body remains facing toward the center of the circle, requiring that the waist turn in toward the center, as the feet step gracefully around slightly on an angle.

A cross-step can be used by way of alternating the stepping.

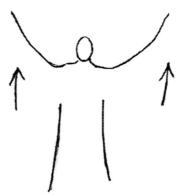

Venus Gesture: On the long gracious curve to the right, the **left** arm is pointed down toward the earth (palm open, arm diagonally back and rotating counter-clockwise):

Stirring the depths of the unconscious and emotional life.

The **right** arm is held at a right-angle (palm open, facing up) and remains still, as though *presenting an offering.*

Now circle in toward the center and move **counter-clockwise** *around* and back to the periphery of the circle.

Venus Sound: "A" ("ah")

The face reflects a quality of wonder as the arms open and rise up to form an open "V" above the head. Palms open in a gesture of *praise and gratitude.*

Complete the "A" sound with the open "V" at the front of the circle.

Circling in, continuing to move toward the right, then around to the left and back around to the right.

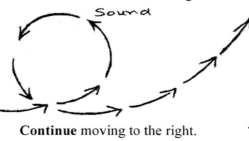

Continue moving to the right.

"This is the human being in his aspect of loving sacrifice."

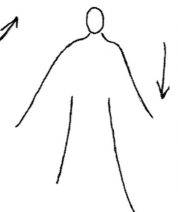

Slowly lower the arms as you complete the circle moving back to the periphery.

Alternately: Form the Venus *gesture* on the long graceful curves and the "A" *sound* circling in toward the center of the circle.

The 6 Petal Lotus Flower

The 6 petal lotus flower (sacral center) corresponds *macrocosmically* to Venus and can be likened to the two interpenetrating triangles of a 6-pointed star:

The form of a 6-pointed star indicates the task of the Venus chakra – which is to bring to expression the balance of body, soul, and spirit. With the *marriage* of the two triangles coming together, we have an imagination of an ascending/descending *movement* in perfect balance. This is *one aspect* of the human being's multi-layered nature endeavoring to maintain *equilibrium*. A musical expression of the search for equilibrium is found in the **interval** of the sixth.

The Venus center (located in the sacral region), which appears to clairvoyant vision as a **6 petal lotus flower**, is responsible for a subtle and continuous activity in support of balance and harmony. This suggests that the health and function of this center requires an *active* participation on the part of the human being to maintain equilibrium (the resonance of the *interval* of the sixth). Daily life constantly demands the activity of maintaining a **balance** in earthly existence, bringing harmony to the dynamic interrelationships between the physical, soul, and spiritual realms.

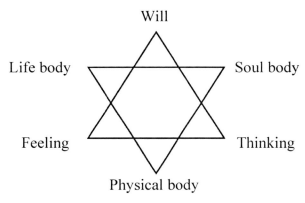

Balance — The Middle Way

The practice of *right standpoint* ("right standing") [272] requires a firm and steady standing in maintaining a balance in earthly life – that is, not "being consumed" by the earthly *temptations* of the senses, which can lead to debauchery or extreme materiality, while at the same time being deeply *devoted* and *caring* for the earthly realm, including of course, Nature herself. This is "right standing" in relation to life on Earth.

Then there is "right standing" with respect to one's spiritual life – that is, taking care not to divorce oneself from the earthly, physical realm or one's own corporeality in the fervent quest for communion with the divine. For the spiritual life also has its challenges: the temptation to use spiritual experience toward egoic superiority (or even "spiritual debauchery") instead of as a *source* of inspiration for the daily walk of life. The practice of *right standpoint* thus entails the "middle way" between the two extremes. Ideally the result of this practice becomes the fulfillment of the words of Christ, "*I am the way, the truth, and the life*" – which is the "I AM" saying corresponding to the 6 petal lotus flower. Perhaps this comes to expression with the glyph for Venus ♀, wherein the circle of life is lifted *up* and *supported* by the cross.

---

[272] See Robert Powell, *Hermetic Astrology*, vol. I, pp. 136-137, 196, 246-248 for further discussion concerning the 6 petal lotus flower and the practice of "right standpoint". See also Appendix III.

Venus — The "Etheric Center" of the Seven Lotus Flowers

The 6 petal lotus flower is located beneath the **Mercury center** (solar plexus/10 petal lotus flower), which is connected through the diaphragm to *breathing*. By contrast, the 6 petal lotus/**Venus center** in the region of the abdomen has an important role in connection with the glandular system and the secretion of fluids in the organism. Each center (chakra) has its own unique function and purpose.

The **Mercury center** is central to the activity of the *astral body* (through the breathing, recalling that the astral body lives in the human being's "air organism"). Similarly the **Venus center** is of central importance in the functioning of the *etheric/life body*. Just as the 6 petal lotus flower is constantly active in trying to maintain equilibrium between the different levels (physical–soul–spiritual), so the etheric body serves as an **_intermediary_** between the *astral* and *physical* bodies (physical–etheric–astral) and is active in relation to the fluidic system which regulates glandular activity in balance and harmony.

The Venus center with its six petals mediates cosmic forces that maintain an *equilibrium* between the physical body and the astral body. And true to the Venus association with the goddess of love, the Venus chakra is also *active* in the bringing together of man and woman, *serving* to harmonize the polarities of masculine and feminine life currents that sustain health within the entire human organism.

In this respect the **Venus chakra** – which, like all the chakras, is an "astral organ" – *serves* as the "**etheric center**" for the **seven** lotus flowers, having a regulating, balancing effect upon the inter-relationships of each of the seven chakras comprising the astral body.

Venus — The Heavenly Consort

In one account of Greek mythology Venus-Aphrodite, the goddess of beauty, harmony, and love, is depicted as having been in *intimate* relationship with Jupiter-Zeus,[273] the son of Saturn-Chronos, a relationship which is mirrored in the working together of Jupiter and Venus in the functioning of the human glandular system (relating to the interdependence of the Venus and Jupiter chakras). There are, however, mythological accounts which suggest that Venus was also in relationship with Mars-Ares, as well as Mercury-Hermes, who was a son of Zeus – *and* each relationship, we are told, was sacred.

Divine Madness vs. Heavenly Perfection

How are we to understand the wisdom and plurality of these relationships, which sought to reveal themselves through the image-making faculty of the imagination, providing *telling* images for the spoken word expressed in mythologies throughout the various ages?

The image of the 6-pointed star, depicting the *marriage* of the ascending/descending triangles (heaven/earth, spirit/soul, masculine/feminine), helps to penetrate the deeper significance of this mystery. This image, as we have seen, applies to the activity of the Venus center *serving* to balance the ascending/descending currents which *mediate* between the *physical* and the *astral* levels (physical–etheric–astral), influencing also the work of the glandular system. In turn, the direction of the flow of life currents in the human being is dependent upon the harmonization of the glandular system and the inner planetary system of the organs (heart, lungs, kidneys, etc.).

---

[273] "*Aphrodite was not the love-goddess's only principal name. She also had the Greek name of Dione… At Dodona she was worshipped together with Zeus in his quality as a god of springs, being regarded as wife of the supreme god…*" – Carl Kerényi, *The Gods of the Greeks*, p. 68.

Against this background the marriage in Greek mythology of Venus-Aphrodite to Jupiter-Zeus can be grasped, especially in view of the Jupiter chakra's influence upon the pituitary gland, the "master gland" of the glandular system. Likewise the marriage of Venus-Aphrodite to Mercury-Hermes can be understood, in *serving* as the mediating balancing force between the *astral* body (which finds its center of connection in the solar plexus/Mercury center) and the physical body. The Venus center, through these interrelationships, plays a balancing role in the functioning of the organs.

How might Mars come into this picture? The answer becomes clear when we consider that Mars governs the larynx chakra, which has to do with "right speech". Remembering that the larynx chakra is not only connected with speech but also with *spiritual listening,* we can begin to understand that the relationship of Venus to Mars is a mutual attraction – as our emotional life (Venus) is largely dependent upon the shaping, forming quality of our thoughts, which are then reflected in the inner *sounding* coming from the Mars center.

Mars – in right relationship with Venus – takes care to shape the internal *sounding* of the thought life with the *gentleness* of a lover, taking care not to cause fear, so as not to upset the emotional life. Now comes the cause for the "mutual attraction" of Mars and Venus. For, in turn, the **balance** in the emotional life (brought about by the caring attention toward the inner realm of thought) is reflected in the outward expression of the spoken word through **moral speech,** *and* in the activation of the higher **will** forces toward right action in the world.

A Cosmic Affair — Hephaestus, Aphrodite, Ares

The alchemy of the divine triangle

In Greek mythology, according to some sources, Aphrodite was married to Hephaestus. Hephaestus was the heavenly blacksmith who brought the divine alchemy of fire to the *shaping* of *iron* (Mars) and was reported to have shaped the *beauty* and *form* of Aphrodite (Venus) into images of pure gold. Now, as the story unfolds, we are told that on one occasion when Hephaestus was absent, Ares (Mars) showed up and Aphrodite (Venus) was *unfaithful* to her husband.

Therein lies the mystery of the challenge of instability (unfaithfulness) in the relationship of the Venus–life center with the Mars–larynx center – for without the *moral* shaping forces of divine love (heavenly blacksmith) applied to the *sounding* of Mars ("right speech"/"spiritual listening") in his relationship with Venus, the divine marriage putrefies, in the realm of speech and also in life itself.

This brings to appreciation the mediating force of the heart, which comes to expression in the Venus gesture with the left arm extended down toward the Earth (stirring the depths of the subconscious soul life), *listening* with the radiating force of the heart's connection to the Sun (the divine fire of "I" consciousness), which becomes the inspiring *source* for the gesture of the right arm and hand – turned heavenward – in offering the subconscious soul life as a gift of devotion to the spiritual world.

The Mystery of Love

Rudolf Steiner, in his clairvoyant viewing of Venus, offers a resolution to this divine mystery – indicating that Venus' *"true love"* is the Earth:

> *Venus is highly responsive to everything that comes from the Earth. The Earth is, so to speak, her only lover. She lovingly reflects whatever comes from the Earth. The truth is that human beings on Earth can do nothing in the secrecy of their souls without it*

being reflected back again by Venus. Venus gazes deeply into the hearts of human beings, for that is what interests her. Thus, the most intimate experiences of earthly life are reflected again from Venus. In the reflection she transforms everything.

She listens attentively to the utterances of Mars. She transforms and illuminates her dreamlike experiences of earthly things with what is communicated to her from the universe through Mars.

All these things have their physical side as well. Impulses go out from these sources into what is done and what comes into existence in the world. Venus receives into herself everything that comes from the Earth and she listens always to Mars. And from this process – only of course the Sun is there to regulate it – spring the forces which underlie the organs connected with the formation of human speech. If one wants to understand the impulses in the universe connected with the function of human speech, one must turn one's gaze to this strange life that weaves between Venus and Mars. When destiny wills it, the relationship of Mars is therefore a factor of great significance in the development of the speech or language of a people.[274]

Botticelli's Painting, *"The Birth of Venus"*

Moving from the macrocosmic to the microcosmic level of understanding, we could say that with Venus *"art imitates life"* and correspondingly *"life imitates art"*, and so it is with Botticelli's exquisite painting, *"The Birth of Venus"*, which is a masterpiece of symbolic imagery. In the painting Venus stands centrally, in the *middle* of the composition, *balanced* on a conch shell, floating on the *reflective* surface of *water*. The conch is a sea creature whose *breathing* mechanism is triggered by copper (the Venus metal). Gusty *wind* forces assail her from the left and also from *below* on the right, but she remains upright, completely *sovereign* in her realm. She is resplendent in her nakedness, declaring the glory of the *embodiment of spirit* – the gift of human corporeality. Through the balance of her gestures, she appears both vulnerable and chaste – her countenance serene (see reproduction on page 134).

In the realm of *"life imitating art"*, what might these images represent symbolically? Venus is associated with the elements of water and air. Correspondingly, the Venus center in the human being serves as *mediatrix* for the **glandular system**, which regulates the *fluids* of the human body, as well as serving as an interface for the element of air, as a *balancing* force toward the regulation of **breathing.**

Mercury is associated with the element of air at work through the human diaphragm. The Mercury center is connected to the navel, and thus to the umbilical cord, through which the human embryo is connected to the mother's breath. Upon birth the umbilical cord is cut and the baby takes its first breath. According to astrology, this is the moment of the birth of the soul, which is *"breathed in"* through the activity of the lungs. Thus, the **mysteries of soul** and those of **destiny** are conceived as belonging to the *air*, permeating the entire human aura surrounding the physical body, which is referred to as the **astral body.**[275] As discussed earlier, the Venus center serves as **mediatrix** between the astral body and the physical body, assuming a mediating role in the balancing of etheric life. The etheric/life body retains the blueprint for the organization of the life forces.

---

[274] Rudolf Steiner, *"The Spiritual Individualities of the Planets"*, <u>The Golden Blade</u>, vol. 40 (1988), pp. 47-48.
[275] Robert Powell, <u>Hermetic Astrology, vol.I</u>, p. 136.

We encounter the reality of the human aura through our ability to feel and to sense subtle realities. For example, we might have the thought, "I can sense that…something is in the *air*", signifying that we can sense an *atmosphere* or a certain "emotional climate" surrounding a person. When the Venus center is challenged, and we feel that we are losing our sense of balance, if we remember to *breathe* and to breathe deeply, to draw the breath deep into the **abdomen**, we can often recover a sense of quietude and not fall prey to the fears which can arise from the *depths* of the subconscious, but rather maintain a sense of sovereignty, which can lead to a certain mastery of the situation.

Fear, Anger, and the Kidneys[276]

The Venus gesture brings to harmony what might be called the alchemy of the *"birthing force"* of spring" – or the *passion,* which describes the effort made to *raise* something *up* from the Earth's gravity. The Venus gesture brings this mystery to expression, with the left arm (relating to the feeling nature) extended down, stirring the depths of the unconscious, and the right arm held in a gesture of devotion, offering up the content of the soul life.

This effort of raising up is the *force* proper to beginnings. In the beginning or *spring* of a new endeavor or direction, the Venus influence might be *prompted*, through the heart's longing toward the fulfillment of destiny, to *serve* the cause by inspiring a good dose of *impetuosity,* or when real change is seeking to break through, the Jupiter influence, in response to wisdom's call for caution in times of impending change, could send a message to the liver that the heart is threatened. Thus the liver might respond in defence of the heart, reacting to the threat with a *stirring*, fiery force that might be experienced as anger.

Herein lies a challenge, for great anger, when not tempered with higher understanding, can cause the life currents to go into a counter-current of resistance, becoming knotted, or to flow in a contrary way. When the kidneys become prey to swelling anger without the power to stop it (higher understanding/Jupiter), then there can be an injury to the *will* forces (Mars), manifesting as the *dampening* effect brought about by an on-going state of fear. Fear can be caused by the counter-current of the Venus center's response to the signal of anger from the liver. It is the liver which *enables* thinking to pass on to reflection, and when this does not occur, anger is frequently the result. However, when anger is mastered or held in check, the organism is *supported* (through the life currents) toward proper thinking, which can overcome fear.

Irresolvable states of fear and anger will take effect upon the **will** forces and impact the faculty of movement. Thus, the circulation of the life currents in the fluidic system, influenced by the Venus center, is essential to the will nature. One might say that the human spirit and the will become *grieved*. In this case the organ of the heart is endangered. Here we see the interrelationship of the kidneys to the heart and the importance of thinking *with* the light and warmth of the Sun forces radiating from the heart center.

Loss of memory is an indication of a kidney imbalance (not being able to contain), which can also cause an injury to the will forces. When one cannot remember what one has just said, this can be a sign that awareness and consciousness are *limited* to the very moment of speaking. This indicates a lack of continuity, which is a feeling for the *duration* of life and a lack of anchorage, grounding, or "right standing".

---

[276] Claude Larre and Elizabeth Rochat de la Valleé, *The Seven Emotions*, p.121.

A weakness in the functioning of the kidneys often takes effect on bodily structure, on the bones and the marrow inside the bones, which normally are in a constant *springtime* of renewal and invigoration through the forces of the kidneys. Strong bones are linked to the suppleness and richness of the bone marrow. An injury to the will forces, which manifests in the malfunction of the kidneys, can thus create problems in the lumbar area and spine, which would indicate the soul condition of feeling a lack of support. Anger stiffens rather than softens, and when anger and fear have become a perpetual irritation, the *balance* of life becomes impossible.

Physical — Etheric — Astral

The kidneys are the *portal* to astral influences and, in turn, have a *mediating* effect upon the etheric body, *filtering* content flowing from the astral body to the physical body. This function of mediation is mirrored in the Venus concern for soul life and the depths of the subconscious.

In this way the kidneys are especially vulnerable to fear. Fear breaks the axis between the kidneys (Venus) and the heart. Remembering that the kidneys are responsible for the functioning of liquids everywhere in the body, including the ability to hold and to contain, there are observable pathologies in the functioning of the kidneys with the presence of overwhelming or long-endured fear.

Either the life force descends and there is no longer the power to contain, hence a condition of physical and/or emotional incontinence becomes manifest, or a condition of cold swells upward, causing what might be called a "frozen heart". Extreme hesitancy and uncertainty are symptomatic of the kidneys affecting the heart with a kind of paralysis of the will. Both are symptomatic of the challenge of the Venus center to maintain a balance in the emotional life – bringing *integrity* to the intimate relationships of body, spirit, and soul. In the case of extreme disequilibrium, the kidney meridian is affected, resulting in panic attacks and the haunting impression of being on the edge of disaster.

Extreme bouts of tears are sometimes indicative of a "blow" to the will – whereby the power of the kidneys to contain liquids no longer functions well. The cause of the problem usually lies between the heart and the will. When there is something wrong and the heart cannot endure some kind of suffering, the kidneys respond. Long-suffering relationships or endeavors which are endured through sheer force of will, but which do not support one's true nature, circumstances, or heart's desire, when taken to the extreme ("aching heart"), are cause for kidney conditions which result in aching bones and flaccidity in the muscles (weakened will).

It is said that normal fear is the "prudence of the wise man", indicating the call for a vigilant watch over the most intimate thoughts and feelings in the emotional life. This is the benevolence of a watchful, caring heart toward the activity of true reflection. Reflective thought *serves* as the relational turning point between the functioning of the kidneys and the heart, in that the ascending/descending currents of the Venus center are turned through such thought activity. Symptomatic to an imbalance in these ascending/descending currents are the conditions of poor circulation (a symptom of diabetes) and/or retention of fluids resulting in swelling, when the power of the water is too strong. The interrelationship of iron (Mars and the proper shaping of thought content) to copper (Venus and the maintaining of balance in the emotional life) is vital for the circulation of the blood.

Through the practice of reflection, entailing an offering up of fearful concerns for the higher perspectives of spiritual thought (Jupiter), the water of the kidneys is free to *nourish* the liver, resulting in an enrichment of the blood, bringing a "springtime" to the organism. In contrast, a lack of Venus nourishment creates an *emptiness* in the liver, which results in fear. This is the counter-current to the innate harmony of life, which requires the presence of love. Herein lies the wisdom of the Venus gesture!

When we understand the **wisdom** of the flow of life currents orchestrated through the mediating function of the Venus center, this can help toward the understanding of how it is that the life force which *enlivens* creation is *intelligent* (when it is not impeded by untempered emotions), as it is the bearer of the divine blueprint of both the physical and soul (astral) levels of existence.

Combinatorial Thinking — Mercurial Thinking / Venus Listening

How is the weather…?

Conditions of heat and chill, dryness and moisture – qualities of temperature and temperament – characterize Venus conditions. How is the weather?…might be an appropriate question for the Venus center in relation not only to one's emotional life, but also concerning the state of one's physical well-being.

The human being is of a sevenfold nature – and Venus, being fully preoccupied with the "nature of things", *listens* – listens to the *weather* (both atmospheric and emotional), listens to the soul conditions, listens for guidance and higher perspectives and – above all – listens with the heart (Venus gesture). She, through her exquisite feeling nature (Venus listening), penetrates through to the "heart of the matter". Then a marriage can take place of Mercury's "*combinatorial thinking*" with Venus' listening, feeling for the truth. Only when Venus is fully *informed* and cared for (nourishment of the soul) can she bring harmony to the whole. Venus listens not as a gossip (like Mars), but rather her listening is for the purpose of bringing harmony to the whole of the organism.

The Promise of "Harmonia"

As mentioned earlier "Harmonia" was the child or divine *offspring* (progeny) of the marriage of Ares/Mars and Aphrodite/Venus. The name "Harmonia" means "the uniter". This is the promise of right relationship between the well-formed, well-honed, well-intentioned word (the work of the divine blacksmith) with the Mars/larynx center and the Venus/life center.

Harmonia, however, requires the wisdom inherent in the Venus glyph ♀ of standing in the middle, holding the balance. Perhaps the names of the other offspring of Ares and Aphrodite reveal a more complete telling of the *tension* inherent in the marriage of these opposites – Phobos and Deimos, "Fear" and "Terror"– and, on the other hand, Eros and Anteros, "Love" and "Answering Love".[277] Clearly these pairs of opposites are calling for the resolution of the **will** of Venus toward balance.

It is interesting that other mythological genealogies attribute **Eros** to have been fathered both by Hephaestus, the heavenly blacksmith in his marriage to Venus/Aphrodite, and also by Mercury/ Hermes, the messenger of the gods, having to do with communication between the spiritual and earthly realms. In any case, the promise of grace in a *springtime* of peace, both to the soul and to the physical health, is determined by the third – the spiritual *presence* of higher perspective (Jupiter).

---

[277] Carl Kerényi, *The Gods of the Greeks*, p. 71.

Venus and the Soul Life

Venus leads the soul into the body and through the body to spirit. (Thomas Moore)[278]

The effect of love's presence upon the balancing faculty of the Venus center, resulting in harmonizing the ascending/descending currents of the life forces, could be likened to the WIND currents in nature, which cleanse, purify, and circulate the currents of the etheric body of the Earth.

Something of the soul qualities of this story of circulation, transition, and mutual attraction are depicted in Botticelli's beautiful painting of Spring, ("*Primavera*"), in which Venus is central. Beautiful in form, supple in standing, and resplendent in Nature, Venus *lifts* her right hand (Ego) in a gesture of receiving and also blessing. She is the divine vessel, the inspiration for the activity that surrounds her, as a blind-folded cupid (Eros) hovers over her head, suggesting that romantic love is blind. (It is, however, also *wise*). In Botticelli's painting there is everywhere a *circulation*.

It is the wind's pursuit that begins the action.[279] This is the *nature* of things. As the earth nymph (Chloris) flees from the wind Zephyr, her *breath* creates flowers and the alchemy of spring *transforms* this *breath* into **Flora**, the herald of spring. We see Flora, clothed with the flowers of spring, emerging at the side of Chloris, appearing as a kind of visual metamorphosis of Chloris. Flora embodies the transformed breath of spring's alchemy – remembering that spring is Venus' season.

The three graces, Chastity, Love, and Beauty (representing the soul friendship of brotherly, sisterly love/philia) are in an all-consuming round dance of perfect harmony.[280] Chastity and Love gaze into each other's eyes with their hands interlocked as in a contest, which has reached the balance point. Beauty looks toward the divine world *lifting* Love's left arm (relating to the feeling nature), while

---

[278] Thomas Moore, *The Planets Within*, p. 142.

[279] In Botticelli's painting, the wind of spring, Zephyr, appears on the far right in pursuit of the Earth nymph Chloris.

[280] The three Graces, often depicted as handmaidens of Venus-Aphrodite, were considered to be daughters of Zeus. Hesiod in the *Theogony* names them Aglaia ("Beauty"), Euphrosyne ("Joy"), and Thalia ("Abundance"). The Florentine humanists saw them as the personification of Beauty, Chastity, and Love.

Beauty's left arm joins hands with Chastity's right arm (relating to the Ego) in a gesture that is earth-bound – a perfect soul picture for the balance necessary for sensual love to reach the promise of spirit.

Now, on the painting's left edge, at the periphery of the dancing circle of feminine beings, young Mercury-Hermes stands pointing up, lifting our soul's vision upwards toward the divine. His hand becomes the fleshly counterpart to the apple-laden trees, which stand like sentinels in the background, waiting to bear the fruits of reason.

Mercury stands solidly on the ground, Chastity gazing wistfully in his direction, while Flora strides forward clasping her pregnant belly with her right hand (Ego), her *unseen* left hand (feeling) hidden in the veil *and* protective mantle of her *garden* (Venus center) of spring.

There is everywhere a mutual attraction, a continuous movement, with Venus' watchful eye holding the balance. She presides over the fertility of the earth, gazing subliminally – as though belonging to a realm between the divine and the human – reminding us that "*love connects us to the gods*" (Plato).

> *There is one continuous attraction, beginning with God, going to the world and ending at last in God, an attraction which returns to the same place where it began as though in a kind of circle.* (Marsilio Ficino)[281]

Botticelli seems to be saying that Venus' gift is, after all, spirit and that a sensual, pleasurable life, when balanced with chastity and the reason of Mercury in the *celebration* of beauty in physical form, as well as in nature, is simply and *naturally* good for the soul!

> *Desire as holy is our <u>sensual</u> connection to the divine world...*[282]

Venus — The Healing of the Seven Lotus Flowers (Chakras)

Venus, through orchestrating the waters of life in the physical body, in her capacity as vessel to mediate the etheric realm (the *living* waters of Christ/the healer of the life body), is important – expressing herself through the 6 petal lotus – as a center for the potential healing of the sevenfold human being through the *divine marriage* of Christ and the human soul. The archetype of the healing of the sevenfold human being is to be found in the seven healing miracles of Christ described in the <u>Gospel of St. John</u>, where each healing miracle relates to one of the seven chakras.

The Words and Healing Miracles of Christ

The Mars Chakra (16 petal lotus, larynx)

> *In the beginning was the WORD — I am the good shepherd — Man does not live by bread alone, but by every word that proceedeth from the mouth of God.*

The healing words of Christ, "*I am the good shepherd*", tell the story of the healing of the challenging aspects of the Mars center.[283] The words of Christ's promise to *serve* as the "good shepherd" at the door of the spoken word (Mars center/"right speech") are powerful and strengthening. The throat center "thirsts" for this *promise* (reflected archetypally in the words of Christ, "*I thirst*", the promise of the shepherding guidance of Christ.)[284]

---

[281] Quote from Thomas Moore, <u>The Planets Within</u>, p. 139.

[282] Robert Sardello, <u>Freeing The Soul From Fear</u>, p. 180.

[283] Robert Powell, <u>Morning Meditation in Eurythmy</u>, pp. 3-4 indicates the correspondence between the chakras, the "I AM" sayings, and the healing miracles of Christ. In the case of the 16 petal lotus flower (Mars center), the correspondences are: "*I am the good shepherd*" and the walking on the water.

[284] Ibid. p. 8 indicates the correspondence between Christ's words from the Cross ("*I thirst*", "*It is fulfilled*"...) and the seven chakras, whereby "*I thirst*" is the saying from the Cross relating to the Mars center (larynx).

Considering the Mars center in relation to the Venus center, there is a sacred marriage between these two centers when the intent is held "to love, honor, and protect" the divine feminine focus of the "etheric center" (6 petal chakra) of the seven lotus flowers.

Also related to the Mars chakra, the healing miracle of the *walking on the water* signifies a demonstration of the overcoming of fear, so as to *lift* one's daily walk from the challenge of being drowned in the emotional waters of life.

The Mercury Chakra (10 petal lotus, movement center)

"*I am the door, the entrance and the exit*" posits the words of Christ as the guardian of this gateway to the astral world, the door of "right judgment" (Mercury center). Of the seven chakras, the Mercury center is particularly the focus of the astral body. One way of schooling the 10 petal lotus is through consciously directing our movements – for example, through our choice of deeds – "right judgment", to bring consciousness into all movement and activity.

The *healing of the paralyzed man* at the pool (water) of Bethesda, in relation to the Mercury center, demonstrates a healing through Christ's guidance to "*stand up*" in the face of the paralyzing effect of fear.

This often manifests in daily life as a fear of "moving forward", making a change, or coming to a decision for fear of taking the wrong step or action. The presence of fear in these instances results in a state of paralysis – one becomes crippled.

As an example here, there is the inspiring story of Hephaestus, the heavenly blacksmith, who *was* crippled and still *learned* the art of forging and shaping thought (Mercury center) with the fire of divine love. The work of the shaping of thought *with* love brings the will and the life forces into right relationship.

The Venus Chakra (6 petal lotus, life center)

"*I am the way, the truth, and the life*" are the healing words spoken by Christ for the Venus center, which acts as an interface (through the *watery* element of the etheric body) between the astral body and the physical body.

The *healing of the nobleman's son* reinstates the Christ-centered connection and thus the <u>return of the "I"-centered consciousness</u> to the *creative* principle of life. (Refer to the story of the healing miracles in the Moon chapter.) In this miracle the son (offspring) of Selathiel, the nobleman's servant, was dying and thus was rendered a "withered vine", due to the servant, Selathiel, having given over his "I" to the hierarchical demands of the *material* world, in the giving of his own son to be adopted by his benefactor, the nobleman. This miracle is a healing for the Venus chakra, having to do with the loss and reinstatement of the Christ-centered consciousness to the balancing organ (6 petal lotus) within the astral body.

The Heart Chakra (12 petal lotus flower, heart center)

Here there is a call to <u>return to heart-centered consciousness</u>. "*I am the bread of life*" are the words of Christ that break the *iron* grip of fear which would drive the human being into the temptation of "*turning stones to bread*" – seeking life-bringing substance from the material driving forces of earthly reality. In this mercurial age, the second half of Earth evolution, humanity has reached a new octave, having come a long way from the shaping of stone for weaponry and utensils to the manipulation of the more subtle driving forces which find themselves as the compelling focus of the technological age. Consider, for example, the awesome realities of the virtual world of forgery and faking – forged (fake) identities, fake *breasts*, fake faces (through *face lifts*), on-line romance between people with created identities, and so on.

The miracle of the *feeding of the five thousand* is the *nourishing* promise of true sustenance. Through the *circulation* which occurs with a conscious reconnection to divine spiritual guidance, truth *enters,* rendering new, revivifying blood – cleansed through the breath and nourished by the liver (detoxifying the blood). A heart that is Sun-centered becomes a radiating presence in the world.

The Jupiter Chakra (2 petal lotus, brow center, Third Eye)

"*I am the light of the world*" are words of Christ which reveal the power of TRUTH through "right thinking" – bringing light to the dark precipices of fear.

The *healing of the man born blind* brings inner sight to the Third Eye – making the *way* clear, bringing clarity and decision.

Physiologically the liver (Jupiter organ) responds to the waters of the kidneys (Venus organ) in nourishing the blood. The blood becomes full-bodied and whole. The brain is then nourished and can think properly and form right decisions.

Moon Chakra (4 petal lotus, center of procreation)

"*I am the true vine*" reveals Christ as the divine *source* of vitality, as is also evident in the healing miracle of the *turning of water into wine* (mystery of purification and renewal). The Virgin Mary was present at this miracle, at the beginning of which Christ spoke the words to her, "*O woman, what have you to do with me,*" which should be translated as, "*O woman, what is it that weaves between you and me.*" For in this weaving lives the promise of the sacred marriage of Christ with the *purity* of the divine feminine, signifying not only the promise of *new* blood (wine) but also a total transformation of the procreative process (4 petal lotus). What one brings into the world through thought, word, or deed ("right deed") becomes the divine progeny of this fructification.

Saturn Chakra (8 petal lotus, crown center)

"*I am the resurrection and the life*" – these words of Christ are the promise of the *restoration* of life, crowned with the *sovereignty* of one's divine "task" of *service* to the world. The archetypal return to sovereignty – with the "I" completely restored – is revealed in the healing miracle of the *raising of Lazarus from the dead*. This healing miracle is also about overcoming the ultimate fear, which is the fear of death. Inner sovereignty renders it possible to experience awe in face of this great mystery, instead of fear. Interestingly, the German word for fear ("*Furcht*") expresses this transformation, since the German word meaning reverential awe is "*Ehrfurcht*", arrived at by *honoring* (the verb "*ehren*" in German means "to honor") God Most High, to whom the human being returns at death. The English expression "fear of God" does not really convey the connotation of reverential awe contained in the German word "*Ehrfurcht*" as the metamorphosis of "*Furcht*" ("fear").

Christ breathed upon Lazarus seven times, infusing into him the *breath* of the Holy Spirit (healing each of the seven chakras), and spoke the words, "*Lazarus, come forth*" – come forth from the cave (the image of earthly life without the light of spirit) into the "light" of your true Selfhood, the "fully upright human being".

Venus — Morning and Evening Star

In ancient times Venus' appearance as morning or evening star was beheld as two distinct stars referred to as a pair of "twin sisters".[285] It was only later that the two stars were recognized as one and the same star. Thus the temple of Venus in Nineveh was originally known as the "*House of the Twins*", and it was only later that the single name **Inanna** was given, implying that the true identity of Venus as a planet had been recognized.[286]

Appearing in the east as morning star, Venus was called "*the herald*", and in the west as evening star, "*our lady*". Both appearances are indications that Venus' planetary dance is in close relationship to the orbit of the Sun. In relation to the Sun, the *elongation* of Venus never reaches beyond 48° *trailing* (morning star) or *leading* (evening star) the Sun in its orbit around the zodiac.

The Venus planetary dance holds true to the planet's reputation for beautiful proportion and form. In the course of eight years her sequence of *inferior* (between the Sun and the Earth) and *superior* (behind the Sun) conjunctions with the Sun complete a pattern of a double 5-pointed star, which has been likened to the unfolding of a 5-petaled rose.

That which the ancient star gazers could only intuit and *reach toward* in grateful awe and wonder through the extension of *spiritual touch* can now be observed through the help of modern computer programs wherein the orbital pattern of Venus in movement appears to the eye as the unfolding pattern of a rose.

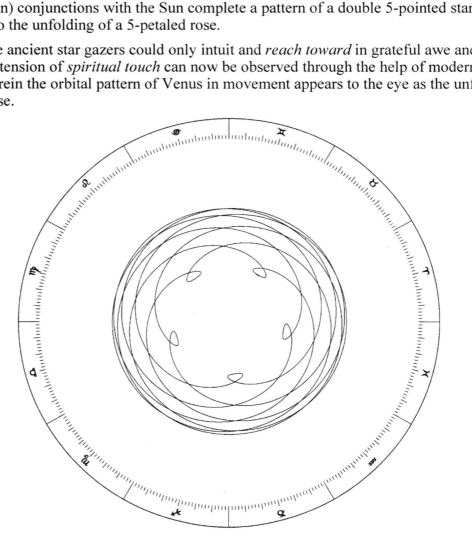

---

[285] According to ancient Akkadian cuneiform texts, see Robert Powell, *History of the Planets,* pp. 11-12.
[286] "Inanna" was the Sumerian name for the goddess of Venus, who was "Ishtar" to the Babylonians.

The Venus cosmic dance form *mirrors* the planet's orbital pattern, moving counter-clockwise around the zodiac and looping in toward the Earth in smaller counter-clockwise circles. The petals of the rose are formed by these smaller circles – with the midpoint of the loop indicating the moment of *inferior* conjunction with the Sun (Earth–Venus–Sun), whereas the *outer superior* conjunctions (Earth–Sun–Venus) can be imagined at the midpoint of the longer sweeping curves of the larger circle.

Venus has Phases (Like the Moon)

Just as the Moon as companion (satellite) to the Earth has phases reflecting the Moon's relationship to the Sun, so too both Venus and Mercury as satellites of the Sun have their phases reflecting their movements in relationship to the Sun as seen from the perspective of the Earth.[287]

By way of analogy with the Moon's phases, "new Venus" occurs at the point of *inferior* conjunction with the Sun, the point when Venus stands *between* the Earth and the Sun, and "full Venus" is when Venus comes into alignment with the Earth and the Sun, orbiting *behind* the Sun, at the time of a *superior* conjunction of Venus with the Sun. To summarize:

<u>inferior</u> conjunction: Earth–**new Venus**–Sun;

<u>superior</u> conjunction: Earth–Sun–**full Venus**

Venus Orbital Dance — The 5-pointed Star

Venus and Mercury are referred to as the "inner planets", because their orbits pass between the Earth and the Sun. As one of the two "inner planets", Venus reveals her influence *within* the human organism as *mediatrix*: Earth–Moon–**Venus**–Mercury–Sun. The form traced out by Venus, that of a 5-pointed star, is an "as above, so below" indication of her sphere of influence, which is the human etheric body, that has the shape of a 5-pointed star.

Unlike the "fleet-footed" planet Mercury, which weaves his 6-pointed star form (which in movement resembles a 6-petaled flower)[288] in less than a year's time, Venus' 225-day orbit of the Sun requires <u>eight years</u> to reveal the full flowering of the 5-pointed rose formation.

Thus, the "quickened" pace of Mercury could be likened to circulation, whereas the slower Venus rhythm reveals the qualities of *duration* and *process,* related more to the growth processes which are important in the creation of form.

Just as lunar rhythms can be seen to pull upon the ebb and flow patterns of the tidal waters in the sea, so too the weavings of the Venus patterned dance can be seen in nature as forms arising from her rhythmic movement – for example, the shape of the starfish, the 5-pointed star surrounding the apple's core or etched on the back of the sea urchin, flowers of five petals, and especially the rose, which is known and appreciated as a symbol of love.

---

[287] Venus is six times nearer the Earth at inferior conjunction than when in superior conjunction (beyond the Sun), and therefore from the perspective of the Earth she appears larger at or around inferior conjunction.

[288] The form of the 6-pointed star traced out by Mercury indicates its sphere of influence, the astral body, which has the shape of a 6-pointed star. See Rudolf Steiner, *From the History and Contents of the First Section of the Esoteric School, 1904-1914*, pp. 182-183 for diagrams of the 5-pointed star (etheric body) and the 6-pointed star (astral body).

The Venus Pentagram[289]

Harmony shines out of the 8-year pentagram dance of Venus. Because of the regularity of the Venus movement, there is an equal-distant 144° *interval* between each inferior conjunction, whereby the intervening superior conjunction (between two inferior conjunctions) falls midway between the zodiacal locations of the two inferior conjunctions, thus giving rise to an alternating 72° distance between each inferior and superior point of the star, so that the resulting inner star formation (formed by the inferior conjunctions) echoes the larger outer 5-pointed star (formed by the superior conjunctions).

Inferior conjunctions of Venus with the Sun, 1980-1988,
in relation to the sidereal zodiac, with the vernal point (VP) at 5½° Pisces during this period

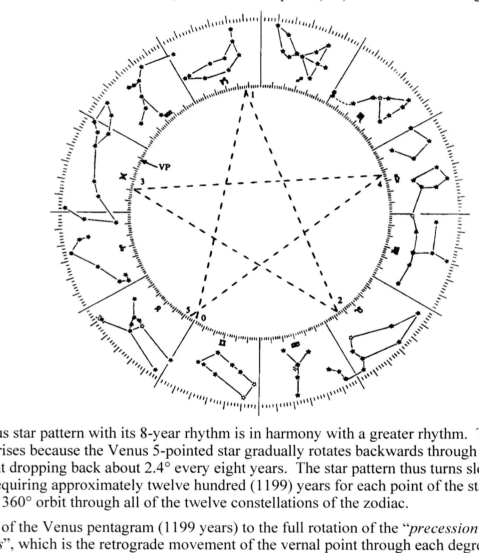

The Venus star pattern with its 8-year rhythm is in harmony with a greater rhythm. This greater rhythm arises because the Venus 5-pointed star gradually rotates backwards through the zodiac, each point dropping back about 2.4° every eight years. The star pattern thus turns slowly *within* the zodiac, requiring approximately twelve hundred (1199) years for each point of the star to make a complete 360° orbit through all of the twelve constellations of the zodiac.

The ratio of the Venus pentagram (1199 years) to the full rotation of the *"precession of the equinoxes"*, which is the retrograde movement of the vernal point through each degree (360°) of the zodiac requiring 25,920 years, is 1 to 21½, which may be likened (approximately) to the ratio of 1 hour to a day (1 to 24).

---

[289] See Robert Powell, *Hermetic Astrology*, vol. I, pp. 58-63.

The Venus Rhythm and the "Astrological Age"

I will give you the morning star...[290]

The beginning of an astrological age signifies when the vernal point enters a new sign in the zodiac. Presently the vernal point is located at 5° Pisces and will regress progressively 1° every 72 years, entering into Aquarius in the year AD 2375. This signals the beginning of the Aquarian Age, the start of a new "astrological age".

It is important to observe that the Venus pentagram rhythm of 1199 years actually marks the <u>completion of an "astrological age"</u>, and thus plays a harmonic role as mediatrix *within* the organic unfoldment of new states of consciousness, which are further reflected in the birth or beginning of a new cultural age.[291]

Parallel Histories in Heaven and on Earth

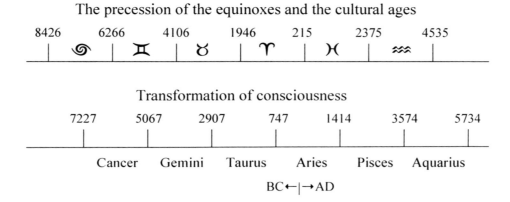

The precession of the equinoxes and the cultural ages

Transformation of consciousness

"As *above, so below...*", there are parallel histories in heaven and on Earth, which can be observed over a period of twelve centuries (1199 years), the time required for the rotating Venus pentagram to regress through the entire zodiac.

At the beginning of each astrological age a new spiritual impulse or level is *sounded* forth. Then with one complete Venus pentagram rotation (1199 years), this new octave of spiritual thought is organically woven and allowed to filter through the cosmic realm – stepping down the cosmic impulse from the spiritual to the cultural (and social) human level.

One example of this "as above, so below" astrological age phenomenon as a stepping-down process is apparent through the written teachings inspired by the Egyptian initiate, Hermes Trismegistus ("Thrice Greatest Hermes"). The Greek original of *Asclepius*, Book III, was written within a year or two of AD 270, some 50 years after the entrance of the vernal point into Pisces in AD 220. Some twelve centuries later, at the time of the Renaissance, these Hermetic writings (including *Asclepius*)

---

[290] The significance of the words of Christ, "*I will give you the morning star...*" (*The Revelation to John* 2:28) is that they reveal the Cosmic Christ, who leads humanity from stage to stage in cosmic evolution. As indicated in Appendix I, the next stage of evolution (Future Jupiter) will take place with humanity on the planet orbiting the Sun in the present orbit of Venus, known as the "morning star". This is the deeper significance of the words, "*I will give you the morning star*".

[291] Robert Powell, *Hermetic Astrology*, vol. I, pp. 55-63 discusses the relationship between the Venus pentagram rhythm of 1199 years and the cycle of astrological ages, each 2160 years long, and the corresponding cultural epochs, which are also 2160 years long, but are shifted back by a time-lag of 1199 years, which is the period of the Venus pentagram.

flowered into a true cultural impulse which flourished in Florence, Italy, largely through the teachings of Marsilio Ficino in the Platonic Academy in Florence. Ficino translated the Hermetic writings to make them available to students at the Florentine Platonic Academy – the publication was in 1471.

It was through the work of translation from the Greek to the Latin that the wisdom of Hermes Trismegistus ignited a Promethean fire within the heart of this inspired genius (Marsilio Ficino), who in turn influenced the "high court" of the Medici family – spawning a plethora of creative activity on the part of painters, musicians, poets, and inspiring works of high spiritual content, bathed in the splendor of Venusian beauty, harmony, and form.

The Tree of Life

"*I will give you the morning star…*" (*The Revelation to John), 2:28*) is revealed as the proclamation of the Cosmic Christ. It is he who leads humanity through the schooling of the twelve – the twelve streams of cosmic nourishment which comprise the "Tree of Life".

In the present astrological age of Pisces, the cosmic streams of nourishment work upon the inner forces of youthfulness (life) and maturity (death), which must be brought into a state of *inner* balance.[292] The present age can thus be likened to the taking in of *substance* from the Cosmic Christ, the "*bread of life.*"

This bestowing of *substance* is such that the organs of the physical body become *capable* of taking up spiritual life.[293] The physical body is emphasized especially in the early stages (childhood) of life and also toward the end of life (old age). In the sense of the words "*not I, but Christ in me*", the bestowing of substance in childhood and in old age mirrors the organic unfoldment of cosmic order in the astrological age of Pisces (lasting until 2375), which has a strong influence upon the physical body.

Mani — The Herald of the Piscean Age[294]

The year AD 215 was the birth year of the spiritual teacher called Mani.[295] Born to the Persian culture, his teachings spread all the way to China, where he was called the Buddha of Light.[296] Mani's teachings brought a *synthesis* between Christianity and the ancient mystery religions.

This was the *seed* impulse for the Age of Pisces, wherein the mystery wisdom of the Taurean/ Egyptian/Babylonian Age is destined to reappear in a metamorphosed way.[297]

---

[292] Robert Powell, *Christian Hermetic Astrology*, pp. 198-204 describes the twelve streams of nourishment comprising the Tree of Life and how the stream of nourishment connected with Pisces – the "*bread of life*" – bestows inner substance and balances the forces of youthfulness and maturity.

[293] See Valentin Tomberg, *New Testament Studies*, Chapter III "*The Beatitudes In the Sermon on the Mount*".

[294] According to the clairvoyant vision of Rudolf Steiner, there was a successive incarnational line proceeding from "The Youth of Nain", who was raised from the dead by Jesus Christ, to the prophet Mani, to Parzifal, the hero of the Grail story – see Rudolf Steiner, *From the History and Contents of the First Section of the Esoteric School, 1904-1914*, pp. 216-217.

[295] Some sources give AD 216 as Mani's birth year – for example, Andrew Welburn, *Mani, the Angel and the Column of Glory*, pp. 9, 67.

[296] Ibid. p. 69.

[297] Rudolf Steiner, *From the History and Contents of the First Section of the Esoteric School, 1904-1914*, p. 216 – "*The store of wisdom contained in the third epoch will be reawakened by the Christ to fructify our fifth epoch*". This signifies a metamorphosis from the third epoch = Age of Taurus (Egyptian/ Babylonian epoch) to the fifth epoch = Age of Pisces (present epoch).

The task is to *awaken* the impulses of ancient mystery wisdom slumbering in the depths of the soul. It is toward this purpose that the Choreocosmos School of Cosmic and Sacred Dance was founded – in particular, to call forth in a metamorphosed way the stream of initiation of the ancient cosmic dances practiced in the temples of antiquity.

Venus — Relationship to the Constellations

Ruler of Taurus and Libra

> *Venus gazes deeply into the hearts of human beings ...*
> *She lovingly reflects whatever comes from the Earth.*   (Rudolf Steiner)[298]

Taurus is an earth sign, feminine in nature – caring for beauty, the human soul, and nature. Each of these qualities mirror the concerns of Venus, as do the decans associated with Taurus, which provide a telling story of Venus' relationship to Taurus as one of the constellations where she has her domicile.

The constellation of **Perseus** is located above the first decan (10°) of Taurus, as a guardian for the astral forces which threaten the soul. Venus is especially strong in this region, reminding us that Perseus rescued Andromeda (representing the divine feminine soul of humanity).

Andromeda is the "Enchained Woman" who is threatened to be swallowed up by **Cetus**, the constellation of the "Sea Monster", representing the sea of the emotional life and the subconscious depths of the human soul.

The Moon is exalted at 3° in the first decan of Taurus at the gateway to the **Pleiades** in the neck of the **Bull**. Let us recall that Taurus is related to the throat/larynx, the center of our speaking and spiritual listening capacity – the archetype of which is indicated in the words: "In the beginning was the WORD." As we have discussed in relation to the mirroring of Venus in human physiology, all of these qualities are of special concern to Venus.

The starry script revealed by the decans which support the etheric body of Taurus tells the story of the work of the soul.[299] The cosmic river **Eridanus**, the constellation of "The River", flows in the central decan of Taurus, which is *ruled* by the Moon. The Moon bears the memory of the soul karma, which is inscribed in the astral body of the human being. This can be especially felt during the 2½ days each month when the Moon resides in Taurus, enhancing the human being's receptivity to astral influences.

When understood in connection with the etheric waters of the *source* of life, which are regulated by the Venus center, in the region of the abdomen, the circulation of the "living waters of life" can be imagined as a "river" of alchemical fire, indicating the *marriage* of fire and water. This describes the activity of Venus ♀, standing in the center, bringing balance and harmony to the streaming of life forces in the human being – through the practice of "right standing" in her realm.

Auriga, "The Shepherd", is located above the third decan of Taurus. This decan is *ruled* by Saturn, indicating a gathering of strength for the Saturn influence. Auriga holds two goat "kids" in a gesture

---

[298] Rudolf Steiner, *"The Spiritual Individualities of the Planets"*, *The Golden Blade*, vol. 40 (1988), p. 47.
[299] Lacquanna Paul and Robert Powell, *Cosmic Dances of the Zodiac*, pp. 25-26 discusses the three constellations associated with the three decans of Taurus, as well as the decans relating to the remaining signs of the zodiac.

of protection. It is interesting to note that the planet Venus was also sometimes referred to as "*The Shepherd*", indicating a special caring for nature and humankind.

On the archetypal level **Taurus** relates to the forming of the **Mars** center (larynx chakra/16 petal lotus). In this connection, contemplating Venus as the *ruler* of Taurus, we can again appreciate the mythological story of the marriage of Mars/Ares and Venus/Aphrodite discussed earlier.

Venus rules Libra

Venus is also considered to be "at home" in **Libra**, "The Scales", which is the sign of balance. The two balance pans of the Libran scales are supported by a central fulcrum, reminding us of the central fulcrum of support represented by the cross in the Venus glyph ♀.

Libra bears the archetypal pattern for the form and functioning of the hips and the entire region of the pelvic girdle of the human being.

To understand the inspiration of Libra, it is important to grasp that the inspiring "ballast" which holds the balance pans in balance is the *spiritual* function of the element of air, the element which brings the "winds of change" to the activities of daily life.

This requires the inner and outer activity of the balance of one's thought life. The up/down, left/right, heaven/earth, levity/gravity relationships of life require a harmonizing of the inner will with the forces of change that pulse through our daily life.

It is in awe and wonder that we contemplate the wisdom that ascribes to Venus the region of the constellation of Libra. This is an "as above, so below" mirroring of the balancing activity of the Venus center (abdomen), which is clearly "at home" in that part of the human being which corresponds to Libra – the region of the hips and pelvic girdle.

The starry script revealed by the decans which support the etheric body of Libra provides us with further *telling* images.[300] **Boötes**, "The Ploughman" (located above the last part of Virgo and the first decan of Libra) leads the way into Libra, breathing the strength of his etheric forces into the air element of "The Scales". The great star **Arcturus**, "The Watcher" (or Guardian), the main star in the Boötes constellation, stands at the threshold 29½° Virgo leading into Libra – reminding us of the Archangel Michael holding the "*Scales of Justice*".

With **Corona**, the "Northern Crown", and **Crux**, the "Southern Cross", gracing the region above and below the central decan of Libra, the heart of Libra is revealed as the work of atonement (cross), and coming into alignment (crown) with truth, building toward the "Life Spirit" (the love-permeated etheric body). An archetype for this is indicated by the Moon's position at the time of the Crucifixion, when the full Moon stood at 13° Libra, in the central decan of Libra. [301]

Centaurus, "The Centaur" (located below the last part of Libra) lends its etheric strength to the final decan of Libra. The "Southern Cross" resides beneath the legs of the Centaur, as a cosmic archetype for the taming of one's animal nature (the challenge inherent in the sensual nature of Venus). With the Centaur it is the upright nature of the human being (the Centaur is depicted with a human head and torso connected to the body of a horse) which is leading the way. Contemplating the traditional image of the constellation of the Centaur, we see that the human figure is holding a lance,

---

[300] Ibid. pp. 62-63 discusses the three constellations associated with the three decans of Libra.
[301] Robert Powell, *Chronicle of the Living Christ*, p. 175.

representing moral speaking, the "Sword of Truth" – reminding us of Longinus, whose spear pierced through the side of Jesus Christ all the way to his heart.

Exaltation of Venus — 27° Pisces

The Fishes

According to ancient myth, **Pisces** was the watery region that birthed the fair planet ***Venus***, the "Star of Aphrodite", the goddess who inspires the form of love associated with Eros.

According to ancient star mythology, Venus was pursued by Neptune, who threatened to take her back to the sea of dissolution into illusion, alluding to the Pisces challenge of taking care to consciously balance the gift of psychic perception with an active engagement with reality.

The constellation of ***Pegasus***, the celestial "Winged Horse" (located above the last part of Aquarius and the first part of Pisces), brings etheric strength to inspire the imagination. In particular, the "Square of Pegasus", the body of the Winged Horse, is in *mystical union* with the ***Lower Fish*** in the region of the first decan of Pisces. The **Lower Fish** is linked by a *cord* from its tail fin to the tail fin of the **Upper Fish**, which is swimming in the opposite direction. The ***Upper Fish*** marks the third decan of Pisces.

Here in the third decan of Pisces is Venus' exaltation point at 27° Pisces. ***Andromeda***, "The Enchained Woman", is above the region of the ***Upper Fish*** (third decan) – and ***Pegasus*** springs from her forehead. This image reminds us of the gift of imagination as a "fluidity" to free the soul's dead thought patterns from the *chains* of rigidity. In Greek mythology, ***Perseus*** (representing the human spirit) saved fair Andromeda (representing the soul of humanity) from being swallowed by ***Cetus***, the celestial "Sea Monster" – representing the blind instinctual forces of the subconscious.

The cord that connects the two fish is the *promise* that perpetuates our connection with heaven. ***Cepheus***, "The Crowned King", resides in this central region of Pisces, representing the promise of the *crowned* king, the "I" of the human being, which is in "*heavenly accord*" with the central concerns of Venus in "right standing". This is the human being's covenant with the spiritual world to uphold "*the way, the truth and the life*" toward the healing of the Venus center in the human being.

The Venus Metal — Copper[302]

The Marriage of Mars and Venus

Venus (copper) and Mars (iron) are found bound together in the depths of the Earth in the form of **copper-iron pyrite**. The copper ore is characteristically sea-green in color, reminiscent of the goddess Venus being born of the sea. The iron threads through the copper ore form a darkened net or web to hold the beautiful ore – as if in an embrace…?

Well, so the mythological story goes – Aphrodite's husband, Hephaestus (the *Heavenly Blacksmith*), upon returning home and finding his wife locked in an embrace with Ares-Mars, had fashioned an

---

[302] See Nick Kollerstrom, *"The Metal-Planet Affinities – Copper,"* – http://www.levity.com/alchemy/kollerstrom-copper.html

157

iron web which he let fall upon the lovers, so that they were caught up in a bound condition. How interesting that the depths of the Earth divulge the truth of the matter – that with Mars and Venus, there is a mutual attraction.

Mirroring this divine attraction, we find that iron and copper levels in human blood are proportioned according to the sexes. Women have 20% more copper serum than men, and correspondingly the iron level in men's blood is one-third higher than in women. As might be imagined, the copper level in women's blood is in tune with the monthly menstrual cycle, rising progressively as the time of menstruation approaches.

During pregnancy the copper serum climbs up to double the normal level, suggesting that copper plays an important role in the reproductive system. When the time of birth draws near, the iron level increases in the fetal blood, causing a copper-iron polarity between mother and child.

The word copper comes from the Latin word "*cuprum*", which in turn is derived from the Greek word "*hyprus*". Cyprus, the Mediterranean isle famed as the birthplace of Venus-Aphrodite, was in antiquity the principal source of copper. In Botticelli's famous picture of the "Birth of Venus", Venus appears balanced on a conch shell, born from the sea off the shores of the island of Cyprus.

Copper reminds us of this sea connection. The copper ore malachite, when cut, reveals the swirling sea-green patterns of the sea – malachite, azurite, turquoise, chalcopyrite, and peacock ore: the entire family of copper ores allude to the colors of the sea – all are hydrated, water-containing, as well as the copper salts, which are sea-green colored and water-soluble.

Architects appreciate the pliability and beautiful aesthetic quality of copper. Often the sea-green color of copper's aging process is preferred and various methods are used to encourage the aging – perhaps on a deeper level we want to be reminded of her rosy glow emerging from the sea!

Copper's soft, pliable character needs to be alloyed (married) to other metals to produce structural strength. Thus, bronze or brass, the marriage of copper (Venus) and tin (Jupiter), has inspired an entire age, the Bronze Age, as well as beautiful forms in art.

Remembering the importance of iron to the breathing process in the human being, it is interesting to note that the breathing process in various sea creatures is by means of a copper rather than an iron process. For example, the conch shell, traditionally associated with Venus, is such a creature, so too are the octopus and the scorpion – creatures which demonstrate the darker side of the feminine nature.

True to the Venus quality of enduring beauty, it is not surprising to find copper in beauty skin creams, as copper apparently plays a vital role in skin repair, stimulating the growth of collagen and elastin – as well as having good anti-inflammatory effects. The copper tones in the skin that result from the bronzing effect of the Sun are due to increased levels of melanin, the copper-based skin pigment.

In the inorganic realm, there is a copper-iron polarity (derived from a Mars/Venus interaction) which has spawned the principle of the electromagnetic current. Iron creates the "*ground*" and copper "*conducts* or *carries*" it, producing the alternating currents which are the basis of the energy powering our modern civilization. Correspondingly, copper is a key material for telecommunications, even finding its way into computer microchips and solar power cells.

Venus — "The Mysterious Veiled Lady"

Of all the planets, Venus at its brightest is by far the most dazzling sight in the night sky. On June 8, 2004 she provided a spectacle, even by the light of the day, as she passed in transit slowly (within the space of 6½ hours) before the face of the Sun. On that day dedicated star gazers were able to follow an actual viewing of the transit at the time of an inferior Venus/Sun conjunction – with the help of a good telescope and the necessary filters to protect the eyes.

As we gazed into the keen eye of our garden telescope from our village hamlet in southern Bavaria – joined by our friends and other curious star gazers – one could not help but feel a certain warmth of heart toward our "sister planet". Admired for her beauty and "starring" role as the brightest in the heavenly array of stars, Venus shares a certain kindred spirit with the Earth.

In fact Venus is often regarded as the Earth's "sister" because she is only slightly smaller than the Earth (95% of the Earth's diameter and 80% of the Earth's mass).

What we know of her supports her reputation for harmony and beauty, gentleness, and the dark mysterious regions of the soul.

The Venus orbit is the most circular of that of any planet and she is one of the most upright – with a mere 3° inclination of her axis.[303] The planet known to astrologers as the "Lesser Benefic" finds her match in eligible dancing partners with Jupiter, the "Greater Benefic", whose noble upright axis also has an inclination of only 3°. Whereas Jupiter has a terrific rotational speed (one rotation in approximately 10 hours) and very gusty winds,[304] Venus takes her royal time, requiring approximately eight Earth months (243 days) to complete her rotational orbit.[305]

Unlike the gusty winds of Jupiter's royal domain, the Venus winds are described as gentle by cosmic standards, circumnavigating the planet in a 4-day rhythm – and rewarding her with a beautifully smooth[306] (relatively young)[307] surface "skin", similar to her sister planet Earth.

While the winds at the top of Venus' cloud layer may reach over 200 miles/hour, at the surface of Venus they are very slow, no more than a few miles/hour.

There is a harmony in the rhythm of the Venus rotation (243 days) and her heliocentric orbit (224.7 days) with the rhythm of the Earth – so that Venus always presents the same face toward the Earth (as does the Moon). Perhaps something of this cosmic resonance lives at the heart of her recognition on Earth as the *bringer of peace*.

Further observation of the nature of Venus, the beautiful planet, reveals her to be quite feminine in nature – that is to say, completely unique, contrary, and mysterious!

Her clockwise direction of rotation about her axis is retrograde to that of the counter-clockwise direction of all the other planets, except Pluto and Uranus, which also rotate clockwise about their axes. Uranus, however, cannot manage the Venus upright balanced stature and presents himself toppled over – with his axis on a fairly horizontal incline, tilted at 98° to the vertical, i.e. pointing more or less toward the Sun. Otherwise the family of planets visible to the naked eye all have a

---

[303] The tilt of Venus' axis is 177.4° (upside down!), so that it is less than 3° from the vertical alignment.
[304] The Giant Red Spot on Jupiter is the spectacle of a great storm, moving in a counter-clockwise direction, which has been raging on Jupiter for several hundred years.
[305] Compared with 24 hours for the Earth to complete one rotation, an approximate Venus comparison implies that one Venus hour is about ten Earth days, which is the length of time for the Sun to pass through one decan (10°) at approximately 1° per day.
[306] Much smoother than the Moon, Mercury and Mars.
[307] The oldest surfaces on Venus seem to be about 800 million years old.

(more or less) vertical axis, the largest divergence from the vertical being that of Saturn, which is less than 27°.[308]

Yet another unique feature of Venus is the lack of a magnetic field (10,000 times weaker than the Earth), possibly due to the slow rotation of the planet, which might be insufficient to stir a liquid iron core – although the composition of her interiority remains unknown.

Until recently, the mysteries of Venus have been rather difficult to penetrate, as she resides in the depths behind thick vapors of water and carbon dioxide, which create an extreme "greenhouse effect" – trapping the heat and gases from the solar radiation and her own thermal radiation in a blanket of protection from the probing eye of voyeuristic inspection, allowing approximately 10° of the light from the Sun to reach her darkened surface, which has been likened by scientists to be similar to a dark, rainy day on Earth.

Venus is Hot!

Due to the heat, the waters of the planetary body of Venus have been lifted up into an evaporated state and held in the vapors of her enveloping cloud body. Moreover, her breath of *exhalation* is rich in carbon dioxide, which creates a dense atmospheric pressure 90 times[309] that of the Earth and surface temperatures up to 930° F – hot enough to melt lead.[310]

Venus' surface is actually hotter than that of Mercury, although she is nearly twice the distance from the Sun. Compared to the Earth, the Venus "greenhouse effect" intercepts twice as much sunlight than reaches the Earth's atmosphere, resulting in a solar absorption of about the same energy as the Earth. The thick clouds of Venus reflect the light of the Sun back into the atmosphere creating the dazzling effects of her fiery "hot-house" aura.

Following this fiery theme, radar images reveal the surface of Venus to be covered with lava flows, indicating an actively volcanic nature (having remained, however, geologically quiet for the past few hundred million years).

When we take into consideration that her striated vapors (many kilometers thick) also contain highly-condensed levels of toxic sulfur dioxide and sulfuric acid, as well as hydrogen chloride and hydrogen fluoride, we have a rather suffocating vision of hell. Romantic as she may seem, Venus may be the least hospitable place for life in the solar system.

The question which arises with the reality of this picture is, "Might this be the future of the Earth?" Given the advancement of the technological age and the expansion of even greater degrees of toxic "greenhouse" gases, the resulting erosion of the protective shield of the Earth's ozone layer, and global warming conditions that we are already observing – we are presented with a call for responsible guardianship of our own precious Earth.

Of course, the question remains a mystery as does Venus, whose mysterious veil has forbidden even our knowing of the composition of her interiority, which *"raises more questions than answers. With her deep, murky atmosphere, she remains a clouded crystal ball".*[311]

---

[308] The tilt of the axis of the planets are: Mercury (0°), Venus (177°24'), Earth (23°27'), Mars (25°12'), Jupiter (3°06'), Saturn (26°42'), Uranus (98°), Neptune (29°36'), and Pluto (122°31').

[309] About the same pressure as at a depth of one kilometer (0.621 miles) in the Earth's oceans.

[310] The average surface temperature of Venus, according to NASA, is 864° F.

[311] *The Solar System, A Scientific American Book*, p.56.

"There Will Be Signs in the Heavens"

As we contemplate the enigma of this beautiful lady, we can return our thoughts to the wondrous event of the "transit of Venus" on June 8, 2004, which is a rare event: the last one was in 1882. The next one on June 6, 2012 will not be repeated until 2117.

Leading toward the Future Venus

Now in this present stage of planetary evolution, the Mercury stage, our task is to grow in our capacity to love one another. In cosmic and sacred dance we celebrate the joy of community in sacrificing our lower egoic self by calling forth our higher self to serve through our gestures and movements in the dance of the communal whole. Just as the honey bees serve the queen bee, the cosmic dance is dedicated to the divine wisdom of the heavenly Queen, Sophia, who bears the divine pattern of creation, both the memory of the involutionary stages of planetary evolution and the fullness of our return home – the evolutionary stages which will lead us toward the Future Venus stage of our development.

Interestingly, the mystery of the life of **bees** points toward **Future Venus** and it is through the communal dance of the bees that we can have an understanding that this future evolutionary stage is *inwardly* connected with the planet now called Venus:

> *In olden times …wise men related the whole wonderful activity within the hive to the life of love, to that part of life which they connected with the planet Venus …Bees surrender themselves entirely to Venus, unfolding a life of love throughout the whole hive …*[312]

> *The consciousness of the beehive, not of the single bee, is immensely lofty. The wisdom of this consciousness will only be attained by the human being in the Venus existence.*[313]

Vulcan — The Seventh Stage of Planetary Evolution

Reference was made earlier to the marriage of Venus-Aphrodite to Hephaestus, the Greek god known as Vulcan to the Romans. Hephaestus (Vulcan) was the heavenly blacksmith whose particular skill had to do with the divine alchemy of fire. The word "volcano" indicates the realm of the sub-earthly fire forces over which the god Vulcan was master. Vulcan presides over the forces active in the interior of the Earth, and this holds the key to understanding the seventh stage of evolution, named after the god Vulcan. Whereas the other stages of evolution – Saturn, Sun, Moon, etc. – are named after visible heavenly bodies belonging to the solar system, there is no planet Vulcan. There is a mystery here, which is only possible to understand if it is grasped that the future stage of evolution known as Vulcan will be the Earth turned inside out. What is now the interior of the Earth will become exteriorized during the Vulcan stage of evolution, which is why this stage is named after the god presiding over the forces of the underworld – forces over which the human being will gain mastery in the far distant future, during Vulcan evolution.[314]

---

[312] Rudolf Steiner, *Nine Lectures on Bees*, p. 4.

[313] Rudolf Steiner, *Foundations of Esotericism*, p. 85.

[314] In the future Vulcan stage of planetary evolution the final transmutation of the physical body into the resurrection body (Atma) will take place. For the Earth as a whole, the spiritualization of matter will extend all the way to the center of the Earth, and the Earth will have become a Sun. See Appendix I for Vulcan Planetary Evolution and eurythmy form discussion.

Appendix I: Planetary Stages of Evolution

The Formation of the Solar System from the Solar Nebula

According to the nebular hypothesis, the asteroids and the planets with their moons gradually crystallized out of the original gaseous solar nebula that was slowly rotating – or rather, they came into existence by way of agglomeration from the rotating gaseous cloud of the primal nebula. At the same time our Sun also took on shape through a process of contraction. It is this principle of contraction that offers a key to understanding humanity's relationship with the solar system.

The whole process of the formation of our solar system can be looked at purely physically, or it can be looked at as an expression of the "incarnation" of Spiritual Intelligences into a "body" that forms into a star – our Sun in the case of our solar system. Viewed from this latter perspective, there is a meaning to the fact that nine planets orbit around the Sun: Mercury, Venus, Earth, Mars, Jupiter, Saturn, Uranus, Neptune, and Pluto.[315] If we accept C.G. Jung's idea of a "collective unconscious", we would expect to find ideas in the realm of mythology which could serve as indicators (so to say, "promptings" from the collective unconscious) pointing to truths not yet at that time known consciously. For example, the Greeks did not know consciously that our Sun has nine planets orbiting around it. Nevertheless, Greek mythology refers to the Sun god, Apollo, with his nine muses. Could this myth of Apollo and the nine muses be a prompting arising from the collective unconscious of that time, indicating the truth we now know consciously – that there are nine planets orbiting around our Sun?

The Cosmogony of Orpheus

Similarly, could it be that mythological ideas concerning cosmogony (the genesis of the cosmos) also contain cosmological truths? If so, then it is a matter of deciphering them correctly. In this spirit, the following is an attempt to decipher the ancient Greek cosmogony of Orpheus.[316] Orpheus described the sequence of cosmic evolution in terms of the planetary gods. As this has been handed down to us, the Orphic cosmology describes the divine rule of six generations of gods: Phanes, Nyx (Night), Ouranos, Chronos, Zeus, and Dionysos.

Dionysos was the son of Zeus and Persephone. While he was but still an infant, Zeus handed over his power to him. In the Orphic cosmogony, therefore, Dionysos was the successor of Zeus. However, who preceded Zeus in this cosmogony? Going backwards in time, the reign of Zeus (Jupiter) was preceded by that of Chronos (Saturn), which, in turn, was preceded by the reign of Ouranos (Uranus). Ouranos (Heaven) was married to his sister Gaia (Earth), and

---

[315] On August 24, 2006 the International Astronomical Union reduced the status of Pluto from that of a planet to that of a "dwarf planet." However, as described in Robert Powell's article on Pluto in the *Christian Star Calendar 2007* (the article is also posted on the Sophia Foundation website), Pluto is nevertheless the representative of an entire cosmic sphere and therefore, despite its small size, can still be considered together with the other eight planets as the ninth planet orbiting the Sun.

[316] W.K.C. Guthrie, *Orpheus and Greek Religion*, pp. 80-82 describes the cosmogony of Orpheus.

from this union Chronos and Rhea were born. (Zeus was the offspring of the union of Chronos and Rhea.)

Looking at each of the planets as a "marker" in the unfolding of this cosmic evolution, since the planet of Zeus is Jupiter, the orbit of Jupiter denotes the orb of the reign of Zeus. This is encircled by the orbit of Saturn, which represents an earlier stage of evolution than that of Jupiter, and this earlier stage of evolution corresponds to the reign of Chronos. Similarly, the orbit of Uranus encircles that of Saturn, and therefore Uranus marks a still earlier stage of evolution than Saturn. Thus, the orbit of Uranus delineates the reign of the god of Heaven (Ouranos). Extending this analogy further, Neptune marks the stage of cosmic evolution preceding that of Uranus, and Pluto is the marker of the evolutionary stage preceding that of Neptune.

Since Orpheus described two stages of cosmic evolution prior to that of Ouranos – namely, that of the reign of Night, and prior to this, that of the reign of Phanes – these correspondingly relate to the orbits of the planets Neptune and Pluto, respectively, if we follow the hypothesis that the planets are markers of various stages of evolution.

The Planet Neptune

Firstly, Neptune: immediately preceding the reign of Ouranos – according to Orpheus – was the reign of the goddess Night (Nyx), the being of supreme wisdom in the cosmos. She corresponds to the Egyptian goddess Nût. The ancient Egyptian depictions of this goddess show her arched across the vault of heaven. She presents the background against which the stars appear and the Sun, Moon, and planets move. Night is the mother goddess from whom Ouranos was born, just as the night sky provides the background against which the stars of heaven (Ouranos) appear. Little is known about the goddess Night, but toward the end of the eighteenth century the poet Novalis wrote his deeply mystical *Hymns to the Night*, which capture something of this mysterious being:

> *Aside I turn to the holy, ineffable, mysterious Night…Dost thou take pleasure in us also, dark Night? What dost thou hold underneath thy mantle that with unseen power affects my soul?…More heavenly than these flashing stars seem to us the infinite eyes which the Night has opened within us. They see further than the palest of those countless hosts: without need of the Light they penetrate the depths of a loving heart, a feat which fills a higher realm with unutterable delight. Praise be unto the world's queen, the high herald of sacred worlds, the fostering nurse of blessed love! She sends thee to me, tender Beloved, lovely Sun of the Night.*[317]

Elsewhere Night is simply referred to as the great goddess:

> *The great goddess, the mother of all the gods, the queen of heaven, ruler over all the gods – in the beginning she entered into existence.*[318]

---

[317] Novalis, *Hymns to the Night*, pp. 3-4.
[318] Josefine Schreier, *Göttinnen, Ihr Einfluß von der Urzeit bis zur Gegenwart*, p. 12.

The reign of the goddess Night, preceding that of Ouranos, was delineated in the planetary system by the orbit of the planet that is now called Neptune. Thus, in the light of Orphic cosmology, Night (Egyptian *Nût*, Greek *Nyx*) would have been an appropriate name for the planet Neptune. The result of naming this planet Neptune is that subconsciously the attributes of the Greek mythological figure Neptune have become associated with the planet instead of the attributes of the goddess Night, the mother of all. Some of the attributes of Neptune, the sea god in Greek mythology, overlap with those of Night. For example, the black depths of the subconscious can be represented by the depths of the ocean as well as by the infinite darkness of outer space beyond the light of the stars. Therefore the mythological associations connected with Neptune are not completely false, but they need to be qualified in light of the correspondence of this planet with the mythological figure of Night.

The Planet Pluto

Secondly, Pluto: in the cosmology of Orpheus – prior to the reign of the goddess Night – there took place, originally, the reign of the god Phanes. Orpheus described Phanes as an androgynous creator god, the source of the primal will, the fire of love that underlies the whole of existence.

> *Phanes is the creator of all, from whom the world has its first origin ...He is imagined as marvelously beautiful, a figure of shining light ...He is of both sexes, since he is to create the race of gods unaided, "bearing within himself the honored seed of the gods" (Orphic Fragment 85) ...He made an eternal home for the gods and was their first king ...Phanes bore a daughter, Night, whom he took as his partner and to whom he gave great power. She assisted him in the work of creation, and he finally handed over his scepter to her, so that she became the next in order of the rulers of the universe ...Night bore to Phanes Gaia and Ouranos (Earth and Heaven) ...To Ouranos Night handed over the supreme power.*[319]

The Planet Uranus

Phanes and Night thus represent in the cosmogony of Orpheus the father and mother of the gods. Similarly, Ouranos represents an aspect of the Intelligence of the Cosmos, whose outer aspect comes to manifestation in the light of the starry heavens.

The domain of Phanes, as the antecedent of Night, corresponds to the realm delineated by the planet that is now called Pluto. In the light of Orphic cosmology, an appropriate name for the planet Pluto would be Phanes. As this planet is called Pluto, in the collective unconscious it has acquired attributes ascribed in Greek mythology to Pluto, the god of the underworld. But as some of the attributes of Pluto overlap with those of Phanes, the associations attributed to Pluto are not entirely wrong.

According to Orphic cosmogony, a divine dynasty of six generations are said to have held in turn the rule of the universe. These six generations of gods are: Phanes, Night (Nyx), Ouranos, Chronos, Zeus, and Dionysos. Each god ruled over a certain stage of evolution. How are the different states of evolution in Orphic cosmology associated with the planets? Here we are still following our basic hypothesis that mythology may be able to offer truth on a level that needs to be deciphered by the conscious mind.

---

[319] W.K.C. Guthrie, op. cit. pp. 80-81.

Looking now at the heliocentric conception of the solar system (see Figure), in light of Orphic cosmology our hypothesis is that the orbits of the planets are markers of various stages of evolution. To borrow a Hindu term, cosmic evolution proceeds by way of a series of *manvantaras*, or planetary periods, each drawing successively closer toward the Sun by way of contraction. The first manvantara in the Orphic cosmology, that of Phanes, took place within the orbit of Pluto. Then there took place a contraction from the orbit of Pluto to that of Neptune.

The second manvantara, that of Night (Nyx), took place within the orbit of Neptune. Here a new evolutionary phase began. A contraction took place from the first to the second stage of cosmic evolution, which is marked in our present solar system by the difference in the orbits of Pluto and Neptune. In between these two manvantaras it can be assumed that there took place a *pralaya* (again using a Hindu term), i.e. a rest period, during which the contraction from the orbit of Pluto to the orbit of Neptune took place. After a second pralaya and a further contraction, the manvantara of Ouranos took place, the third period of cosmic evolution according to the cosmology of Orpheus. With the third manvantara, the cosmos arrived at a three-fold foundation – through Phanes, Night (Nyx), and Ouranos – each laid down successively during the manvantaras taking place within the orbits of the planets Pluto, Neptune, and Uranus.

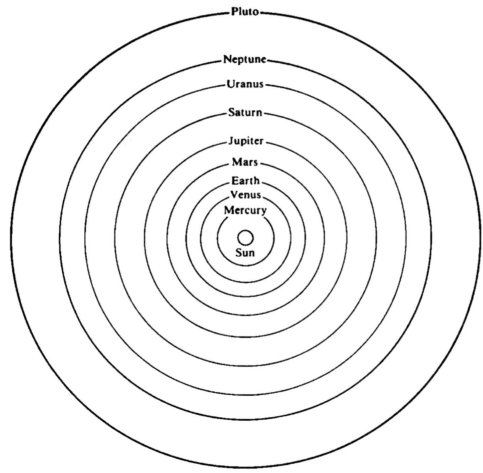

Continuing further, the cosmology of Orpheus then describes the cosmic reign of Chronos (Saturn) as following on from that of Ouranos. Accordingly, a further contraction took place, in which cosmic evolution became circumscribed by the orbit of Saturn. In the light of Orphic cosmology, the Saturn period of cosmic evolution is the fourth manvantara, but there are grounds, as we shall see, for regarding this as the **first stage of cosmic evolution** – in the sense that human evolution began during the Saturn manvantara.

In Orphic cosmology, the Earth manvantara (= the present period of cosmic evolution, associated with the planet Earth) would be the seventh period of cosmic evolution, but in terms of human evolution, the Earth period can be regarded as the fourth stage of evolution (see Table below).

Looking at the heliocentric planetary system, according to our hypothesis successive manvantaras are indicated by the orbits of the planets around the Sun, each stage of cosmic evolution – by a process of contraction – drawing nearer toward the Sun.

The manvantaras of Orphic cosmology

manvantara: orbit of Pluto (Phanes)	
manvantara: orbit of Neptune (Night)	
manvantara: orbit of Uranus (Ouranos)	The stages of human evolution:
manvantara: orbit of Saturn (Chronos)	1st stage: orbit of Saturn
manvantara: orbit of Jupiter (Zeus)	2nd stage: orbit of Jupiter
manvantara: orbit of Mars (Dionysos)	3rd stage: orbit of Mars
manvantara: orbit of the Earth	4th stage: orbit of the Earth
manvantara: orbit of Venus	5th stage: orbit of Venus
manvantara: orbit of Mercury	6th stage: orbit of Mercury
manvantara: orbit of the Sun	7th stage: orbit of the Sun

The above Table contains our hypothesis, based initially on the cosmogony of Orpheus, that the structure of our heliocentric solar system reveals a plan of evolution. The basic supposition is that, following the contraction of our Sun that formed long ago from the primal gaseous nebula, humanity is also engaged in an evolutionary process proceeding from planet to planet, drawing ever closer to the Sun. According to this hypothesis, cosmic evolution began with Pluto – or with the entire Kuiper belt of which Pluto is a part – and began contracting from there. Pluto and all other objects belonging to the Kuiper belt are, so to say, "relics" of this first stage of evolution, reminding us of the origins of our solar system from the primal giant nebula that filled the entire space extending out to the limits of the Kuiper belt.

According to modern astronomy, the Kuiper belt is the outermost region of our solar system, except possibly for the Oort cloud (named after Jan Oort). However, the existence of the Oort cloud is purely hypothetical. Modern astronomers – following Kuiper's original hypothesis – regard the Kuiper belt as a reservoir of comet nuclei, orbiting together with Pluto, the asteroids and other objects there. But because the nuclei of comets are so small, they are undetectable at such vast distances. It is supposed that occasionally gravitational influences dislodge comet nuclei from this comet reservoir (Kuiper belt) resulting in a comet making its appearance, sometimes penetrating into the inner region of our solar system. Some comets, after orbiting around the Sun, disappear back into these outermost reaches of the solar system, never to be seen again. Other comets are "captured" by the gravitational pull of the larger planets (Jupiter, Saturn, Uranus, Neptune).

One description of Saturn suggests that in the early phases of formation of our solar system, Saturn was comet-like, with a tail, and it was only after the settling down of the solar system, that the tail became "wrapped around" Saturn to form its ring system.

> *Had we been able to observe Saturn at a very early condition of our earth evolution, we would have seen that in its orbit it had a sort of nucleus and a sort of comet's tail, which passed out into cosmic space ...That is, in the primeval periods of our earth, Saturn would have been seen circling round its orbit with its tail pointing outwards ...At a later period ...that which had formerly gone out into cosmic space was so drawn together that the tail became an enclosed ring. Through the power of attraction of the planetary system the ring was formed ...If you were to take the ring of Saturn as it circles around Saturn and open it out, you would have a comet's tail.*[320]

Steiner put this forward as a fact that he beheld clairvoyantly, looking back into the past of our solar system. From a scientific standpoint, until proven true it remains a hypothesis, which we shall refer to in the following as Steiner's hypothesis. Support for this hypothesis has come from the 2004/2005 flight of NASA's Cassini spacecraft to explore Saturn and its largest moon, Titan. A study of data and images transmitted by Cassini has revealed that the strands of Saturn's F-ring – initially interpreted as concentric ring segments – are in fact connected and form a single one-arm trailing spiral winding at least three times around Saturn.[321] This is indirect confirmation of Steiner's observation quoted above that, "*If you were to take the ring of Saturn as it circles around Saturn and open it out, you would have a comet's tail.*"

It is now known that not only Saturn but also Jupiter, Uranus, and Neptune have ring systems. The rings of Jupiter, Uranus, and Neptune are much thinner and darker than Saturn's rings, which is why they did not become discovered until fairly recently. Saturn's rings were discovered by Galileo in the year 1610, when he began his exploration of the heavens with a telescope. If Steiner's hypothesis is correct that Saturn's ring system was originally a kind of comet's tail, then the same should hold true for the ring systems of Jupiter, Uranus, and Neptune. This hypothesis, unusual as it first may sound, perhaps offers a key to understanding the formation of our solar system from the primal nebula.

As indicated in *Hermetic Astrology*, vol. I, Chapter 10, Rudolf Steiner had perfect recall not only of his previous incarnations, but also of earlier stages of cosmic evolution. These seven stages of evolution through which the human being evolves are described by Rudolf Steiner in his book *Occult Science: An Outline*.[322] Thus, by means of his spiritual faculties of perception, he was able to behold and describe not only the history of Earth evolution going

---

[320] Rudolf Steiner, *The Spiritual Beings in the Heavenly Bodies*, pp. 199-200.
[321] Robert Roy Britt, "*Saturn's Surprise: One Ring is Actually a Spiral*" – www.SPACE.com article from November 28, 2005 – writing about the research of Sebastian Charnoz at the University of Paris, reported in the November 25, 2005 issue of the journal *Science*. Saturn's ring system – identified by letters from the inside out – is in this order: D, C, B, A, F, G, E.
[322] Rudolf Steiner, *Occult Science – An Outline*.

back through various cultural epochs (see *Hermetic Astrology*, vol. I, Chapter 3) to Atlantis and even earlier, but also the history of each of the preceding stages of evolution, identified with the orbits of Saturn, Jupiter, and Mars. He named these stages of evolution according to his clairvoyant perception. For example, he described the stage of evolution which took place within the orbit of the planet Jupiter as the Sun period; because the entire sphere bounded by the planet Jupiter was like a giant Sun.[323] Similarly, the stage of evolution which took place within the orbit of the planet Mars he described as the Moon period of evolution, because of the moonlike globe that revolved around the orbit which is now occupied by Mars. These four stages of evolution – the three former evolutionary periods and the present Earth period – were therefore named by Rudolf Steiner: Saturn, Sun, Moon, and Earth. These are to be followed by three evolutionary periods, which Rudolf Steiner named: Jupiter, Venus, and Vulcan. Thus, according to Rudolf Steiner's cosmology, these seven stages of evolution relating to the development of the human being are:

> Saturn (took place within the orbit of the planet Saturn);
>
> Sun (took place within the orbit of the planet Jupiter);
>
> Moon (took place within the orbit of the planet Mars);
>
> Earth (taking place <u>now</u> in the orbit of the Earth around the Sun);
>
> Jupiter (will take place within the orbit of the planet Venus);
>
> Venus (will take place within the orbit of the planet Mercury);
>
> Vulcan (will take place in the sphere of the Sun).

These seven stages of the human being's evolution, together with the names given to them by Rudolf Steiner, are listed in the Table alongside the manvantaras of Orphic cosmology.

The stages of human evolution are indicated by the names for the days of the week, where the present Earth evolution is divided into two halves: Mars (prior to the Mystery of Golgotha) and Mercury (post-Christian era), Saturday (Saturn), Sunday (Sun), Monday (Moon), Tuesday (Mars), Wednesday (Mercury), Thursday (Jupiter), Friday (Venus), and lastly Saturday (Vulcan) being the "higher octave" of the Saturn stage. The Anglo-Saxon names for the days of the week are partly derived from the names of the Germanic gods: Tiw = Mars, Wotan = Mercury, Thor = Jupiter, Freya = Venus. It should be noted that in the heliocentric system the orbit of the Earth lies between that of Mars and Venus, where Mars represents a continuation from the past Moon stage and Venus leads into the future Jupiter stage of human evolution. According to Rudolf Steiner's esoteric cosmology, the names of the planets Venus and Mercury became interchanged, so that esoterically considered, the orbit of the Earth lies between that of Mars and Mercury. In the light of this consideration the validity of the designation of the two halves of Earth evolution as "Mars" and "Mercury" can be seen. For further details concerning the naming of the weekdays by the Egyptians in relation to the stages of cosmic evolution, see Appendix II: *Musical Tones and the Planets*.

The Vulcan stage of evolution will take place where the Sun is currently located. Looking up to the Sun, one beholds the location of the future Earth, where humanity shall be at the seventh stage of evolution. In other words, at the Vulcan stage the Earth will become reunited with the

---

[323] Rudolf Steiner, *Spiritual Hierarchies and their Reflection in the Physical World*. According to Rudolf Steiner's description, in the Sun period of evolution a giant Sun filled the orbit that is now traced out by the planet Jupiter. At that time, however, Jupiter as a planetary body did not exist.

Sun – or rather, the Earth will be a Sun. This signifies for human beings the creation of the resurrection body, where the power of the spirit transmutes the physical body into the resurrection body. For the Earth as a whole it means that the spiritualization of matter will extend all the way to the center of the Earth and that the interior of the Earth will become exteriorized during this process. In the process of exteriorization all that which is presently negative within the interior of the Earth will become transformed into the Good. For no evil will be possible within the Sun radiance of Vulcan, where the power of resurrection will prevail.

Vulcan represents the octave of the ancient Saturn evolution, when the first rudiments of the physical body were established. During Vulcan evolution the final transmutation of the physical body into the resurrection body (*atma*) will take place. In terms of the stages of planetary evolution described in this book – Saturn, Sun, Moon, Mars, Mercury, Jupiter, Venus – Vulcan follows on from Venus and is the metamorphosis of Ancient Saturn, just as Future Venus is the transformation of Ancient Sun, and Future Jupiter is the transfigured Ancient Moon.

In a certain respect the present Mercury stage (second half of Earth evolution) is a metamorphosis of the Mars stage (first half of Earth evolution). During the Mars stage the foundation of the human "I" was given, then with the coming of Christ there began the Mercury stage with the commencement of the spiritualization of the "I" in the sense of the words of St. Paul: "*Not I, but Christ in me.*" Similarly, during the Ancient Moon the rudimentary form of the astral body was given, and the metamorphosis of this during the Future Jupiter stage will give rise to the transfigured astral body, known as the Spirit Self (*manas*). Likewise, during the Ancient Sun the rudimentary form of the etheric body was given, and the metamorphosis of this during the Future Venus stage will give rise to the transformed etheric body, known as the Life Spirit (*buddhi*). Lastly, the Ancient Saturn stage was that during which the rudimentary form of the physical body was given, which will be metamorphosed during the Future Vulcan stage into the resurrection body (*atma*), the stage of the human being's resurrection, representing the goal of evolution.

Appendix II: Musical Tones and the Planets

Although lacking in extensive explication, the following is written as an offering or stimulus to further reflection on a theme that has occupied Western humanity at least since Pythagoras (sixth/fifth centuries BC). In order to do justice to "musical tones and the planets", an entire book would need to be written. Hopefully the reader will bear this in mind when reading the following, which can serve only as a brief introduction, whereby the reader is invited to "fill in the gaps" in order to make sense of the brief descriptions.

As a starting point it may be noted from indications given by Rudolf Steiner that there are at least *two* correspondences between the seven tones of the scale and the seven planets.

The first correspondence is indicated by Rudolf Steiner in his answer to a question put after his lecture "*Erden und Menschheitsentwickelung*" ("*The Development of the Earth and Humanity*").[324] He relates the seven tones to the seven metals and these, in turn, to the seven planets – correspondence (1):

C	Iron	Mars
D	Quicksilver	Mercury
E	Tin	Jupiter
F	Copper	Venus
G	Lead	Saturn
A	Gold	Sun
B	Silver	Moon

The first thing to notice about this list is that it follows the sequence of the planets according to the days of the week, as described in Appendix I in connection with the stages of cosmic evolution. There the sequence begins with Saturday (the day of Saturn). However, in the above tabulation the sequence starts with Tuesday (the day of Mars), followed by Wednesday (the day of Mercury), then Thursday (the day of Jupiter), then Friday (the day of Venus), then Saturday (the day of Saturn), then Sunday (the day of the Sun), and lastly Monday (the day of the Moon). The planetary week originated in Egypt and was transmitted to Rome around the time of the emperor Augustus, and then spread throughout the civilized world.[325] There are different levels of significance to the planetary week, the most outstanding one being that it indicates the stages of planetary evolution, as discussed in Appendix I, where the sequence begins with Saturday: Ancient Saturn, Ancient Sun, Ancient Moon, Earth (the 1st half of Earth evolution being associated with Mars, and the 2nd half of Earth evolution being associated with Mercury), Future Jupiter, and Future Venus.[326] In the context of the correspondence between the seven tones and the planets, the fact of beginning correspondence (1) with Mars is considered below (see the paragraph prior to the summary at the end of this appendix).

---

[324] Rudolf Steiner, *Erden und Menschheitsentwickelung* ("*The Development of the Earth and Humanity*"). Fragenbeantwortung ("Answers to Questions"). Nachrichtenblatt der Rudolf Steiner Nachlassverwaltung, vol. 26 (Rudolf Steiner Verlag: Dornach/Switzerland, Summer 1969).

[325] Robert Powell, *History of the Planets*, pp. 18-19.

[326] Robert Powell, *Hermetic Astrology*, vol. II, chapter 8 discusses the stages of cosmic evolution in relation to the naming of the planets in our solar system.

The second point to note in relation to the above list is the association of the metals with the planets. This is a very ancient correspondence, first mentioned by the Greek astrologer Vettius Valens (second century A D), with the exception that Vettius Valens gives electrum (an alloy of gold and silver) as the metal corresponding to Mercury, instead of quicksilver.[327] However, Arabic alchemical texts give quicksilver as the metal corresponding to Mercury, and agree with Vettius Valens with respect to the six other planetary metals.[328] It is not surprising that quicksilver is not mentioned by Vettius Valens, as its distillation became established only later – at some time around the fourth century A D.

The idea of a correspondence between the seven tones and the seven planets is even more ancient, evidently going back to Terpander (seventh century BC), and possibly being even older – perhaps stemming originally from Orpheus and his mystery school. Pythagoras is credited with having added the eighth tone, the octave, to the seven belonging to the heptachord of Terpander, thus creating the octachord. The Pythagorean Nicomachus of Gerasa, who lived between 50 and 150 A D, discusses the heptachord of Terpander, arranged in seven descending tones. From his description it can be deduced that the descending sequence is A, G, F, E, D, C, B.[329] If this deduction is correct (which is by no means certain), it follows from Nicomachus' description[330] that there is a definite correspondence between the tones and the planets.[331]

However, it has to be pointed out that an actual correspondence between tones and planets based on the heptachord of Terpander is nowhere specified by Nicomachus; it is a conclusion drawn from the writings of modern authors. In fact, none of the ancient authors give an explicit correspondence between the seven tones and the planets. Despite all the speculation about the nature of this correspondence, it was not even clear *whether according to the doctrine of the ancient Pythagoreans the outermost of the planet spheres, namely that of Saturn, or the innermost, that of the Moon, gave forth the deepest tone.*[332] In this respect, Rudolf Steiner's indication (1) above is historically the first one clearly stated by a known person concerning a correspondence between the seven tones and the planets that is not simply a speculation about what the Pythagoreans might have believed.[333]

The second correspondence is derived from the statement made by Rudolf Steiner that "C = 128 Hz = Sun".[334] Here, since the Sun is taken as the starting point, it seems to imply that this indication is assuming a *heliocentric* view of the solar system, with the Sun at the center.

---

[327] Vettius Valens, *Anthologiarum* I, 1.
[328] E.J. Holmyard, *Alchemy*, pp. 18-19.
[329] Maria Renold, *Von Intervallen, Tonleitern, Tönen und dem Kammerton c = 128 Hertz*, pp. 40-41. This book is now available in English translation: *Intervals, Scales, Tones and the Concert Pitch c=128 Hz*.
[330] Joscelyn Godwin, *The Harmony of the Spheres: A Sourcebook of the Pythagorean Tradition in Music*, pp. 10-11.
[331] Assuming that Maria Renold's interpretation is correct, the sequence based on the heptachord of Terpander is: A Moon; G Venus; F Mercury; E Sun; D Mars; C Jupiter; B Saturn.
[332] Albert Freiherr von Thimus (1806-1878) quoted in Godwin, op. cit., p. 376.
[333] There is a poem written in the late eleventh or early twelfth century AD entitled "*The Natural Concord of Notes with Planets*", which assigns A to the Moon and then ascends as follows: A Moon; B Mercury; C Venus; D Sun; E Mars; F Jupiter; G Saturn. Alas, it is unknown who the author of this poem is, which was included in a manuscript of Boethius' *De Institutione musica*. Cf. Godwin, op. cit., pp. 123-125.
[334] Cf. Renold, op. cit., p. 109. Hz is the abbreviation for Hertz, which is the number of vibrations per second of any given tone.

The sequence of planets, moving outwards from the Sun in the center (not including the Earth), starting with C corresponding to the Sun, is:

Sun – Mercury – Venus – Mars – Jupiter – Saturn
C   D   E   F   G   A

In terms of the seven classical planets, the Moon is missing from this sequence.

Adding in the Moon, and assigning the remaining tone B to the Moon, correspondence (2) is:

Sun – Mercury – Venus – Mars – Jupiter – Saturn – Moon
C   D   E   F   G   A   B

In so far as the Moon reflects the entire heavenly realm, it is not entirely illogical to place the Moon after Saturn in this sequence. In antiquity the sphere of the starry heavens was placed beyond Saturn, and thus the Moon – like a pure mirror reflecting the entire sphere of the starry heavens – could be thought of as occupying this position, at least symbolically, even though the Moon is not physically located beyond Saturn.

The naming of the days of the week according to the stages of planetary evolution is discussed in Appendix I, and above it was pointed out that this is the sequence underlying the correspondence (1). The stages of planetary evolution are also relevant to understanding the correspondence (2). For the positions of the planets in the heliocentric system offer a picture of the evolution of our solar system. The picture that emerges is that the planet Saturn indicates the extent of the expansion of the primitive solar nebula at the Ancient Saturn stage of evolution. When the solar nebula contracted, the planet Saturn was left behind, marking the previous extension of the solar nebula. The solar nebula contracted and then filled the space extending up to the region where the planet Jupiter now orbits around the Sun. At this stage the solar nebula was called the Ancient Sun, one reason for this designation being the sun-like nature of this giant globe that filled the entire space extending up to Jupiter.[335] A further contraction of the solar nebula then took place, leaving behind the planet Jupiter. The orbit of the planet Jupiter thus delineates the extent of the solar nebula at the Ancient Sun stage of evolution, just as the orbit of the planet Saturn demarcates the extent of the solar nebula at the Ancient Saturn stage of evolution.[336] The next contraction of the solar nebula that took place signified a contraction of this giant globe to the size delineated by the orbit of Mars around the Sun. At this stage the solar nebula was called the Ancient Moon. With the subsequent contraction of the solar nebula, contracting to the size denoted by the Earth's orbit around the Sun, the planet Mars was left behind as a marker reminding us of the extent of the solar nebula at the time of the Ancient Moon stage of evolution. Then, early during the present Earth stage of evolution, the solar nebula contracted further to the size of our present Sun, leaving behind the planet Earth – together with Mars, Jupiter, and Saturn – orbiting around the Sun. The planets Uranus, Neptune and Pluto were also part of our solar system at

---

[335] At the Ancient Sun stage of evolution, the giant solar nebula could be compared to the star Betelgeuze at its maximum. Betelgeuze, the reddish star marking the right shoulder of the hunter or giant Orion, is an irregularly pulsating red supergiant whose diameter, when at its minimum, is believed to be at least the size of the orbit of Mars, and at its maximum is thought to be equal in diameter to the orbit of Jupiter. In volume Betelgeuze exceeds the Sun by a factor of at least 160 million, and thus in contemplating Betelgeuze we can begin to gain a conception of the size of the Ancient Sun in comparison to the Sun's present size.

[336] Robert Powell, *Hermetic Astrology, vol. II*, chapter 8 considers the earlier stages of evolution prior to the Ancient Saturn stage. The planets Uranus, Neptune and Pluto are markers of three earlier stages of cosmic evolution preceding Ancient Saturn. See also Appendix I.

that stage, as discussed in Appendix I.[337] Later during Earth evolution the planets Venus and Mercury separated out from the Sun and took up their orbits around the Sun. Also, the Moon separated out from the Earth and began to orbit the Earth, this being the final stage of the formation of our solar system as we now know it.

The orbits of the planets Venus and Mercury point to future stages of evolution: the orbit of Venus denotes the Future Jupiter stage (comprising a further stage of contraction toward the Sun), and the orbit of Mercury indicates the Future Venus stage (a later stage of contraction drawing even closer to the Sun). This conception of the orbits of the planets Venus and Mercury delineating the stages of evolution known as Future Jupiter and Future Venus is confirmed by Rudolf Steiner who, instead of referring to the stages of evolution (as he usually did) as Saturn, Sun, Moon, Earth, Jupiter, Venus, once referred to the stages of evolution as: Saturn, Sun, Moon, Earth, Venus, Mercury.[338]

Evidently the ancient Egyptians were aware of the structure of our solar system in relation to the stages of evolution. For this reason they named the planet that we call Mercury "Venus". For them this planet delineated the Future Venus stage of evolution and was thus appropriately called "Venus", this planet signifying the demarcation of the "Friday" (Venus) stage of evolution following the "Thursday" (Jupiter) stage in the naming of the days of the week. Similarly, the planet we call Venus was called by the Egyptians "Mercury" – as the planet leading to, and indicating the demarcation of, the Future Jupiter stage of evolution.[339] If we honor the Egyptian naming of the planets, then correspondence (2) is:

C	Sun
D	"Venus"
E	"Mercury"
F	Mars
G	Jupiter
A	Saturn
B	Moon

This is precisely the planetary sequence given by Rudolf Steiner in his cosmic poem known as "*The Twelve Moods*", which he wrote for performance in eurythmy.[340]

Comparing correspondences (1) and (2), it can be seen that B = Moon and D = Mercury (remembering that the planet the Egyptians called "Venus" is the planet now called Mercury) in both sets of correspondences, and that these are the only common tones between the two sequences. The question is: What is the significance of these two correspondences of the seven tones with the planets?

---

[337] For reasons that are apparent against the background of the description elucidated in the book referred to in the previous footnote. See also Appendix I.

[338] Rudolf Steiner, *Die Rosenkreuzer-Esoterik* (lecture held in Nijmegen/Holland on March 10, 1908; *Beiträge zur Rudolf Steiner Gesamtausgabe*, volume 60; Rudolf Steiner Verlag: Dornach/Switzerland, Christmas 1977), pp. 30-32.

[339] For further details, see Robert Powell, *Hermetic Astrology*, vol. II, chapter 8.

[340] Cf. Lacquanna Paul and Robert Powell, *Cosmic Dances of the Zodiac*, p. 115 for an English translation of "*The Twelve Moods*" by Rudolf Steiner, together with an indication as to how to work with this poem in the cosmic dance of eurythmy.

The following thoughts are intended as a stimulus toward understanding the two correspondences (macrocosm = the cosmic world; microcosm = the human being):

- (1) and (2) relate to two different levels.

- (1) relates macrocosmically to the level of the *astral plane*.

- (2) relates macrocosmically to the *spiritual (devachanic)* level associated with the Sun.

- (2) works microcosmically in the seven lotus flowers (*chakras*) corresponding to the planets, as follows:

C	heart *chakra*	12 petal lotus flower	Sun
D	solar plexus *chakra*	10 petal lotus flower	Mercury ("Venus")
E	sacral *chakra*	6 petal lotus flower	Venus ("Mercury")
F	larynx *chakra*	16 petal lotus flower	Mars
G	third eye *chakra*	2 petal lotus flower	Jupiter
A	crown *chakra*	8 petal lotus flower	Saturn
B	root *chakra*	4 petal lotus flower	Moon[341]

- In this correspondence indicated above, the *present-day* names of the planets Mercury and Venus are used and the Egyptian names (written "Venus" and "Mercury") are indicated in parentheses.

- (1) works microcosmically in the seven organs corresponding to the planets, as follows:

C	Gall-bladder	Mars
D	Lungs	Mercury
E	Liver	Jupiter
F	Kidneys	Venus
G	Spleen	Saturn
A	Heart	Sun
B	Brain	Moon[342]

- According to the above, there are two different levels in the human being, and the planetary tones work differently according to level. For example, the tone C works upon the heart *chakra* (*astral body*), but the same tone C works upon the gall-bladder organ (*etheric body*). And whereas C works upon the heart *chakra*, A works upon the *heart* itself. This distinction is particularly important for the therapeutic application of musical tones in healing. If a heart problem is primarily on the soul/astral level, it can be healed best by using the tone C, whereas

---

[341] Cf. Robert Powell, *Hermetic Astrology*, vol. I, pp. 133-139 for a description of the seven lotus flowers corresponding to the seven planets. This correspondence holds particularly on the level of the astral body, since the lotus flowers (*chakras*) are organs in the astral body. Along the same lines, Rudolf Steiner's sketch from the year 1923 "*Der Mensch in Beziehung zu den Planeten*" ("*The Human Being in Relation to the Planets*") shows the correspondence between the lotus flowers and the planets, also indicating the colors of the lotus flowers. See also Appendix III.

[342] Rudolf Steiner, *Occult Physiology* gives a description of the correspondence between the seven organs and the planets. This correspondence holds on the level of the etheric body, since the organs are primarily etheric (but also manifesting physically).

if it is more on the etheric/physical level, the tone A is most helpful. An understanding of (1) and (2) enables healing through musical tones to be applied. For example, if someone's respiratory system is suffering, it can be healed through the person repeatedly singing or hearing the tone D, or hearing music in which the tone D is repeated often.

This healing application of the correspondences between the musical tones and the planets signifies a practical application of the Pythagorean *harmonies of the spheres*.

☐ Finally, there is the consideration as to how the tones, resounding in their pure essence upon the *spiritual (devachanic)* plane of existence, work down onto the *astral plane*.

The pure spiritual tones become "translated" into color, when they take effect on the *astral plane*. In terms of the translation of tone into color on the astral plane, C is red, D is orange, E is yellow, F is green, G is blue, A is indigo, and B is violet.[343] Returning to (1), the correspondence of Mars to the color red is universal, from which it follows that "C = red" applies here. Further, Rudolf Steiner indicated the colors of the planets in eurythmy: Mars–red; Mercury–yellow; Jupiter–orange; Venus–green; Saturn–blue; Sun–white; Moon–violet. Looking at sequence (1), it can be seen that these colors fit the tones in the case of four of the planets: Mars (C–red), Venus (F–green); Saturn (G–blue); Moon (B–violet), and that the colors for Mercury (yellow) and Jupiter (orange) are interchanged in the sequence given in (1). This is interesting in light of the mythological relationship between Jupiter (Zeus) and Mercury (Hermes), the latter being the scribe of the former. In terms of the color for the Sun (white), this color could also be represented by gold, the metal of the Sun. Here there is a relationship with indigo, in so far as indigo is complementary in color to gold. Indigo is the sacred color associated with Krishna, who is regarded in the Hindu tradition as the avatar of the Sun. Further, indigo is often associated with the Virgin Mary who, in turn, is often depicted as *"clothed with the Sun"* (*The Revelation to John* 12:1).

☐ The entire subject of the correspondences between the planets and the tones *and* the colors is both interesting and complex. At any rate, given the correspondence C = red, and that Mars is called the "red planet", it is apparent why the correspondence of C with Mars *begins* the sequence (1), for C is at the beginning of the scale of seven tones, and red is usually taken as the starting point of the color spectrum of seven colors.

---

[343] Isaac Newton, *Opticks: or, a Treatise of the Reflections, Refractions, Inflexions and Colours of Light*, pp. 154-155, indicates a relationship between tone and color, albeit different from the one given above. He places red between the tones D and E, orange between E and F, yellow between F and G, green between G and A, blue between A and B, indigo between B and C, and violet between C and D, so that *"from D to E be all degrees of red, from E to F all degrees of orange, from F to G all degrees of yellow, and so on"*. Here Newton goes against the almost universal traditional correspondence between the tone C and the color red. For an extensive historical investigation of the relationship between tone and color from Aristotle to Goethe, cf. Jörg Jewanski, *Ist C = Rot? Eine Kultur- und Wissenschaftsgeschichte zum Problem der wechselseitigen Beziehung zwischen Ton und Farbe*. ["*Is C=Red? A Cultural and Scientific History Concerning the Problem of the Interchangeable Relationship between Tone and Color*"].

Summary of the two correspondences
between the seven tones and the planets

Clearly there are other approaches to this topic and that there are many websites on the Internet dealing with this subject and with related themes.

However, the point of departure here are **Rudolf Steiner's two indications**:
the first being *correspondence (1)* listed at the start of this article and given again here below;
the second being the statement *"C = 128 Hz = Sun"* from which *correspondence (2)* is derived.

Summarizing these two sequences of correspondences:

Correspondence (1)

C	Iron	Mars
D	Quicksilver	Mercury
E	Tin	Jupiter
F	Copper	Venus
G	Lead	Saturn
A	Gold	Sun
B	Silver	Moon

This is the first correspondence between the tones and the planets given by Rudolf Steiner – in the sequence of the days of the week, beginning with the red planet Mars. It works upon the organs of the human being, which are primary centers in the *etheric body*; however, these organs also manifest physically. Expanding correspondence (1) to include the organs and also the colors associated with the seven tones, we arrive at the following tabulation:

Red	C	Iron	Mars	Gall bladder
Orange	D	Quicksilver	Mercury	Lungs
Yellow	E	Tin	Jupiter	Liver
Green	F	Copper	Venus	Kidneys
Blue	G	Lead	Saturn	Spleen
Indigo	A	Gold	Sun	Heart
Violet	B	Silver	Moon	Brain

Correspondence (2)

C	Sun
D	Mercury ("Venus")
E	Venus ("Mercury")
F	Mars
G	Jupiter
A	Saturn
B	Moon

This second correspondence between the tones and the planets is derived from Rudolf Steiner's statement: "C = 128 Hz = Sun". When using the original Egyptian names for the planets Mercury and Venus ("Venus" and "Mercury"), the above sequence is precisely the planetary sequence indicated by Rudolf Steiner in his cosmic poem *"The Twelve Moods"*, for performance in eurythmy. This sequence of tones works upon the seven lotus flowers (*chakras*) of the human being, which are primary centers in the *astral body*. Expanding correspondence (2) to include the lotus flowers (*chakras*) and also the frequencies of the tones, we arrive at the following tabulation:

128	C	heart *chakra*	12 petal lotus flower	Sun
144	D	solar plexus *chakra*	10 petal lotus flower	Mercury ("Venus")
162	E	sacral *chakra*	6 petal lotus flower	Venus ("Mercury")
170⅔	F	larynx *chakra*	16 petal lotus flower	Mars
192	G	third eye *chakra*	2 petal lotus flower	Jupiter
216	A	crown *chakra*	8 petal lotus flower	Saturn
243	B	root *chakra*	4 petal lotus flower	Moon

Here it should be noted that the frequencies of the tones listed above are according to the Pythagorean mode of tuning, which yields slightly different frequencies than those given by the usual *natural intervals*.[344] For example, the interval between the tone C=128 and the tone A=216 is a major sixth. However, the *natural interval* of the major sixth is defined by the ratio 5:3, and if 128 is multiplied by 5 and divided by 3 the result is 213⅓ (not 216). The value 216 for the tone A is derived from 128 by multiplying by 27 and dividing by 16, expressed by the ratio 27:16, and this ratio is the Pythagorean major sixth.[345] Since Rudolf Steiner indicated that recorders should be tuned according to a^1=432,[346] he thus firmly endorsed the Pythagorean intervals (rather than the natural intervals or any other kind of intervals). For a^1=432 is simply the octave of a=216. Taken together with his indication that c=128, the conclusion is inescapable that he assumed Pythagorean intervals. In the words of Maria Renold:

> *How do the two concert pitches c=128 Hz and a^1=432 Hz relate to one another? They are an octave plus a **major Pythagorean sixth** apart, thus in the ratio 27:8. The tone c=128 Hz has revealed itself in the course of our considerations to be the foundational prime tone for our time. As the c major scale, it is central to – and is the archetype for – all the major scales in the circle of fifths. The c major scale, and correspondingly all the major scales, stand in a direct relationship to **Christ** and to the Mystery of Golgotha ...Now, Rudolf Steiner gives a^1=432 as the second concert pitch ...Since ancient times – and also in the case of Rudolf Steiner – the tone A is regarded as the Sun tone and is thus also used as the tuning tone. However, the regent of the Sun is the Archangel Michael, who is the Spirit of our time. So we can also designate a^1=432 Hz as the **Michael tone**.[347]*

---

[344] The reader is referred to Maria Renold's book for a comprehensive discussion of the difference between Pythagorean and natural intervals. This book is now available in English translation: *Intervals, Scales, Tones and the Concert Pitch c=128 Hz*.

[345] The term *Pythagorean intervals* is used by Maria Renold (op. cit., German edition, p. 19) to indicate the intervals resulting from the tuning of "Apollo's lyre" in fifths. The Pythagorean intervals are cosmic in nature, underlying the *harmony of the spheres* spoken of by Pythagoras, whereas the *natural intervals* underlie the natural harmonies heard by the earthly ear.

[346] Maria Renold, op. cit. (German edition), p. 238.

[347] Maria Renold, op. cit., p. 238 (German edition – translation of this quote by RP). Note that it was in the region of a^1=432 Hz that was the tuning tone used for tuning the instruments of orchestras in the days of Mozart and Beethoven, but that nowadays it is generally a^1=440 Hz, a^1=442 Hz, a^1=444 Hz or even higher, signifying that modern music consciousness has fallen out of step with the *cosmic tuning* implied by a^1=432 Hz. The Italian composer Verdi recognized a^1=432 Hz as the true value and managed to establish this at a conference held in Milan in 1881. Verdi subsequently wrote a letter to the Italian government recommending that all orchestras should use the tuning tone a^1=432 Hz. This persuaded the Italian government's Ministry of War to decree in 1884 that a^1=432 should be the tuning tone used by all military brass bands in Italy.

That a¹=432 Hz expresses the *cosmic tuning* can be recognized from the following simple consideration. The vernal point regresses through the zodiac at a rate of one degree in 72 years, which is approximately the average length of a human life. Thus, 25,920 years is the time period (known as a *Platonic year*) required for the vernal point to make a complete cycle of precession through the 360 degrees of the zodiac, since 72 x 360 = 25,920. Now, the unit Hertz (Hz), named after the German scientist Heinrich Hertz, is a measure of the frequency or number of vibrations (oscillations) per second, and so a¹=432 Hz signifies 432 vibrations per second. Multiplied by 60, this yields 432 x 60 = 25,920 vibrations per minute, the same figure as the cosmic number underlying the Platonic year! In this way *a¹=432 Hz* can be seen to be the *cosmically aligned tuning tone*. Similarly, the tone c=128 Hz arises naturally when we consider that the octave is given by doubling (or halving) the value, e.g. c¹=256 is twice the value of c=128. By continually halving c=128 Hz, we find the frequencies of the tone C to be: 1, 2, 4, 8, 16, 32, 64, *128*, 256, 512, etc. Beginning with one vibration per second, yielding a tone C well below the limit of audibility for the human ear, and deriving the octave by doubling the frequency of vibration each time, it is clear that c=128 Hz arises quite naturally.

Maria Renold's linking the Sun tone a¹=432 Hz with the Archangel Michael and the tone c=128 Hz with Christ, known in the early days of Christianity as the *Sun Spirit*, offers a new perspective on the two sets of correspondences (1) and (2). For Christ, the Logos ("Word") is obviously connected with sound, and there was a time – before the Incarnation upon the Earth – when Christ worked from the Sun. And correspondence (2) does indeed relate to a Sun-centered (heliocentric) perspective – or rather, it relates to the Egyptian hermetic perspective that was later elaborated as an astronomical system by the Danish astronomer Tycho Brahe.[348]

In the Tychonic (hermetic) system, the planets are conceived of as orbiting around the Sun, and the Sun and Moon are thought to revolve around the Earth. This is the astronomical system underlying the sequence Sun, "Venus", "Mercury", Mars, Jupiter, Saturn, Moon in correspondence (2), where the Egyptian names for Mercury ("Venus") and for Venus ("Mercury") have been substituted for the usual astronomical names of these two planets. The spiritual reality of this astronomical system is that it acknowledges Christ as the Sun Spirit and, at the same time, that Christ – through his Incarnation upon the Earth – has made the Earth the center of his activity. For this reason the tone c=128 Hz is indeed the foundational prime tone for humanity and the Earth, having been carried over from the Sun to the Earth by Christ.

---

[348] The Tychonic (hermetic) system of Tycho Brahe is discussed at length in Robert Powell, *Hermetic Astrology*, vol. I, chapter 2.

Appendix III: Correspondences to the Seven Classical Planets

The correspondences, given in the three tables below, are used in the Choreocosmos School of Cosmic and Sacred Dance – in particular when working with the planets in cosmic dance. They are listed here as a stimulus to further thought and research concerning the planets. One could write a whole treatise about each set of correspondences, and obviously this is not possible. For example, Appendix II elaborates on the correspondences between the tones and the planets, and each set of correspondences listed in the three tables below deserves an extensive treatise like the one in Appendix II. Thus it needs to be borne in mind that any particular set of correspondences is simply a summary of a vast background to which it pertains. The list of correspondences is therefore the "bare bones" of something fuller and more all-encompassing, which can be used as material for deep and profound meditation – and, moreover, for a complete spiritual schooling such as the Sophia Foundation offers in its various courses.

Where some explanation is called for is with regard to the colors indicated for the planets. These are listed in the first table, and are the colors indicated by Rudolf Steiner for the planets in eurythmy. They are the *objective* colors of the planets as seen by way of clairvoyance. The pure white light of the Sun is at the center of the tabulation. Mercury, as the planet closest to the Sun, has the brightest color: yellow. In terms of the usual color spectrum, red and orange are on the side of the upper planets (above the Sun in the tabulation) and yellow and green are on the side of the lower planets. Then follow blue (uppermost planet: Saturn) and violet (lowest planet: Moon). Note that in this color spectrum indigo is not present – however, white is, so that the color spectrum for the planets is: white, red, orange, yellow, green, blue, violet, in the order: blue (Saturn), orange (Jupiter), red (Mars), white (Sun), yellow (Mercury), green (Venus), violet (Moon).

In his sketch *Der Mensch in Beziehung zu den Planeten* ("*The Human Being in Relation to the Planets*"), Rudolf Steiner indicates the colors of the chakras in relation to the planets. From this sketch it is apparent that the colors of the chakras are, in part, complementary to the colors of the planets. (See the first row of the first table below for the correspondence between the chakras and the planets, and the fifth row for the objective colors of the planets.) For example, the color of the larynx (Mars) chakra is green, which is complementary to the color red for Mars. Similarly, the color of the sacral (Venus) chakra is red, which is complementary to the color green for Venus. Likewise, the color for the third eye (Jupiter) chakra is blue, which is complementary to the color orange for Jupiter. The color of the heart (Sun) chakra, however, is yellow, which is *not* complementary to the color white for the Sun. Here it has to be borne in mind that the Sun is actually a fixed star and not a planet, and that, interestingly, the color of our Sun as determined by spectral analysis is yellow. In the case of the heart (Sun) chakra, therefore, the color is the same as that of the intrinsic color of the Sun according to spectral analysis. Moreover, the color of the solar plexus (Mercury) chakra is orange, which is *not* complementary to the color yellow for Mercury. In addition, the color of the crown (Saturn) chakra is violet, which again is *not* complementary to the color blue for Saturn. Finally, the color of the root (Moon) chakra is peach blossom, which is the color of the etheric, as may be seen in beholding the peach blossom hue on the cheeks of a healthy face, where the etheric (life) body "bleaches through" the physical body in the case of a healthy person. Here again, in the case of the root (Moon) chakra, the color peach blossom is *not* complementary to the violet color of the

Moon. Summarizing the color spectrum of the chakras according to Rudolf Steiner's sketch, it is: peach blossom (root), red (sacral), orange (solar plexus), yellow (heart), green (larynx), blue (third eye), and violet (crown), whereby in the case of the sacral chakra, larynx chakra, and third eye chakra their colors are complementary to the colors of the corresponding planets. (See Figure below for Rudolf Steiner's color indications for the chakras.)

The question arises: Why is Rudolf Steiner's color spectrum for the chakras different from the usual sequence given: red, orange, yellow, green, blue, indigo, violet?

First it has to be recalled, as indicated in Appendix II, footnote 343, that Newton in his book on optics published in 1704 was the first person to describe the color spectrum in this way, which is now the standard color spectrum accepted by modern science. Secondly, this is how the colors of the chakras appeared to the clairvoyance attained by Charles W. Leadbeater of the Theosophical Society, as presented in his book *The Chakras: A Monograph*, published by the Theosophical Publishing House in Adyar, Madras, India in 1927. It was this book, more than any other, that introduced the chakras into the West, and at first sight it appears as if the views that Leadbeater put forward in his book concerning the chakras are drawn from the Hindu tradition. To a certain extent they *are* drawn from the Hindu tradition, but there are also elements within this book that are original to Leadbeater – the colors of the chakras being one of them. Thus, different color indications for the chakras

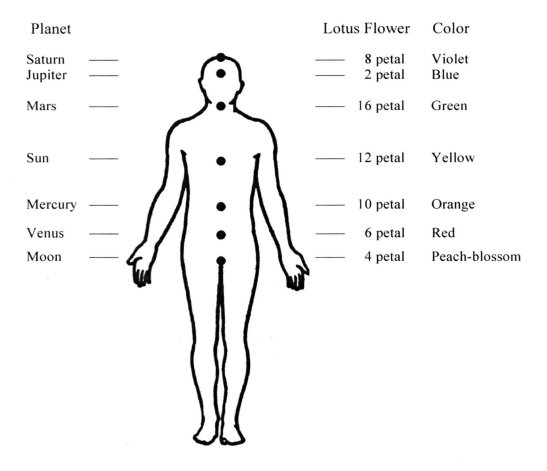

Planet			Lotus Flower	Color
Saturn	——		—— 8 petal	Violet
Jupiter	——		—— 2 petal	Blue
Mars	——		—— 16 petal	Green
Sun	——		—— 12 petal	Yellow
Mercury	——		—— 10 petal	Orange
Venus	——		—— 6 petal	Red
Moon	——		—— 4 petal	Peach-blossom

are given in the book published in 1919 by Sir John Woodroffe (alias Arthur Avalon) entitled *The Serpent Power*, which was the primary source upon which Leadbeater drew his knowledge of the seven chakras. In this book, the first serious work on the chakras to be published in the West, Woodroffe includes a translation of the Sanskrit texts *Paduka-Pancaka* and *Sat-Cakra-Nirupana.* The latter was written by an Indian pundit, Purnananda Swami, around 1577. These texts belong to the Tantric Shakta tradition.[349] Since the texts translated by Sir John Woodroffe were all written prior to the publication of Newton's work on optics (1704), which was the first time that the color spectrum red, orange, yellow, green, blue, indigo, violet was formulated, it is clear that the assignment of this (now standard) color spectrum to the seven chakras is a Western innovation and, in fact, it was Charles W. Leadbeater who was responsible for this. In fact the colors given for the chakras in the *Sat-Cakra-Nirupana* are: root (crimson), sacral (vermilion), solar plexus (the color of heavy laden rain clouds – perhaps indigo), heart (the color of the Bandhuka flower, i.e. pink), larynx (purple), third eye (white), crown (radiant white).

Rudolf Steiner's sketch referred to above, from the year 1923, was based on his own clairvoyant perception of the chakras in relation to the planets. When describing the difference between his clairvoyance and that of Madame Blavatsky, founder of the Theosophical Society, Steiner responded that Blavatsky's clairvoyance reached up to the level of the Moon, whereas his extended to the level of the Sun – and beyond the Sun to Saturn.[350] Perhaps the same can be said of Leadbeater's clairvoyance, that – as in the case of his mentor, Madame Blavatsky – it extended up to the level of the Moon. This would account for the difference in his perception of the colors of the chakras in relation to the clairvoyant vision of Rudolf Steiner, who from the vantage point of his solar clairvoyance saw the color spectrum for the chakras as peach blossom (root), red (sacral), orange (solar plexus), yellow (heart), green (larynx), blue (third eye), violet (crown). At any rate, since, as described above, Steiner's color indications for the chakras reveal some interesting complementary color relationships between the planets and the chakras, there is obviously a level of truth in his color assignments that needs to be further explored. However, these colors assigned to the chakras by Rudolf Steiner have not been included in the table of correspondences below, in order not to confuse those who are used to Leadbeater's color indications for the chakras – now widely accepted in the West – which correlate with the standard color spectrum formulated for the first time by Newton in the year 1704.

---

[349] For an online translation of the *Sat-Cakra-Nirupana* see *www.lightmind.com/jung/seminar/kundaline.html* and for a summary of the traditional colors of the chakras according to the Tantric Shakta tradition, see *www.kheper.net/topics/chakras*

[350] Rudolf Steiner, *True and False Paths in Spiritual Investigation*, p. 174: "*Everything to be found in the writings of H.P. Blavatsky is determined by her association with the Moon sphere...When I wrote my book Occult Science: an Outline in the years between 1906 and 1909, I described the Earth in its earlier incarnations of Moon, Sun, and Saturn. My description did not end with the Moon incarnation. I traced the Earth as far back as the Saturn incarnation.*"

Here is a tabulation of the colors indicated for the chakras by both Steiner and Leadbeater for the sake of comparison:

		Rudolf Steiner (1923)	Charles W. Leadbeater (1927)
crown	(Saturn)	violet	violet
third eye	(Jupiter)	blue	indigo
larynx	(Mars)	green	blue
heart	(Sun)	yellow	green
solar plexus	(Mercury)	orange	yellow
sacral	(Venus)	red	orange
root	(Moon)	peach blossom	red

One further point that needs some elucidation is the number of petals attributed to each chakra (see the first row in the first table below). In the tabulation below the number of petals indicated for each chakra is the same as in the Hindu tradition except for the crown chakra. As indicated in the Tantric Shakta tradition concerning the seven chakras, made known in the West through Sir John Woodroffe's book *The Serpent Power*, the crown chakra is said to have one thousand petals.

However, according to the Russian esotericist and Sophiologist Valentin Tomberg in his *Lord's Prayer Course* (distributed by the Sophia Foundation): *"The 8 petal lotus flower: above the head, it is that which creates the connection with the spiritual world. To those who can see it, it appears to light up in 1000 violet scintillations..."* (Week 71 of the *Lord's Prayer Course*). In other words, because the eight petals of this lotus flower are in such rapid movement, it appears to have one thousand petals. Also in the spiritual classic *Meditations on the Tarot* the crown chakra is referred to as having eight petals: *"Concerning the crown center (the 8 petal lotus flower)...it is the center of liberation"* (p. 228). For this reason, in the table below, the crown chakra is indicated as having eight petals (rather than one thousand). However, in both the *Lord's Prayer Course* and *Meditations on the Tarot* the number of petals indicated for the six remaining lotus flowers (chakras) is the same as given in the Tantric Shakta tradition, and this agrees also with the number of petals of the six lower lotus flowers indicated by Rudolf Steiner.[351]

---

[351] Rudolf Steiner, *Knowledge of the Higher Worlds* (Rudolf Steiner Press: London, 1972). Note that Rudolf Steiner did not indicate the number of petals of the crown chakra.

Correspondences to the seven classical planets

	SATURN	JUPITER	MARS	SUN	MERCURY	VENUS	MOON
Sign	♄	♃	♂	☉	☿	♀	☽
Chakra *Lotus* ✿◊	Crown 8 petal	Third eye 2 petal	Larynx 16 petal	Heart 12 petal	Solar plexus 10 petal	Sacral 6 petal	Root 4 petal
Gland †△	Pineal	Hypo-thalamus	Thyroid	Thymus	Adrenals	Pancreas	Gonads
Cosmic Quality ✿◊	memory *gateway to Father*	thought *I AM center*	speech *higher will*	love *self (I")*	intelligence *movement*	harmony *balance*	instinctual will *gateway to Mother*
Sound ◊	U "oo"	O "oh"	E "eh"	AU ("ow")	I ("ee")	A ("ah")	EI ("eye")
Color ◊	Blue	Orange	Red	White	Yellow	Green	Violet
Mediating organ †◊	Spleen	Liver	Gall Bladder	Heart	Lungs	Kidneys	Brain
Tone ◊ ☆ *Geocentric* *Heliocentric*	G A=216	E G=192	C F=170⅔	A C=128	D D=144	F E=162	B B=243
Day of week †	Saturday	Thursday	Tuesday	Sunday	Wednesday	Friday	Monday
Metal †◊	Lead	Tin	Iron	Gold	Mercury (quicksilver)	Copper	Silver
Wood ◊	Fir, beech, cypress	Maple	Oak	Ash	Elm	Birch	Cherry
Grain * ◊	Corn	Rye	Oats	Wheat	Millet	Barley	Rice

*Note that the grains oats and barley are sometimes interchanged.

† = traditional
◊ = Rudolf Steiner
✿ = Valentin Tomberg
△ = Alla Selawry (anthroposophical medical doctor)
☆ = Robert Powell

Correspondences to the seven classical planets

	SATURN	JUPITER	MARS	SUN	MERCURY	VENUS	MOON
Eurythmy quality ◊	Contemplative being	Wisdom-filled being	Aggressive being	The whole human being	Egoistic being	Loving devoted being	Creative being
Creative principle ◊	Physical foundation	Freeing the "I"	Leading into incarnation	Eternal growth and development	Leading out of the life of the senses	Ascending in love	Holding fast and firm
Words from Gospel ☆	I and the Father are one	Glory to God in the heights	Thy will be done on earth as it is in heaven	Love the Lord thy God, with all thy heart, all thy soul and all thy strength	Be ye perfect as your Father in heaven	Love thy neighbor as thyself	Not my will, but thy will be done
Relation to the Godhead ◊	Resting in the Godhead	Embrace of the Godhead	Reverence for the Godhead	Beholding the Godhead	Seeking the Godhead	Majesty of the Godhead	Holy awe for the Godhead
7 gifts of Holy Spirit † ☆	Wisdom	Understanding	Counsel	Courage	Knowledge	Piety	Holy awe
Cardinal Virtues † ☆	Temperance	Wisdom	Courage	Righteousness	Hope	Love/ Compassion	Faith
Seven Virtues † ☆	Zeal	Goodness	Kindness	Humility	Generosity	Purity	Temperance
Seven deadly sins † Δ ☆	Sloth (laziness)	Envy	Anger (wrath)	Pride (arrogance)	Avarice (greed)	Lust	Gluttony

Robert Powell's indications given in the rows of the above table and the next table regarding the SEVEN DEADLY SINS, the SEVEN ARCHETYPES IN FAIRY TALES, the PYSCHOLOGICAL TYPES, and the TEMPERAMENTS, are essentially the same as those indicated by the anthroposophical doctor, Alla Selawry in her book on the seven planetary metals (available only in German), except for some minor variations.

Reference: Alla Selawry, METALLFUNKTIONSTYPEN IN PSYCHOLOGIE UND MEDIZIN ("The Metal-Functional Types in Psychology and Medicine")
(Haug Verlag: Heidelberg/Germany, 1991).

† = traditional
◊ = Rudolf Steiner
✿ = Valentin Tomberg
Δ = Alla Selawry
☆ = Robert Powell

Correspondences to the seven classical planets

	SATURN	JUPITER	MARS	SUN	MERCURY	VENUS	MOON
Seven original sins ✿	Death/ separation from God	Shame/deceit Spiritual blindness	Fear	Egotism (false communion)	Grasping (trespassing)	Desire	Doubt
Christ's gifts of salvation ✿	Overcoming death	Restoring spiritual sight	Overcoming fear	True communion	Overcoming trespassing	Overcoming desire	Faith
Life process ◊	Life of the senses	Life of nerves	Life of breathing	Life of circulation	Life of digestion	Life of movement	Life of reproduction
Inner movement ◊	Uprightness	Thinking	Speech	Blood circulation	Movement of breathing	Glandular movement	Movement of reproduction
Impulse ◊	Instinctual life	Inclinations (dispositions)	Moral impulses	Spiritual will	Cleverness, combinatorial thinking	Love	Fantasy, memory
Individuality ◊	Memory of past, historian	Spiritual presence, thinker	Agitator, talker	Harmony, freedom	Coordinative thinking, intellect	Secrets of soul, poetry	Mirrors everything, primal wisdom
Soul quality ◊	Melancholic, suffering, at rest in oneself	Forceful, leading, directing	Passionate, compelling, aggressive	Giving Bestowing, warming	Mediating, conciliating	Loving, mild, gentle	Receiving one, mirroring
Temperament △☆	Melancholic	Jovial	Choleric	Harmonious	Sanguine	Aesthetic	Phlegmatic
Psychological type △☆	Serious and conscientious	Philosophical, good overview	Willful, ready to act	Radiant, open-hearted	Quick, intelligent, communicative	Strong feelings, artistic nature	Strong instincts, connection to nature
Fairy tale Archetype △☆	Hermit, sage	Wise and good king	Courageous knight	Solar hero	Messenger, intelligent, nimble	Beautiful maiden	Nurturing mother
Tarot Card ☆	High priestess	Emperor	Charioteer	Magician	Pope	Lover	Empress
World Mood ◊	Gnosis	Logicism	Voluntarism	Empiricism	Transcendentalism	Mysticism	Occultism*
Archangel †◊	Oriphiel	Zachariel	Samael	Michael	Raphael	Anael	Gabriel

*Occultism (esotericism) is the science, both theoretical and applied, of the hidden invisible realms.

Correspondences to the seven classical planets

(Note: Mercury and Venus are reversed)

	SIGN	7 YEAR PERIOD †◊	SPIRITUAL HIERARCHY †◊			GREEK GOD †
Saturn	♄	56-63	Seraphim	Spirits of Love	All-consuming fire of love	Chronos
Jupiter	♃	49-56	Cherubim	Spirits of Harmony	Outpouring fount of wisdom	Zeus
Mars	♂	42-49	Thrones	Spirits of Will	Seats, Ophanim (Divine Wheels)	Ares
Sun	☉	21-42	Kyriotetes Dynamis Exusiai	Spirits of Wisdom Spirits of Movement Spirits of Form	Dominions, Lords, True authority Mights, Virtues, Godlike energy Powers, Elohim, Supermundane power	Apollo
Venus	♀	14-21	Archai	Time Spirits	Principalities, Spirits of personality, Bearers of intelligence	Aphrodite
Mercury	☿	7-14	Archangeloi	Folk Spirits	Archangels, Fire Spirits, Bearers of warmth	Hermes
Moon	☽	0-7	Angeloi	Guardian Angels	Angels, Sons of Life, Bearers of life	Artemis

† = traditional
◊ = Rudolf Steiner

Appendix IV: Music and Verses for the Seven Classical Planets

In Choreocosmos workshops there is generally live music (usually piano or violin) accompanying the eurythmy for the cosmic dances of the planets. As mentioned in the Introduction, concert pianist Sylvia Karpe has recorded two CDs (available from the Sophia Foundation): one of the two series of music – listed below – used for the planets, and one used for the Four Elements together with the music by Schubert for the Prayer Sequence in Sacred Dance. In the case of the Planet CD, the music has been chosen on the one hand relating to the planetary quality of the music (e.g. Beethoven's *"Moonlight Sonata"* for the Moon) and on the other hand relative to the rhythmical form of the choreography of the cosmic dance for that planet.

Piano Music for the Planets: 1ˢᵗ Series

Saturn	Bach, "Air" from the Orchestra Suite no. 3, D major (piano transcription) Andante (BWV 1068)
Jupiter	Bach, Prelude in C major from the Well-Tempered Clavier, Vol. I
Mars	Beethoven, "Minore" from the 3ʳᵈ movement in E♭ minor of Sonata no.4 in E major, op.7 Allegro
Sun	Bach, Chorale "Jesus, Joy of Man's Desire" from the Cantata in G major (piano transcription) Poco mosso, ma tranquillo
Venus	Chopin, "Raindrop Prelude" in D♭ major Sostenuto
Mercury	Mozart, "Alla turca" from Sonata no.11 in A major (KV 331) Allegretto
Moon	Beethoven, "Moonlight Sonata", 1ˢᵗ movement in C# minor (op.27, no.2) Adagio sostenuto

Piano Music for the Planets: 2ⁿᵈ Series

Saturn	Chopin, Prélude no.6 in B Minor, op.28, no.6 Lento assai. {1-24} + {3-26}
Jupiter	Beethoven, from the 3ʳᵈ movement of Sonata no.30 in E Major, op.109. Play all repeats. Andante molto cantabile ed espressivo
Mars	Beethoven, "Bagatelle" in A♭ Major, op.33, no.7 Presto. Repeat {17-20}, {61-64}, {73-76}, {117-120}, {129-132}
Sun	Bach, "Pastorale" in F Major Piano transcription: Dinu Lipatti Andantino tranquillo
Venus	Beethoven, from the 2ⁿᵈ movement (in A♭ Major) of Sonata no.8 in C Minor, op.13 ("Pathétique") Adagio cantabile
Mercury	Chopin, Etude no.1 in A♭ Major Allegro sostenuto. Medium tempo
Moon	Chopin, "Berceuse" in D♭ Major Andante. Play slowly to fit the Moon eurythmy form

In addition to the above music for the seven classical planets, the following piano music is used for Vulcan, which is the future stage of evolution following the Jupiter and Venus stages. As described in Appendix I, Vulcan is the octave of the Ancient Saturn stage of evolution.

Vulcan	Bach, Prelude XXII from the Well-Tempered Clavier, Vol. II: B♭ minor

Violin Music for the Planets

Saturn	Bach	"Air" from the orchestra suite no.3 (first violin) "Andante" (BWV 1068)	D major
Jupiter	Mozart	"Ave Verum" (transcription for violin and piano) (KV 618)	D major
Mars	Corelli	"Allegro" from "La Follia" (Variation in time signature of 12/8) play twice	D minor
Sun	Bach	Chorale "Jesus, Joy of Man's Desire" (transcription of this cantata) Poco mosso, ma tranquillo	G major
Venus	Mozart	"Adagio" (KV 261) (first violin from this orchestral piece)	E major
Mercury	Händel	"Allegro" from the 3rd violin sonata	F major
Moon	Bach	"Adagio" from Sonata no. 4 for violin and harpsichord (BWV 1017)	C minor
Vulcan	Bach	"Double" from Partita no. 1 (from "Tempo di Borea") (BWV 1002)	B minor

For the planets **Saturn** and the **Sun** the violin pieces are the same as the corresponding piano pieces for these planets (refer to Sylvia Karpe's "*Planet Music*" CD). The violin simply plays the melody line (of the piano transcription in the case of the **Sun**).

The role of Vulcan as the octave of Saturn is key to grasping the cosmic dance of Vulcan which, however, is not discussed in great detail here, as it entails a group form, rather than the individual forms described for the other planets.

The eurythmy form adopted for this cosmic dance is known as the "crown form", which is a group form, usually for seven people, that represents a metamorphosis of the Saturn form. It is best to learn this form at a Choreocosmos workshop.

For those who know the crown form and the eurythmy gesture for the octave, and are also familiar with the piano or violin music, four steps are made to the music when moving forward or backward

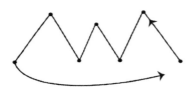 on the crown form, always beginning with the left foot – except for the "connecting way" of the crown form (the lower arc in the diagram), where one begins with the right foot, moving swiftly to the right, to complete this way in time to recommence the first way of the crown form with four steps moving diagonally forward to the left. With the first four steps the Saturn gesture is made from above down. Then, with the next four steps the "U" gesture (Saturn sound) is made from below up. Following this, with the next four steps the octave gesture is formed, in consciousness of Vulcan as the octave of Ancient Saturn evolution.

The sequence of these three gestures is repeated throughout the movement to the music, requiring one gesture for each way of the crown form (from one point to the next). The cooperation as a group in shaping the crown form is a powerful experience, representing something completely new in relation to the circle dance forms for the other planets.

Seven Planetary Verses

The following seven verses can be used in conjunction with the eurythmy forms for the planets. The verses have been chosen on the one hand on account of their planetary quality (e.g. Goethe's "*To the Moon*" for the Moon) and on the other hand because of the appropriate concordance between the rhythm of the poem and the choreography (form) of the cosmic dance for that planet. The verses are arranged so that each line fits either the whole form or (as in the case of Mars) half the form once. For example, in the case of the cosmic dance for the Sun – "*You appear in the heavenly blue …*" – this is in the anapest rhythm of "short, short, long". Stepping this rhythm while doing the form for the cosmic dance of the Sun, as the rhythm is repeated three times in each line, if one adds in an extra "short, short, long" at the end of each line, it is possible to complete the first "figure 8" of the form with twelve steps, whereby the "long" is always a cross-over step. The "figure 8" form is repeated twelve times corresponding to the twelve lines of "*You appear in the heavenly blue …*" These seven planetary verses provide a possibility of working with the cosmic forms for the planets in a situation when there is no musical accompaniment – for example, if one is by oneself. Apart from "*You appear in the heavenly blue …*" for the Sun, which is an adaptation of Akhenaten's "*Hymn to the Sun*",[352] and with the exception of Rudolf Steiner's verse "*The Sun behold at the midnight hour …*", all the verses are translated from – or rather are loosely based upon – poems by Goethe.

Sun

You appear in the heavenly blue,
And bestow on the earth your great light,
Your full warmth – it embraces the world,
Which, O Sun, you created yourself.

You arise like a flower in spring.
You appear like a falcon on high,
Who with heavenly eyes beholds all,
When you set, then the world becomes blind.

Human beings arise to your rays,
And the gods jubilate at your sight,
And all beings pay homage to you,
When they see you in heavenly might.

---

[352] Of comparatively late date – from the time of Akhenaten (eighteenth dynasty, circa 1350 BC) – this *Hymn to the Sun* retains the imagery and style of more ancient hymns to the Sun god Ra. This version is adapted from Akhenaten's *Hymn to the Sun*. It has an anapest rhythm.

Venus

The beauty of Venus has captured my senses,
Her fullness of blessing I feel with my heartbeat,
At spring's new begin she appeared in her glory,
I saw her, she touched me, she held me in ecstasy,
She banished all sorrow by gazing upon me,
And showed me the depths and the heights of existence.

In holy apparel she radiates beauty,
And harmony streams from her wondrous appearance,
In thousandfold form she descends from the heavens,
She flows through the aether, she rays out her presence,
To all who behold her majestic effulgence:
To sing of her splendor is each poet's duty.

Mercury

Mighty Apollo, the Sun god, and Hermes, the swift-footed messenger,
Disputed strongly in contest; each wanted the wonderful prize –
Apollo desired the lyre; the lyre was sought also by Hermes;
Yet in vain did each hope for their heart's fulfillment.
For suddenly Ares appeared, and ended the dispute with force –
Striking the golden lyre, severing it in two with his sword.
Hermes laughed aloud at the sight of the damage,
But Apollo was filled with pain, smitten to the core of his being.

Mars

Fire is ignited now,
Lightning is flashing down,
Mars in his chariot,
Burning red warrior,
Sends down his bolts of flame,
Calling aloud by his name,
Shaking his mighty fist,
Thundering through smoke and mist,
Wild and untamed.

Jupiter

In the infinite realm of Jupiter,
Ethereal clouds are eternally flowing,
And manifold archetypes are astir,
Heaven's witness to all that is growing –
Blessing rays from each and every star,
And joy of life pours down from above,
Wisdom and harmony prevail near and far,
And hearts are filled with the warmth of love.

Saturn

The Sun behold at the midnight hour,
In depths untold, build with stone's power.

In this night of death is found from decay,
Creation's new breath, and dawning of new day.

The powers on high reveal the Eternal Word Divine,
The depths below conceal peace in their sacred shrine.

In darkness thou livest, a new Sun creating;
In matter thou weavest, Spirit-Bliss anticipating.

Moon

Lumine thou each hill and vale,
Shining Moon above,
Light the way for my own soul,
Fill my heart with love.

Turn upon my inner life,
Lovingly thy gaze,
Like a friendly eye so kind,
Bless me through thy rays.

With the above seven verses, the seven pieces of music for violin, and the two series of seven pieces of piano music, there are four possibilities of working with the cosmic dances of the seven planets described in this book. Of these four, the seven verses offer an opportunity – particularly if one learns them by heart – of practicing the planetary forms by oneself, without any musical accompaniment. In stepping the verses while reciting them, it is good to pay attention to the rhythm in which they are written (carried over, as far as possible, in the translation), particularly in the Sun, Venus, Mars and Moon verses. The Sun verse is in the rhythm of anapaest or anapest ("short, short, long") – a metrical foot originally used in classical Greek poetry – which means two short (or unstressed) syllables followed by a long (or stressed) syllable, as in the word "seventeen".

The rhythms of the planetary verses are:

Sun	anapest ("*short, short, long*")
Venus	amphibrach ("*short, long, short*")
Mercury	dactylic hexameter (not adhered to strictly in this poem)
	("*long, short, short - long, short, short - long, short*")
Mars	dactyl ("*long, short, short*")
Jupiter	a mixture of anapest, dactyl, trochee ("*long, short*"), iamb ("*short, long*")
	and iambic tetrameter ("*short, long - short, long - short, long - short, long*")
Saturn	iamb and dactyl (not adhered to strictly in this poem)
Moon	trochee ("*long, short*")

Everyone is born of the planets, as expressed in this verse from the mysteries celebrated at the temple of Artemis of Ephesus – a planetary verse addressed to the human soul:

Planets in the order of the days of the week	
	Offspring of worlds,
	Thou in form of light,
Sun (Sunday)	Empowered by the Sun,
Moon (Monday)	With Luna's might,
Mars (Tuesday)	Endowed with Mars' creative sounding,
Mercury (Wednesday)	And Mercury's limb activity abounding,
Jupiter (Thursday)	Illumined by Jupiter's radiant wiseness,
Venus (Friday)	And Venus bearing beauty and lovingness,
Saturn (Saturday)	That Saturn's age-old spirit inwardness
	Thee unto the world of space and time hallow.[353]

---

[353] Rudolf Steiner, *The Easter Festival in the Evolution of the Mysteries*, is the source for this verse which is given here in a new translation by Robert Powell.

Appendix V: The Galactic Center

What is the Galactic Center?

When we look up to the constellation of Sagittarius, the Archer is aiming his arrow directly at the Galactic Center (at 2° Sagittarius), where an extraordinarily intensive point of infra-red light has been discovered.[354] This energy source, approximately 50 light years in diameter, has been identified as the actual center of our Milky Way galaxy. Located some 25,000 light years from our solar system, it is estimated that this energy source is about 500 million times more powerful than our Sun. From here emanates the power that holds our galaxy of more than 100 billion stars together. This is the Central Sun.

All the stars that we see in the heavens are Suns, like our Sun. All of them rotate slowly in a clockwise direction around the Central Sun *"Like a wheel that is evenly moved by the love that moves the Sun and the other stars"* (Dante, *The Divine Comedy: Paradise* 33: 144-145).

In light of Dante's words: Could it be Divine Love emanating from the Central Sun that supports and sustains all the Suns/stars in the heavens such that it is literally *"Love that makes the world go round"*?

To gain an idea of the immensity of the Central Sun at the galactic center (which is NOT a *"black hole"* as modern astronomy teaches), imagine a second Sun alongside our Sun. And then add a third Sun, and a fourth Sun, and a fifth Sun … and so on, until there are 500 million Suns there. This imaginative exercise can offer us a glimpse of the majesty and grandeur of the Central Sun at the Galactic Center, which holds 100 billion Suns/stars in their orbits around it.

The Russian poet and mystic Daniel Andreev once had a vision of the Galactic Center, which he describes in his book *The Rose of the World*:

> I remember seeing a glowing mist of stunning majesty, as though the creative heart of our universe had revealed itself to me in visible form for the first time.
> It was Astrofire, the great center of our galaxy.[355]

Appendix VI: Planetary Positions at Events in Christ's Life

The following table indicates positions of the planets – both geocentrically and heliocentrically – at major events during the life of Christ, based on the research presented in Robert Powell's *Chronicle of the Living Christ*. Contemplation of these events, which are of an archetypal nature, can help toward a deeper understanding of the working of the planets.

Most of the planetary positions at events in the life of Christ listed in the Table are from Robert Powell, *Chronicle of the Living Christ* – see also the *Christ Chronology* database in the *Astrofire* program.

In the Table the following abbreviations are used:
Ø = Conception;   ✶ = Birth;   † = Death.

Heliocentric planetary positions are italicized and marked *. Otherwise all positions are geocentric.

---

[354] The two-dimensional image of the Archer aiming his arrow at the Galactic Center has to be thought of in three dimensions in order to grasp that it is an optical illusion, since the visible stars making up the constellation of Sagittarius are relatively close to our solar system (the most distant stars being not more than a few thousand light years away), whereas the Galactic Center is located at a distance of about 25,000 light years.

[355] Daniel Andreev, *The Rose of the World*, p. 198.

Planetary Positions in the Sidereal Zodiac

	☉	°	♀	°	☿	°
♈			_Feeding of 5000*_	7		
			Ascension	8½		
	Transfiguration	14			Transfiguration	11
	Crucifixion	14			_Adoration of Magi*_	12
	Resurrection	15½	Pentecost	17	Feeding of 4000	14
♉					_2nd raising of Salome*_	2½
			☆ _Solomon Mary*_	9	Discourse with Nicodemus	5
	Ascension	23	Transfiguration	21½		
♊	Pentecost	2½			_Baptism*_	8
			Healing of Nobleman's Son*	20½	Ascension	9
			Healing of two blind men	21		
			Healing of ten lepers	24	Pentecost	25
♋			_Wedding at Cana*_	1½		
			Healing of Nobleman's Son	20		
			Transfiguration*	21	Raising of Lazarus	23
	☆ Nathan Mary	25			_Wedding at Cana*_	24½
♌					_Ascension*_	2
	Raising of Lazarus	3	☆ _Nathan Mary*_	17½	_Feeding of 4000*_	6½
	Healing of Nobleman's Son	10½	Raising of Lazarus	18		
			☆ _Nathan Jesus*_	21½	☆ Nathan Mary	21
♍			_Raising of Lazarus*_	9½	Healing of Nobleman's Son	7
					Baptism	12½
	☆ Solomon Mary	16	Raising of pagan child	23	_Pentecost*_	13½
			Triumphant Entry*	28½	☆ Solomon Mary	28½
♎	Baptism	0½	Raising of Nazor	4	☆ _Nathan Jesus*_	2
			Healing of Manahem	9		
			Crucifixion*	22½	Healing of Manahem	14
			Resurrection*	25	_Transfiguration*_	17
♏			☆ Nathan Jesus	2	☆ _Nathan Mary*_	2
			Appearance to 7 Disciples*	11		
			Appearance to 500 Disciples*	13		
	Raising of Youth of Nain	22	Baptism	15	_Triumphant Entry*_	20½
			Raising of Youth of Nain	27	☆ Nathan Jesus	25
♐			1st raising of Salome	4	☆ _Solomon Jesus*_	6
			Raising of Youth of Nain*	4½	Raising of Youth of Nain	10
	☆ Nathan Jesus	16	Stilling of Storm	8	_Healing of Nobleman's Son*_	15
					1st raising of Salome	17
			2nd raising of Salome	20	_Feeding of 5000*_	25
			Ascension*	27	2nd raising of Salome	25
♑	Wedding at Cana	8	_Pentecost*_	12½	_Last Supper*_	2
			Raising of Essene Daughter	15	_Crucifixion*_	4½
			Wedding at Cana	26	_Resurrection*_	10
			Baptism*	27½	Feeding of 5000	26½
♒	Healing of Paralyzed Man	0½	☆ Solomon Jesus	4	_Raising of Youth of Nain*_	0½
	Feeding of 5000	10½	_2nd Conversion of Magdalene*_	12	☆ Solomon Jesus	9
			ø _Solomon Mary*_	19	_Raising of Lazarus*_	21½
			Healing of Paralyzed Man	21½	Healing of Syrophoenician	21
					1st raising of Salome*	22½
♓			Feeding of 5000	4	_Stilling of Storm*_	7½
	☆ Solomon Jesus	15½	_Adoration of Magi*_	21	Last Supper	18½
			Resurrection	24	Crucifixion	19½
			Crucifixion	24½	Resurrection	22
			Last Supper	25		

Planetary Positions in the Sidereal Zodiac

	♂	°	♃	°	♄	°	☽	°
	*Raising of Youth of Nain**	8½	Feeding of 5000	9	Adoration of Magi	2		
	Raising of Lazarus	11						
♈	Feeding of 5000	15					Ascension	17
	*☆ Solomon Jesus**	17½						
	*2nd raising of Salome**	19	Transfiguration	23				
	Feeding of 4000	14	*Adoration of Magi**	5			Feeding of 4000	8
♉	*Feeding of 5000**	20	☆ Nathan Mary	28				
	Transfiguration	26			☆John the Baptist	27		
	Crucifixion	10	Raising of Lazarus	14½	Baptism	13		
	Resurrection	11	Crucifixion	17				
♊	*Feeding of 4000**	12	Resurrection	17½			Peter's Confession	19
			Ascension	25	Transfiguration	22		
	*Transfiguration**	21	Pentecost	27				
	Ascension	4½	*Ascension**	0½				
	Pentecost	10½	*Pentecost**	1	Crucifixion	18½		
♋	*Crucifixion**	10½			Resurrection	19	2nd raising of Salome	11
	*Resurrection**	11			Ascension	21		
	*Ascension**	28½			Pentecost	22		
	*Pentecost**	3					Raising of Lazarus	5
♌	☆ Nathan Mary	5	☆ John the Baptist	9				
	☆ Solomon Mary	14					Baptism	16
	*Baptism**	18					Pentecost	25
	Baptism	4					Feeding of 5000	7
♍	*Adoration of Magi**	6	☆ Nathan Jesus	12½			☆ Solomon Jesus	15
	*Wedding at Cana**	2½						
♎	*☆ Nathan Jesus**	8			☆ Solomon Mary	9½	Crucifixion	12
	End of Temptations	18						
	☆Nathan Jesus	3					Resurrection	3
♏	Wedding at Cana	5½						
	*Cleansing of Temple**	24			☆ Nathan Mary	19	Raising of Youth of Nain	11
	Raising of Essene Daughter	2			†Solomon Mary	1½		
							Raising of Nazor	9
♐			Ø Solomon Mary	18½			Healing of ten lepers	23
			☆ Solomon Mary	1			☆ Solomon Mary	4
♑	Cleansing of Temple	7						
	*Blessing of children**	15	*☆ Solomon Mary**	12			Transfiguration	23
	Healing of Nobleman's Son	26						
	*Healing of Nobleman's Son**	6½						
♒								
	Raising of Youth of Nain	26	Baptism	28			Healing of Nobleman's Son	27
	*Raising of Lazarus**	29						
	2nd raising of Salome	7	Wedding at Cana	3½			Wedding at Cana	3½
	*Healing of Manahem**	16	*Baptism**	4				
♓	Healing of two blind men	17	*Wedding at Cana**	13			Healing of Syrophoenician	22
	Healing of ten lepers	19			☆ Solomon Jesus	26½		
	*Raising of Nazor**	22						

Bibliography

Richard Hinckley Allen, *Star Names: Their Lore and Meaning* (Dover Public Publications: New York, 1963).

Daniel Andreev, *The Rose of the World* (Lindisfarne Press: Gt. Barrington/MA, 1997).

Anonymous, *Meditations on the Tarot: A Journey into Christian Hermeticism* (Putnam/Tarcher: New York, 2002).

Astrofire – see below, at the end of this bibliography.

Arthur Avalon, *The Serpent Power: A Translation from the Sanskrit of Sat-Cakra-Nirupana and Paduka-Pancaka* (Dover Publications: New York, 1974 – originally published in 1919). Arthur Avalon was the pseudonym of Sir John Woodroffe.

Robert O. Becker and Gary Selden, *The Body Electric* (William Morrow & Company: New York, 1985).

Georg Blattmann, *The Sun: The Ancient Mysteries and a New Physics* (Steiner Books: Great Barrington/MA, 1985).

Robert Roy Britt, "*Saturn's Surprise: One Ring is Actually a Spiral*" – www.SPACE.com article from November 28, 2005 – writing about the research of Sebastian Charnoz at the University of Paris, reported in the November 25, 2005 issue of the journal *Science*.

Jacques Dorsan, Le *veritable sens des maisons astrologiques* ("*The Twelve Astrological Houses Must Be Counted Clockwise*") (Editions du Rocher: Monaco, 1984). An English translation of this book is in preparation – contact Botton Books, Botton Village, Danby, Whitby, Yorkshire, YO21 2NJ, England, tel: (+44) 1287-661279.

Beinsa Douno, *Dans le Royaume de la Nature Vivante* ("*In the Kingdom of Living Nature*") (Le Courrier du Livre: Paris/France, 1966).

Ormond Edwards, *The Time of Christ* (Floris Books: Edinburgh/Scotland, 1986).

Masaru Emoto, *The Hidden Messages in Water* (Beyond Words Publishing: Hillsboro/OR, 2004).

Agnes Fyfe, *Die Signatur Merkurs im Pflanzenreich* ("*The Signature of Mercury in the Plant Kingdom*") (Verlag Freies Geistesleben: Stuttgart/Germany, 1973).

——, *Die Signatur der Venus im Pflanzenreich* ("*The Signature of Venus in the Plant Kingdom*") (Verlag Freies Geistesleben: Stuttgart/Germany, 1978).

Joscelyn Godwin, *The Harmony of the Spheres: A Sourcebook of the Pythagorean Tradition in Music* (Inner Traditions International: Rochester/VT, 1993).

W.K.C. Guthrie, *Orpheus and Greek Religion* (Princeton University Press: Princeton/NJ, 1993).

E.J. Holmyard, *Alchemy* (Dover Publications: New York, 1990).

"*Hubble Gets Superb View of Saturn and Rings*" (*http://www.space.com/scienceastronomy/hubble_030909.html*).

Jörg Jewanski, *Ist C = Rot? Eine Kultur- und Wissenschaftsgeschichte zum Problem der wechselseitigen Beziehung zwischen Ton und Farbe* ("*Is C=Red? A Cultural and Scientific History Concerning the Problem of the Interchangeable Relationship between Tone and Color*") (Berliner Musik Studien, volume 17; Studio: Sinzig/Germany, 1999).

Adalbert von Keyserlingk, *The Birth of a New Agriculture: Koberwitz 1924 (Includes "Twelve Days with Rudolf Steiner" by Johanna von Keyserlingk*) (Temple Lodge Press: London, 1999).

Nick Kollerstrom, "*The Alchemy Website: The Metal-Planet Affinities*" (*http://www.levity.com/alchemy/sevenmetals.html*).

——, *Planting by the Moon* (Prospect Books: Totnes/England, 1998).

—— , "*Zodiac Rhythms in Plant Growth*," *Mercury Star Journal*, vol. III, no. 2 (Temple Lodge Press: London, 1977), pp. 50-53.

Lili Kolisko, *The Moon and the Growth of Plants* (London, 1938).

Claude Larre and Elisabeth Rochat de la Vallée, *The Secret Treatise of the Spiritual Orchid* (Monkey Press: Cambridge/England, 1992).

——, *The Seven Emotions* (Monkey Press: Cambridge/England, 1996).

Charles W. Leadbeater, *The Chakras: A Monograph* (Theosophical Publishing House: Adyar, Madras, India, 1927).

Jacques Lusseyran, *Against the Pollution of the I* (Parabola Books: New York, 1999).

Thomas O. McCracken and Richard Walker, *Der 3D-Anatomie-Atlas* (Bechtermünz – distributed by Weltbild Verlag: Augsburg/Germany, 2000). The original English edition of this book: *New Atlas of Human Anatomy* (Barnes & Noble Books: New York, 1999).

James Miller, *Measures of Wisdom: The Cosmic Dance in Classical and Christian Antiquity* (University of Toronto Press: Toronto, 1986).

Thomas Moore, *The Planets Within* (Lindisfarne Press: Gt. Barrington/MA, 1990).

Isaac Newton, *Opticks: or, a Treatise of the Reflections, Refractions, Inflexions and Colours of Light* (London, 1704).

Novalis, *Hymns to the Night* (trsl. C.E. Passage; Liberal Arts Press: Indianapolis-New York, 1960).

Jacquanna Paul and Robert Powell, *Cosmic Dances of the Zodiac* (Sophia Foundation of North America: Palo Alto/CA, 2003).

Robert Powell, *Christian Hermetic Astrology*, (Steiner Books: Gt. Barrington/MA, 1998).

——, *Chronicle of the Living Christ* (Steiner Books: Gt. Barrington/MA, 1996).

——, *Divine Sophia, Holy Wisdom*, (Sophia Foundation of North America: Palo Alto/CA, 1997).

——, *Hermetic Astrology, vol. I* (Hermetika: Kinsau/Germany, 1987 – distributed by the Sophia Foundation of North America).

——, *Hermetic Astrology, vol. II* (Hermetika: Kinsau/Germany, 1989 – distributed by the Sophia Foundation of North America).

——, *History of the Planets* (Astro Communications Services: San Diego/CA, 1985).

——, "*Lunar Calendar for Farmers and Gardeners*," *Mercury Star Journal*, vol. III, no. 2 (Temple Lodge Press: London, 1977), pp. 54-63.

——, *Morning Meditation in Eurythmy* (Sophia Foundation of North America: Palo Alto/CA, 2005).

Maria Renold, *Von Intervallen, Tonleitern, Tönen und dem Kammerton c = 128 Hertz* (Verlag am Goetheanum: Dornach/Switzerland, 1998) - English translation: *Intervals, Scales, Tones and the Concert Pitch c=128 Hz.* (trsl. Bevis Stevens; Temple Lodge Press: London, 2004).

Valerie J. Roebuch, *The Circle of Stars: An Introduction to Indian Astrology* (Element Books: Rockport/MA, 1992).

Robert Sardello, *Freeing The Soul From Fear* (Riverhead Books: New York, 1999).

Josefine Schreier, *Göttinnen, Ihr Einfluß von der Urzeit bis zur Gegenwart* ("*Goddesses: Their Influence from Ancient Times to the Present*") (Verlag Frauenoffensive: Munich, 1977).

Joseph Seiss, *The Gospel In The Stars* (Kregel Publications: Grand Rapids/MI, 1972).

The Solar System: A Scientific American Book (Freeman & Company: San Francisco/CA, 1975).

Rudolf Steiner, *Concerning the History and Content of the Higher Degrees of the Esoteric School, 1904-1914* (Steiner Books/Etheric Dimensions Press: Gt. Barrington/MA, 2006). The Steiner Books edition has the title, *"Freemasonry" and Ritual Work: The Misraim Service. Texts and Documents from the Cognitive Cultic Section of the Esoteric School, 1904-1914*, which is different than that of the Scottish edition published in 2005 by Etheric Dimensions Press with the title given above; however, the translation is the same. (Note that the page numbering of quotes from this work given in various footnotes above are from the Scottish edition.)

——, *The Easter Festival in the Evolution of the Mysteries* (Steiner Books: Gt. Barrington/MA, 1988).

——, *Erden und Menschheitsentwickelung* ("*The Development of the Earth and Humanity*"). Fragenbeantwortung ("Answers to Questions"). *Nachrichtenblatt der Rudolf Steiner Nachlassverwaltung*, volume 26 (Rudolf Steiner Verlag: Dornach/Switzerland, Summer 1969).

——, *Eurythmy as Visible Speech* (Anastasi: Weobley, Herefordshire/England, 2005).

————, *Foundations of Esotericism* (Rudolf Steiner Press: London, 1983).

————, *Human Questions and Cosmic Answers* (Anthroposophical Publishing Company: London, 1960).

————, *Knowledge of the Higher Worlds* (Rudolf Steiner Press: London, 1972). A more recent edition is available from Steiner Books under the title *How to Know Higher Worlds*.

————, *Life Between Death and Rebirth* (Steiner Books: Gt. Barrington/MA, 1975).

————, *Man in the Light of Occultism, Theosophy, and Philosophy* (Rudolf Steiner Press: London, 1964).

————, *Man: Hieroglyph of the Universe* (Rudolf Steiner Press: London, 1972).

————, *Nine Lectures on Bees* (St. George Publications: Spring Valley/NY, 1964). A more recent edition is available from Steiner Books under the title *Bees*.

————, *Occult Physiology* (Rudolf Steiner Press: London, 1962). A more recent edition is available from Steiner Books.

————, *Occult Science – An Outline* (Rudolf Steiner Press, London, 1979).

————, *Die Rosenkreuzer-Esoterik* ("*Rosicrucian Esotericism*") (lecture held in Nijmegen/Holland on March 10, 1908; *Beiträge zur Rudolf Steiner Gesamtausgabe*, volume 60; Rudolf Steiner Verlag: Dornach/Switzerland, Christmas 1977), pp. 30-32.

————, *The Spiritual Beings in the Heavenly Bodies* (Rudolf Steiner Press: London, 1951).

————, *The Spiritual Hierarchies and their Reflection in the Physical World* (Rudolf Steiner Press: London, 1980).

————, "*Spiritual Individualities of the Planets,*" *Golden Blade*, vol. 40 (1988) (Hawthorn Press: Stroud/England, 1988), pp. 43-49.

————, *True and False Paths in Spiritual Investigation* (Rudolf Steiner Press: London, 1969).

————, "*The Twelve Moods,*" trsl. Robert Powell (Lacquanna Paul and Robert Powell, *Cosmic Dances of The Zodiac*, Sophia Foundation of North America: Palo Alto/CA, 2003, p. 115).

Hazel Straker, *Astrosophy – Introduction to a Quest for a New Star Wisdom* (Anastasi: Weobley, Herefordshire/England, 2000).

Willi Sucher, *Cosmic Christianity and the Changing Countenance of Cosmology* (Steiner Books: Gt. Barrington/MA, 1993).

Curt Suplee, "*The Sun: Living with a Stormy Star,*" *National Geographic*, vol. 206 (July, 2004), pp. 2-33.

Pierre Teilhard de Chardin, *Le Milieu Divin: An Essay on the Interior Life* (Perennial Classics: London, 1964).

Maria and Matthias Thun, *The Biodynamic Planting and Sowing Calendar* (Floris Books: Edinburgh/Scotland, yearly).

Valentin Tomberg, *Inner Development* (Steiner Books: Gt. Barrington/MA, 1992).

————, "*New Testament Studies*" republished in: *Christ and Sophia: Anthroposophical Meditations on the Old Testament, New Testament, and Apocalypse* (Steiner Books: Gt. Barrington/MA, 2006).

Peter Treadgold, *Astrofire* (see below, at the end of this bibliography).

Vettius Valens, *Anthologiarum* (ed. W. Kroll, Berlin, 1908).

Ernst Weidner, *Gestirn-Darstellungen auf babylonischen Tontafeln* ("*Representations of the Stars on Babylonian Cuneiform Tablets*") (Vienna, 1967).

Andrew Welburn, *Mani, The Angel and the Column of Glory* (Floris Books: Edinburgh/Scotland, 1988).

John Whitfield, "*Solar Storms Trip Magnetic Flip,*" *Nature News Service* (November 24, 2003).

John Woodroffe – see Arthur Avalon.

Astrofire Computer Program for Charts and Ephemerides

With grateful acknowledgment to Peter Treadgold, who wrote this computer program that includes a research module, star catalog of over 4000 stars, and database of birth and death charts of historical personalities, and which is capable of printing out geocentric and heliocentric/hermetic sidereal charts and ephemerides throughout history.

With this program one can:

- compute birth charts in a large variety of systems (tropical, sidereal, geocentric, heliocentric, Tychonic/hermetic[356]); calculate conception charts using the hermetic rule, in turn applying it for correction of the birth time; produce charts for the period between conception and birth, and print them out in color
- print out an "astrological biography" for the whole of life with the geocentric, heliocentric (and even lemniscatory) planetary system
- work with the sidereal zodiac according to the definition of your choice (Babylonian sidereal, Indian sidereal, unequal-division astronomical, etc.)
- work with planetary aspects with orbs of your choice

Included are eight house systems and a variety of chart formats, as well as an ephemeris program with a search facility. This program runs under Microsoft Windows.

If you are interested in *Astrofire*, please contact the Sophia Foundation of North America (see contact information at the beginning of this book).

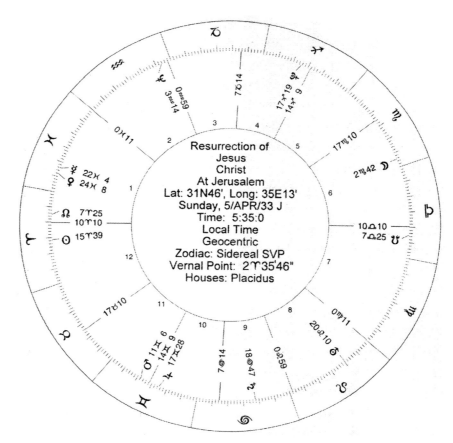

---

[356] The hermetic birth chart is computed on the basis of the astronomical system of the Danish astronomer Tycho Brahe (1546-1601) and is also referred to as the Tychonic chart.

Choreocosmos Experiences

For most of my adult life, I have had a habit of taking a pre-dawn walk or run at the time of the full Moon to some place where I have a clear view of the eastern and western horizons, so that I might stand between the disks of the rising Sun and the setting Moon. With my arms outstretched, it feels like I am holding these twin orbs in the palms of my hand, balancing and weighing them, and experiencing their raying forces within me.

Cosmic Dance affords this deep feeling of oneself as the microcosmic image of the Macrocosm, going beyond Sun and Moon to place into one's bones the other heavenly wanderers, set against the awesome canvas of the zodiacal constellations.

☆ ☆ ☆

At first, I am dancing, feeling the forms, the gestures, and the music, allowing them to work in me, and feeling them working in me. Then after a while, as I become more attuned, it is as if I am not dancing any more, but I am being danced! And sometimes I can even see that others in the circle are being danced too, because our movements are exactly synchronized, though perhaps not only in time – but in some element that I can almost see, and can certainly feel. It is as if we are moving in the same etheric current and are united in it. It is quite a joyful, peaceful experience.

Cosmic Dance balances me in the fullest way. It makes me feel more alive – more aware of others, including the beings in nature. The cosmic dances of Leo and the Sun are two of my favorites. Both of these enliven my heart, though each in its own way. My heart has softened, and opened. I see and feel more beauty in the world. I am more grateful, compassionate, and caring. But what is most intriguing is that it seems as though my body is full of wisdom and that the cosmic dances have put me in touch with that wisdom. I am able to understand things on deep levels; dormant capacities within me are awakening. But the ultimate gift of Cosmic and Sacred Dance, one that I have been given repeatedly by grace, is the experience of Divine Sophia. Her Grace, her Strength, her Wisdom, is the sweetest, most precious experience I could ever have. My faith is growing.

☆ ☆ ☆

I am not a dancer, and need help to remember forward/backward, right/left, and many other things! But after attending a Choreocosmos workshop given by Robert last summer, I couldn't stop dancing. Although at that workshop we had danced the planets in Libra, Scorpio and Sagittarius, I was drawn to the dance of the Sun in Gemini, which we had done in the workshop two years previously. I would take the opportunity when alone at home to push back the furniture and dance, sometimes several times a day - at times trying other dances, but always coming back to the Sun in Gemini - using a tape of the music (Pachelbel's Canon) or else in silence, recalling the music and imagining the whole dance as I danced the sign and the planet in turn. After about a week, as I danced, an unexpected and overwhelming feeling I have not experienced before came over me. It was as if my heart had softened and expanded, and I was enveloped in wave after wave of warmth and love. I sat down and gave myself up to experiencing this feeling, which must have lasted for several minutes. As the days passed, so did my need for this particular dance - but I believe I am beginning to have a new awareness, not only in myself, but also of the special nature of these cosmic dances.

☆ ☆ ☆

Choreocosmos

School of Cosmic and Sacred Dance

Cosmic and Sacred Dance is a schooling through music and movement, engaging the body, soul and spirit, with the intention of aligning oneself harmoniously with the spiritual-cosmic world. It leads to a living experience of the earth and cosmos expressed in the inner life of Nature (four elements), and through the movements of the planets against the background of the zodiac.

Cosmic dance (cosmic eurythmy) is a renewal of the ancient temple dances where the pupils were instructed in the mysteries of the elements relating to Mother Earth, then the mysteries of the planets in relation to the Cosmic Soul, and finally the mysteries of the zodiac pertaining to the World Spirit. _Introductory courses_ of the School of Cosmic and Sacred Dance introduce these three levels of cosmic consciousness through the dances of the four elements, the seven planets, and the twelve signs of the zodiac, which correspond to the "body, soul, and spirit" of the human being. 12 + 7 + 4 = 23, signifying that there are 23 forms (choreographies), each with corresponding music and gestures, to be learnt as a foundation for cosmic dance. _Advanced courses_ weave the dances of the planets and zodiac into a living experience of the cosmic tapestry of the heavens, bringing to expression the planets in relation to the zodiacal signs. This entails 84 possibilities (7 x 12 = 84) for the seven planets in each of the twelve signs of the zodiac. Through cosmic dance, it is possible to find a deeper relationship with the earth, the planets and the zodiac, and thus with Sophia – the Soul of the Cosmos. Cosmic eurythmy aspires to lead one to an experience of the Harmony of the Spheres, culminating in "cosmic communion".

Sacred dance (devotional eurythmy) is meditative movement to prayers and sacred texts. Through gestures and sacred forms, the heart's offering in prayer weaves an ethereal fabric between the individual and the spiritual world which sustains an inner field of spiritual activity. Sacred dance unites the soul of the individual with higher realms of consciousness through an expression of love offered through one's whole being. Sacred dance, whether done individually or in a group, serves to open one to spiritual and religious dimensions of experience.

Eurythmy: Alongside the words attributed to Apollo "Know thyself", Christ spoke the words "Heal thyself". A path toward self-healing can be found through the hidden power of gesture and sound – which form the basis of eurythmy. Eurythmy means "harmonious rhythm" and is applied therapeutically to healing through movement. The body, soul and spirit are harmonized through wisdom-filled eurythmy gestures.

Study and Ideal

In addition to cosmic and sacred dance, there is the study aspect of the schooling: entering into an understanding of the new star wisdom as belonging to the Mysteries of Sophia, the Divine Wisdom of the cosmos. The study activity entails learning about the planets, the signs of the zodiac, and the four elements (Fire, Air, Water and Earth). It also involves becoming acquainted with spiritual exercises – complementary to the cosmic and sacred dances – that can help open the way to knowledge and experience of the star mysteries of Divine Sophia.

Entering into these star mysteries, one comes to experience that there is a continual exchange of divine energy between the cosmos, the Sun and the Earth. This cosmic energy is Divine Love which weaves throughout the entire universe. The cultivation of love is the spiritual ideal of the School of Cosmic and Sacred Dance. In doing the cosmic and sacred dances, we seek to connect our hearts and minds with Divine Love and with the Supreme Consciousness that pervades all existence.

The Choreocosmos School of Cosmic and Sacred Dance, while based in America (under the auspices of the Sophia Foundation of North America), offers the training also in other countries. As a "moving school", with an underlying cosmic language as its basis, it seeks to be universal in scope. The stars belong to everyone and they are united with us all. Our image of the heavens is of a world working in beauty and divine harmony, and the more we enter into communion with the world of stars, the more our gestures and our whole lives begin to correspond to the harmony of the heavens. The cosmic dances, when moved in harmony, serve to create a vessel receiving higher spiritual impulses flowing down from the heavens into earthly life. At the same time, we learn through cosmic dance to "speak to the stars". This work can be seen as a spiritual training and discipline to take into one's daily life and practice. In due course of time it is anticipated that there will be an increasing number of qualified teachers of cosmic and sacred dance. For further information, please contact the Sophia Foundation of North America or visit the Sophia Foundation's website.

Lacquanna Paul

Lucky is a teacher of Qigong, the ancient Chinese form of healing movement. She is also a graduate of the Choreocosmos School of Cosmic and Sacred Dance and has discovered astonishing correspondences between the ancient healing art of Qigong and the modern healing movements of Eurythmy, both working with the flow of life force (*prana* or *chi*). Together with Robert, she has co-authored *Cosmic Dances of the Planets, Cosmic Dances of the Zodiac,* and *The Prayer Sequence in Sacred Dance.*

Robert Powell, Ph.D.

Robert is an internationally known lecturer, author, eurythmist and movement therapist. He is founder of the Choreocosmos School of Cosmic and Sacred Dance, and co-founder of the Sophia Foundation of North America. He received his doctorate for his thesis on the *History of the Zodiac*, now available as a book from Sophia Academic Press. His published works include: *The Sophia Teachings*, a six-tape series (Sounds True Recordings), as well as the following books: *Divine Sophia-Holy Wisdom, The Most Holy Trinosophia and the New Revelation of the Divine Feminine, The Sophia Teachings, Chronicle of the Living Christ, Christian Hermetic Astrology, The Christ Mystery, The Sign of the Son of Man in the Heavens, The Morning Meditation in Eurythmy,* and the yearly *Christian Star Calendar.* Robert teaches the cosmic dances of the planets and signs of the zodiac and facilitates sacred celebrations dedicated to the Divine Feminine. He offers workshops in Europe and North America, and leads pilgrimages to the world's sacred sites (1996 Turkey; 1997 Holy Land; 1998 France; 2000 Britain; 2002 Italy; 2004 Greece; 2006 Egypt; 2008 India).

Sophia Foundation of North America

Email: sophia@sophiafoundation.org
Website: www.sophiafoundation.org

LaVergne, TN USA
17 August 2009
155002LV00001B/84/A

9 781597 311502